Hustling Hinkler is mandatory reading for everyone who loves flight.

A gripping story of an intrepid country boy who followed his dreams, designed, built and tested aircraft, set world records and as a result changed the world's expectation of global travel from months at sea to less than fifteen days via air.

Hinkler's trailblazing achievements match those of Kingsford Smith and Lindbergh, except that Bert operated as a one-horse team, without radios and alone!

Superbly written (with a surprising end-twist), *Hustling Hinkler* shows how unbridled passion for man, machine and humanity trumps fear, doubt and complacency.

I am proud to fly Qantas' tenth A380 named 'Bert Hinkler', honouring his legacy, overflying his route in just sixteen hours and proving his forecast that planes would 'fly the ships off the sea'.

Richard de Crespigny, author of
QF32 – the Captain's extraordinary account of how one of the world's worst air disasters was averted.

People travel to wonder at the height of mountains, at the huge waves of the seas, at the long courses of rivers, at the vast compass of the ocean, at the circular motion of the stars; and they pass by themselves without wondering.

St Augustine, 354–430

★HUSTLING★ HINKLER

THE SHORT TUMULTUOUS LIFE OF A TRAILBLAZING AUSTRALIAN AVIATOR

D.R. DYMOCK

hachette
AUSTRALIA

To Cheryl, who always believes in me, but keeps my feet on the ground

QUEENSLAND WRITERS CENTRE

Hustling Hinkler has been written with the encouragement of the Queensland Writers Centre (QWC). Darryl Dymock participated in the 2010 QWC/Hachette Australia Manuscript Development Program, which received funding from the Queensland Government through Arts Queensland.

hachette AUSTRALIA

Published in Australia and New Zealand in 2013
by Hachette Australia
(an imprint of Hachette Australia Pty Limited)
Level 17, 207 Kent Street, Sydney NSW 2000
www.hachette.com.au

10 9 8 7 6 5 4 3 2 1

National Library of Australia
Cataloguing-in-Publication data:

Dymock, D.R.
Hustling Hinkler: the short tumultuous life of a trailblazing Australian aviator/D.R. Dymock

978 0 7336 2983 9 (pbk.)

HInkler, Bert, 1892–1933.
Air pilots – Australia – Biography.
Aeronautics – Flight – History.

629.13092

Cover design by Luke Causby/Blue Cork
Author photograph © Sublime Photography
Chapter head illustration by Cheryl Orsini
Text design by Bookhouse, Sydney
Typeset in 12/18 pt Simoncini Garamond
Printed and bound in Australia by Griffin Press, Adelaide, an Accredited ISO AS/NZS 14001:2009 Environmental Management System printer

MIX Paper from responsible sources FSC www.fsc.org FSC® C009448

The paper this book is printed on is certified against the Forest Stewardship Council® Standards. Griffin Press holds FSC chain of custody certification SGS-COC-005088. FSC promotes environmentally responsible, socially beneficial and economically viable management of the world's forests.

Contents

Prologue

It was still several hours before a wintry dawn on Saturday, 7 January 1933 when the sound of a small plane's engine rippled across the misty flats of London's Great West Aerodrome, cutting through the silence. The noise came from a silver Puss Moth DH.80A sitting in dim yellow light outside a maintenance hangar, its single propeller a blur of white, its body trembling, as if anxious to be on its way – just like its pilot. The plane's Canadian registration, CF-APK, was emblazoned in red along each side of the fuselage and under the wings. Looking down from the cockpit, Bert Hinkler gave the thumbs up to the two men staring unsmilingly back at him, and in response, each raised a hand in quick farewell, then turned and headed towards their cars parked nearby.

A moment later, two pairs of headlights pierced the gloom as both vehicles bounced over the edges of the airfield and headed towards the distant perimeter, before sweeping around in opposing arcs halfway along to position themselves on either side of the runway, their lights spraying feebly across the take-off path. While the cars were manoeuvring, Hinkler sat quietly in the cockpit, his eyes closed, as if in prayer. He was thinking of his mother in Bundaberg, however, and how excited she would be to see him after an absence of more than four years, and of Nance, poised in New Zealand to board a ship to Australia as soon as she knew he was about to arrive in his home country. As the engine settled into a steady rhythm, the sound drumming on the adjacent hangar walls, he thought of the telephone conversation he'd had with Katherine not long before, and wished she were there to see him off. He was glad though that the inquisitive press were nowhere around. They'd get their story soon enough. Afterwards.

When Hinkler opened his eyes, he saw Harris, the caretaker, looking up at him. The Australian stepped down from the cockpit to shake his host's hand and asked him to thank Mrs Harris for her hospitality. He then climbed aboard again, and the caretaker pulled the wheel chocks away. Hinkler gave him a wave of thanks and headed the Puss Moth through the darkness towards the top of the airstrip, the whine of the plane's Gipsy engine sharp in the frosty air. As he reached the start point, a fog drifted nonchalantly across and settled itself, obscuring the runway. He throttled the motor back and sat impatiently in the cockpit, shrugging his neck into the collar of his flying jacket, but thankful that this time he was in an enclosed cabin.

After forty minutes, the fog vanished as suddenly as it had appeared. He glanced at the gold watch on his wrist – 3.10 am – and pulled his goggles over his eyes. Seconds later, the high-wing monoplane was trundling rapidly down the runway between the gaping headlights of the waiting cars. As the Puss Moth gathered speed, Hinkler made the now familiar pull on the control stick, and CF-APK was soon climbing steeply through patchy cloud, London somewhere below. It wasn't his Ibis 'dream machine' lifting him into the sky, as he had hoped for, but at least he was on his way to Australia. Again.

He set a course across the English Channel. Although his maps for this first day were already spread out on his knees, he'd been this way before. Soon he was passing over Le Bourget Aerodrome in Paris, where Charles Lindbergh had touched down almost six years earlier, after his celebrated Atlantic crossing. The sun had not yet penetrated the darkness of the winter morning as Hinkler continued across France, but he knew that somewhere below were the forests and vineyards of Burgundy, and then the picturesque Rhone valley. If he went east, he would be in Switzerland, but he stayed on his south-easterly track, towards Italy.

The Alps soon loomed up before him, clothed in their winter white, and he was forced to take the Puss Moth up to 8000 feet. Immediately he could feel the cold channelling itself beneath the three layers of clothing he wore, and at the higher altitude the winds were much stronger too, buffeting the plane. He thought he felt a tremor run through the aircraft, and looked anxiously at the lengths of gleaming wing stretching either side of him. The recent fatal Puss Moth crashes had concerned him, and he hoped the modifications had fixed the structural problems with the design.

He pushed on, heading for the pass known as the Colle di Moncenisio, close to where some historians think the Roman general, Hannibal, crossed from France into Italy in 218BC. As Hinkler flew across the border, he knew he was not far from Turin, where he'd landed in the Avro Baby at the end of his first record-breaking flight almost 13 years before. This time, if he could reach Brindisi, in the far south of the country, on the first day, it would be a great start for the record. He knew that his alternative destination, Athens, was now a city too far.

After what seemed like an eternity of winds and cold, the Alps finally slipped behind him and he flew into an area he knew – the north-west coast of Italy – and he was cheered when the cloud thinned enough to afford him a glimpse of the blue arc of the harbour at La Spezia. Hinkler followed the coast for a little way then turned inland across the plantations of Tuscany, the olive trees standing in line to salute the little silver plane as it passed overhead on its south-east track.

He sucked some coffee from his flask and devoured one of Mrs Harris's tongue sandwiches. They tasted good, but his head was buzzing from the constant pounding of the wind on the cabin and the concentration needed to keep the plane on course. When he passed over the city of Florence around 10 am local time, he was already behind the schedule he'd mapped out. By now he'd been in the air for seven hours, and he was weary from the drone of the engine and battling the elements. Hinkler wished he'd been able to leave London three months earlier, as he'd originally intended, when the weather – and Air Ministry officials! – might have been kinder to him. He could see cloud on the mountains distantly ahead, and the thought of diverting to Rome attracted him for a moment, but just as quickly he dismissed the idea – any diversion would mean less chance of breaking the record, and his future depended on achieving that goal. He continued south towards Brindisi.

As soon as he had made the decision to go on, patchy cloud began to snatch at the cockpit, and he could feel the cold drilling deeper into his bones. Sharp fingers of wind continued to push and pull at the plane, and for a moment Hinkler wondered if he sensed another tremor through the wings, but dismissed the thought as he wrestled with the controls.

Up ahead, through the clouds, he glimpsed the snow blanketing the Pratomagno mountains. He knew the highest point of the range, the Croce di Pratomagno, the Cross of Pratomagno, was just over 5000 feet, but that held no fears for him – after all, he'd crossed the much higher Italian Alps earlier in the day. Just so long as the winds were not too violent, and the plane held together . . .

* * *

I have long been interested in what makes some people persist, even against the odds, when others fall by the wayside. What persuades long-distance runners to pursue their solitary goal, for example, even when their bodies should have given up, and how do aid workers helping some of the world's most desperate people continue to labour day after day in the face of seemingly insurmountable difficulties and often at risk to their own lives? So, when I rediscovered Bert Hinkler through a chance reference a few years ago – decades after first seeing his green and silver biplane hanging from the vaulted ceiling of the old Queensland Museum, like a giant moth dangling on the sticky strands of a spider's web – I was immediately intrigued.

I wondered what inner urge spurred a country boy from Queensland to pursue a career in aviation as passionately as he had, flitting across the world in flimsy planes not much bigger than the average family car, eventually to his own destruction at the age of 40. What hopes and dreams did Hinkler have, and what ambitions were cut short, when his plane fell from the sky while he was on his way to Australia in January 1933? The fact that there are streets, parks and even an English pub named after him, and that other aviators have more recently retraced all or part of his 1928 England–Australia record flight – David Cyster, Dick Smith, Lang Kidby – only added to the mystique of the man.

After lengthy research in Australia and across the world, I discovered a story that is part adventure, part mystery, part romance and part tragedy. The image above of the moth dangling, or in this case, struggling, in a spider's sticky strands, is perhaps an apt one for the story of Bert Hinkler – while he spent his whole adult life trying to assert his independence as a pilot, inventor and aircraft designer, external circumstances and his own temperament combined to frustrate some of his most heartfelt ambitions. Nevertheless, his outstanding mechanical skills, his nerve, determination, and sheer instinct for flying, ensured that there were times when he broke free of the constraints and blazed a solo trail across the sky, amazing and delighting the world.

On the ground, however, Hinkler struggled to discern a career for himself, puzzled the press, had a mixed-up romantic life, and was constantly short of money. He lived at a time when the British Empire was arguably at its zenith, in a world that had emerged from the depths of World War I into the optimistic exuberance of the Jazz Age, only to be confronted from the middle of the 1920s by the gloom of economic decline that would lead to the Great Depression and its aftermath.

I am not a pilot, nor an expert in aviation – what I wanted was a better understanding of Bert Hinkler, the man. *Hustling Hinkler* not only chronicles how a boy from Bundaberg, Queensland became the 'hero of the day', as a popular song of the time labelled the record-breaking pilot, but also shows how he responded to the other opportunities and challenges that came his way in his relatively short life, while he tried to find a place for himself in a rapidly changing world.

D.R. Dymock
2013

CHAPTER 1

'A local flying man'

The two brothers flipped a coin to see who would go first. Wilbur, at age thirty-six the elder by four years, won the toss. Watched by five intrigued bystanders, they idled the motor for a few minutes to check it was running smoothly. Then Wilbur clambered aboard the flimsy structure of wooden struts and angled wires. With its 40-foot wings wrapped in unbleached muslin, the contraption might have looked from above like a giant seagull perched on the edge of a sand dune, peering out to the distant sea.

Once Wilbur was settled in the specially built wooden cradle on the lower wing, he released the restraining wire. The machine started quickly down the guide rail, its home-made 12-horsepower engine roaring, the twin propellers thrusting it forward. After sliding some 40 feet, it lifted into the air. But the rise was only momentary. Within seconds the primitive craft hit the ground and twisted itself to one side. It lay there awkwardly, like a fledgling that had left its nest too soon, to the disappointment of the handful of onlookers on Kill Devil Hill in North Carolina.

The team repaired the damage and three days later tried again. This time younger brother Orville got his chance. The wind was much stronger than before, but they decided to take the risk, and ran the engine a few times to warm it up in the sharp cold of the December day. Under a pale winter sun, Orville settled himself in the cradle, stretched out full-length, and gripped the two control levers. Ahead of him, broad sand flats reached out to touch the rolling waves of the Atlantic Ocean. He could taste the salt in the wind.

When the craft was released, it slid slowly along the wooden guide rail, against the wind, Wilbur running alongside to steady it. The motor was at full bore, echoing across the dunes. Suddenly, ethereally, the flimsy creature lifted into the air – staying there for twelve seconds and covering some 120 feet – before it bumped back gently to earth on its skids, Orville still cradled on the wing.

Not long, not far, but that little event was to have an immense impact on the history of the world.

* * *

Bert Hinkler had just turned eleven when Orville Wright lifted the 'Flyer' from the beach at Kitty Hawk, North Carolina, on that morning of 17 December 1903 and flew into history with the world's first powered aircraft flight. In those days of limited international communications, it would have taken some time for word of the feat to reach Hinkler's hometown of Bundaberg, in coastal south-east Queensland. Within a few years, however, if anyone asked Bert what he intended to be when he grew up, his answer would have been: 'I want to be a pilot.'

Like the Wright brothers, he had no formal engineering training, but that didn't stop him from wanting to build his own aeroplane and forge a career in aviation, even though he would be almost twenty before he saw his first real plane. His mother claimed that when Bert was just five years old, he pointed at a bird in the sky and said he wanted to fly like that.

Born in Brisbane in 1866, Frances Bonney was aged twenty-five when she married a 36-year-old Prussian immigrant named John Hinkler in the nearby mining town of Gympie. Ten months later, on 8 December 1892, she gave birth to Herbert John Louis, who quickly became known as Bert. The couple settled into Woodbine Villa, a cottage in Gavan Street, North Bundaberg, where they raised Bert and the four children who followed: Beatrice (known as Mayme or May), John (otherwise known as Jack), George and Frances (who was called Queenie).

At the turn of the twentieth century, North Bundaberg (as it was then known) was a small settlement, with fewer than 1000 residents, and surrounded by sugar cane farms. Until the opening of a traffic bridge across the Burnett River in 1900, a pedestrian walkway along the railway bridge was the only link with the slightly larger village of South Bundaberg. In 1903, the year the Wright brothers took off, North Bundaberg had a sawmill, a sugar factory and distillery, five general stores, five hotels, two butchers' shops, a Methodist church and the Anglican equivalent, and a lock-up. The Hinkler children attended the local primary school, which had some 160 students on its roll, and went to the Anglican Sunday school.

Young Bert was short and slim, with large brown eyes in a round, inquisitive face shaded by dark hair. He did well at his studies and, despite his short stature, played in the school cricket and football teams. His inclination to be careful with his cash led to him being given the nickname of 'Spondulix' or 'Sponny', a slang term for money. After school, he worked part-time in a bicycle shop, and also had a vacation job at a photographic studio in Gympie, where his grandmother lived.

The Hinklers were a working-class family. His father, John, was an itinerant labourer, employed variously in the sawmill, at the foundry, on the railways, and on farms in the Bundaberg area. Known around town as 'Papa', the heavily bearded John Hinkler liked an afternoon drink at the Musgrave Hotel with his mates. Mrs Hinkler kept a couple of cows in a nearby paddock to provide milk, butter and cream for her growing family. The small timber house on Gavan Street featured a high-pointed corrugated iron roof and a low front verandah trimmed with iron lace and white lattice. A white picket fence bordered the grassy footpath next to the gravel road, and there was a woodshed out the back.

From an early age, there were signs that the Hinklers' eldest son had an inventive turn of mind that must have distinguished him from the other boys in his North Bundaberg schoolyard. 'He was always a boy for machinery, trying to make engines and boiler tubes,' his mother would later tell the *Brisbane Courier*. 'When he was 12 years old he installed electric lighting in every room [at Woodbine Villa]. He studied chemistry through his boyhood years. I can never forget the first time he tried it. He had four jars for the electric lighting, but they were not the right kind, and they were eaten away with the chemicals. He got others, and sent to Brisbane for globes, and he got some lovely ones.'[1]

In his mid teens, Hinkler began to cut snippets about aviation inventions and achievements from newspapers and magazines, and paste them into a school exercise book. Pride of place, across the two middle pages, went to a photo of Frenchman Louis Blériot's monoplane making the first flight across the English Channel, in July 1909.

Like many of his generation, Bert Hinkler left school as soon as he could, at the age of fourteen, which would doubtless have helped the family's stretched finances. He worked briefly as a newsboy at the local newspaper, then as a labourer at the nearby foundry, but his out-of-work hours were spent poring over aviation magazines and dreaming up ways of getting himself into the air. It was an obsession that was to dominate his life.

His first effort was not promising. Taking over the woodshed in the backyard, he developed what he called an 'aviette' – a pair of wings with arm sockets that slipped on like a coat. Once he'd donned the garment, young Sponny galloped flat out on his short legs across a paddock (possibly the foundry green near the family home), flapping his outstretched arms, hoping to generate enough lift to launch him into the air. If he didn't actually fall flat on his face, his idea did – amid laughter from his mates – and he quickly discarded it.

He moved on to something he'd seen in the aviation magazines: a glider – not one of those paper planes that schoolboys launch behind the teacher's back, or a flimsy balsa model with a wind-up propeller, but a full-size glider, one that might even carry a person through the air. Hinkler studied the drawings published in *The Aero* and similar magazines of the day, followed intently the movements of the slow-flapping flying foxes in the skies around his hometown, and lay for hours watching seagulls. 'He would make little models with wire and string,' his mother recalled, 'and pull them to pieces, and put them together again in the backyard.'[2]

Among the birds, he particularly liked the grace and power of the ibis, the long-legged wading bird with white plumage and curved black bill that nested nearby in large colonies. He decided the only way to learn the secrets of their seemingly effortless flight was to study the birds close up. So, long before anyone worried much about conservation and the environment, young Bert used his catapult to knock a few out of the sky.

'It seemed to me that the slower flying Ibis possessed all the secrets I needed and offered the safest line of research,' he would later reason in his unpublished memoir, *Eighteen Years of Flying: Dips into My Diary*. 'So [the] poor Ibis was stripped of everything but his chassis and wings, and was stretched out on a board to dry in the sub-tropical sun.'[3]

From the stiffened frame of the bird, Hinkler taught himself some of the rudiments of flight – 'as one begins his alphabet',[4] he wrote afterwards. Already he was showing signs of the intense single-mindedness that became a hallmark of his life in aviation.

He was not alone in his experimentation. Leonardo da Vinci had designed his winged Ornithopter on paper back in the fifteenth century, but it wasn't until the Montgolfier Brothers' development of hot air balloons 300 years later that a person was actually carried into the air. The nineteenth century saw the successful launch in Australia of Lawrence Hargrave's box kite, and a spate of international attempts to build large gliders of various sorts, including those by a German engineer, Otto Lilienthal. One commentator said that Lilienthal's success in making more than 2000 sustained and replicable glider flights in the early 1890s moved the idea of developing heavier-than-air craft from the province of 'dreamers and fools'[5] to a serious possibility. It may also have helped inspire Hinkler's boyhood experiments. Lilienthal died after a glider crash in 1896, but the Wright brothers readily acknowledged that his research and experiments on wing aerodynamics, published in *Birdflight as the Basis of Aviation*, helped them design the machine that amazed the world seven years later. In a parallel with Hinkler's early experiments with ibis, Wilbur Wright recognised the significance of wing warping by watching buzzards correct their lateral balance.

Young Hinkler wasn't fazed by the failures of these pioneers of flight, but stimulated by their successes. In 1911, the then eighteen-year-old enrolled in a correspondence course in aviation, and soon afterwards put together a full-size glider. His job at the local foundry gave him access to many of the materials he needed, and in his spare time he cast sockets for fitting the timber spars together, which were then covered in calico; the 'dope' needed to keep the calico taut he made from ordinary flour paste. Through trial and error, Hinkler and his mates – George Macklin, Charlie and Johnny Laffan, and Charlie Griffin – managed to launch his creation into the air at a nearby beach.

From Christmas 1911 onwards, Hinkler began work on a more substantial glider, putting the frame together under the mulberry tree in the backyard at Woodbine Villa. 'It is easy to put more tail on a diving or wobbling kite, but this glider business was no child's play,' he observed later.[6] His new craft measured 20 feet in length, and the front wing was 32 feet across. The undercarriage comprised two borrowed bicycle wheels. Bert recruited his brothers and sisters to help George, Charlie and the Laffan siblings in the support team, and with the aid of a horse and sulky, they trundled the contraption along the road to nearby Mon Repos Beach. Frances Hinkler, always one of her son's biggest supporters, went along to oversee the operation.

Today Mon Repos Beach is best known as the site of a significant turtle rookery, but on that day, to the amusement of some of the locals, Hinkler and his team experimented with projecting the glider into the air, pulling it across the dunes with guy ropes. Sometimes the air caught under the bleached calico wings and the craft rose briefly above the sandhills, and their hopes rose with it; more often, it struggled for lift, or wobbled briefly in the air before thumping back down. The team persisted, though, with Hinkler making adjustment after adjustment until at last it stayed aloft. But would it carry a man?

Hinkler wanted to give it a go.

There was no seat on the glider, so he fitted a plank lengthways, shaped like an ironing board, and strapped himself to it, face-down. His feet controlled a rocking pedal for the steering and, like Orville Wright, he used hand-held levers to manipulate the elevators he hoped would help the glider rise smoothly into the air. In this case, being short and slim was an asset.

The youthful team waited for the wind to come from the desired direction, their hearts doubtless beating a little faster as they prepared to launch their brother and friend. When the wind was right, they strained on the tow ropes. Slowly the frail craft lifted as they hauled it forward, then the ropes pulled taut. The team let go.

Moments later, the glider soared 30 feet into the air over the sands of Mon Repos, as graceful as the ibis that had helped shape its design. Strapped to the plank, Hinkler worked frantically on the controls and managed to keep the contraption airborne for a short time before it floated back to earth, bouncing to a stop on its thin wheels. He was ecstatic.

The *Bundaberg Mail* called him 'a local flying man'.[7] This was the first of many mentions Bert Hinkler would receive in the newspapers of the world over the next twenty years, although he came to develop a love–hate relationship with the press. Typically, what he remembered most of the experience on Mon Repos Beach that day was what he learned about lift and load balance.

* * *

Hinkler's success with the glider made him hanker to fly a powered aircraft. The only trouble was that there was no motor small enough to suit a glider, and he was sure no one in Australia at that time had an aeroplane engine anyway. Even if they had, how would he pay for it? He'd pasted an advertisement in his scrapbook for a British plane engine costing £125 – not the sort of money his family had readily available.

The first two powered aircraft in Australia – a Wright biplane and a Blériot monoplane – had arrived by ship in 1909. In December that year, George Taylor became the first Australian to make a 'heavier than air' flight, in a series of glider flights at Narrabeen, New South Wales.

During this period, there was a burst of aviation activity in the recently federated nation, including the establishment in Sydney of the Aerial League of Australia, in April 1909. The first powered flight in the country is thought to have taken place that December, in a Wright Flyer piloted by Colin Defries, who crashed after 100 metres at Sydney's Victoria Park Racecourse – reportedly while trying to grab his hat as it blew off his head. Yet the Aerial League wouldn't recognise Defries' attempt as an authentic powered flight because, they said, the plane was not sufficiently *controlled*.

Sources differ, but the first recognised powered flight in Australia was made in March 1910 either by Bill Wittber or Fred Custance at Bolivar, north of Adelaide, or by the world-renowned escapologist Harry Houdini, while on tour in Australia with his celebrated act. At Diggers Rest, 30 kilometres north-west of Melbourne, Houdini almost clipped a gum tree as he lifted his Voisin biplane off the ground, but he managed to make a circle of the paddock before gracefully bringing the plane in to land.

The following year, the Aerial League of Australia awarded the nation's first pilot's licence to a Sydney dentist, William E. Hart, who shortly afterwards set up an aviation school at Penrith, New South Wales. Hart faced challenges unknown to modern-day pilots, including crash-landing on the railway line near Mount Druitt with an overweight pupil, and being forced to pay compensation to a dairy farmer who sued him for stampeding the herd when his plane passed over. On another occasion, Hart landed at the Sydney Showground after a flight from Penrith and found himself dodging poles and hopping the plane over signboards, 'like a ride over hurdles'.[8]

To stimulate the local aviation industry, the Australian Government in 1910 offered £5000 for an Australian-made aircraft that could be used for military purposes. The successful machine had to fly at no less than 20 miles an hour, take off and land safely without special launching apparatus, and carry two people, along with enough fuel to allow it to remain aloft for at least five hours. Inventors from France, Britain, America, Switzerland and Russia, as well as Australia, rushed to submit designs. After considering the submissions, the government declined to award the prize because, it said, none of the designs was better than those being developed overseas. Taking their cue, in late 1910 the Blériot company in France sent Gaston Cugnet to demonstrate one of their aircraft in Australia, and the British and Colonial

Aeroplane Company despatched Joe Hammond and two Bristol Box Kites for the same purpose.

It is very likely that if he'd had the money, young Bert Hinkler would have been one of the entrants for the government's prize, but he was still in Bundaberg, by now working at the Millaquin sugar mill. His career direction was about to change, however, thanks to the arrival in Australia in 1912 of an American aviator, Arthur Burr ('Wizard') Stone.

Stone was one of an increasing number of fliers, often called 'barnstormers', who made a living by giving flying demonstrations, sometimes by competing in the air against a car around a racetrack, and drawing large crowds in the process. On occasions, these activities were supplemented with joy flights for paying passengers willing to take a chance in these new-fangled machines. And it was a chance – because the aircraft builders were still learning their trade, and the pilots were still learning how to control their pernickety charges, and crashes were common. In one incident, in November 1910, Gaston Cugnet reportedly hit a cow when landing his Blériot monoplane at Altona, near Melbourne. A month later, the same plane and pilot failed to clear a boundary fence on take-off at the Melbourne Cricket Ground and the aircraft ended up wrecked on a nearby tennis court.

Wizard Stone was a sort of early-days Evel Knievel, having already made a name for himself in the United States, first as a track cyclist, then a motorcycle track racer, and also as a motorcycle 'Globe of Death' rider. The latter involved Wizard riding inside a latticed steel cage, with his wife on the pillion, 'at a speed which rendered them almost invisible to the audience', according to a promotional leaflet.[9] He claimed to be the third person in the world after Wilbur and Orville Wright to fly a powered aircraft, and had been a test pilot in America, where he once fell from a plane into a lake from 600 feet.

In June 1912, Stone challenged dentist Hart to Australia's first air race, from Ascot in southern Sydney to Parramatta and return. Local knowledge prevailed when Stone lost his way and was forced to land. At the time, Hart held the Australian record for a long-distance flight – 47 miles, which he covered in fifty-five minutes. It was hardly a long flight in today's terms, but a significant feat in the days of unreliable aeroplanes and trial-and-error flying. In the previous sixteen years, almost 150 pilots or would-be pilots across the world had died, and 200 were injured. Those figures were to look miniscule just a couple of years later, when opposing pilots scrambled to knock each other out of the sky in the fierce battles of World War I.

In 1912, however, Australia was hardly prepared for war, let alone an aerial one, although the government's recent attempt to stimulate the local industry showed that it was at least aware of the deficiency. There were calls for Australia to be defended by a fleet of planes, with airstrips built at intervals along the national coastline – 'At least one thousand military aeroplanes could be equipped for practically the cost of one battleship,' one proponent claimed.[10] And this was a long time before Australia had a border protection policy.

Under pressure from the Aerial League, and after a visit in 1911 by Australia's Minister for Defence, Senator George Pearce, to the British aviation training facility at Brooklands, in the south of England, the federal government decided to establish a flying school within the Defence Department. The first course began in August 1914. This was the beginning of the Australian Flying Corps, which would later become the Royal Australian Air Force.

One army pilot's account of his early training underlines the primitiveness of both the machines and the instruction: 'The pupil leaned over and placed his hand over the instructor's on the top of the control column to feel how the plane moved up and down and balanced sideways. The horizon was our only guide as to whether we were flying straight and level or going up and down. We had no instruments to fly by, not even a compass, so we never went out of sight of the aerodrome.'[11]

For Hinkler, these developments were still to come, however, as he laboured away at the Millaquin sugar mill in Bundaberg. The highlight so far in 1912 had been the April launch of his glider, but, as he recorded later in *Eighteen Years of Flying*, 'It was not the kind of flight to which my mind aspired.'[12] He had been reading about international aviation pioneers such as A.V. Roe from Britain, the British pilot Gustav Hamel (who famously looped the loop fourteen times in the sky above King George V), and the Frenchman Henri Farman, 'all of whom had more than floated on air – they had been propelled through it,' Hinkler said, and nothing less would satisfy him. Given that the only planes he had seen to that time had been in magazines and newspapers, however, his prospects of going aloft in one seemed rather slim. 'I resigned myself to patience,' he said later, 'till resources and opportunity joined hands.'[13] That convergence would not be long in coming.

CHAPTER 2

The birdman and the Wizard

Two weeks before that Sydney air race with William Hart, Arthur Burr Stone had toured Queensland coastal towns as part of an entertainment troupe sponsored by a theatre entrepreneur, Philip Lytton. One of the stopover towns was Bundaberg, and it was there, in May 1912, that Stone lit the fuse that launched Bert Hinkler's aviation career.

After completing the midday to 8 pm shift at the Millaquin Sugar Mill, Hinkler led his mother Frances, brother George and sister Mayme past the band playing outside the theatre and along to the marquee where Stone's Blériot was on display. Excitedly he paid for the four tickets and led the group inside. It was the first time any of the Hinklers, along with most of the sugar town's 3000 residents, had ever seen an aeroplane.

No doubt Hinkler could feel his heart pattering. After all that reading, all that experimentation with gliders, here was a real flying machine with its own engine, and a proper seat for the pilot.

The sort that Louis Blériot had flown across the Channel. The crowd around Hinkler must have blurred into the background as he imagined himself in the cockpit.

When Bert came back to reality, Wizard Stone himself had appeared. Urged on by his mother, Hinkler self-consciously introduced himself and told Stone about the gliders he'd built. Realising Hinkler had a genuine interest in aviation and not just in the novelty of flying machines, Stone told the young Queenslander about the occasional instability of the Blériot caused by a problem with its wings.

The nineteen-year-old's eyes lit up. He knew how to fix the problem because only recently he'd been reading about it in an issue of his precious *Flight* magazine. Taking a deep breath, he nervously told Wizard of a report from England that the top wire stays for the wings needed to be almost as strong as the lower ones.

Stone, the experienced pilot and world traveller, looked the diminutive teenager up and down – at little over 5 feet 3 inches in height, Hinkler could never have been the most imposing of sights. No doubt Stone was wondering whether he should take notice of someone who until then had never seen a plane, let alone flown in one. But what did he have to lose? Next day, the American did as Hinkler suggested, and the problem was solved.

Impressed by the young man's technical knowledge and the fact that he had built two gliders (Bert probably didn't mention the aviette), Stone asked him if he'd be interested in travelling with him as his mechanic. 'It was as if heaven had opened its gates,' Hinkler later wrote.[1] For over five years he'd been teaching himself about the theory of aviation, and had applied it to his gliders. Arthur Burr Stone promised the next, and most exciting step: the chance to experience powered flight.

His mother wasn't as keen; she was happy to support her eldest son when he was building gliders to fly over the local beach, but wasn't so sure about his moving away to become involved in what she regarded as an unpredictable and often dangerous pursuit. For Hinkler, it was too good an opportunity to miss, however.

* * *

There seems to have been some uncertainty about when the mechanic's position with Wizard Stone would eventuate, so Hinkler initially headed to Brisbane, armed with references from leading Bundaberg citizens. He'd heard about the plan to form an Australian Army Aviation Corps and applied to join, complete with a recommendation from the commandant at Brisbane's Victoria Barracks. However, Cyril Brudenell Bingham White, the army's Director of Military Operations, said in reply that such a corps was only under consideration, and the regulations still had to be drafted. Notice of the corps' establishment would appear in the press, he added, and Mr Hinkler was welcome to apply then.

Mr Hinkler decided instead to take a job as a plumber's assistant with the Metropolitan Water Supply and Sewerage Board. He also joined the Queensland branch of the Aerial League of Australia.

Hinkler's move to Brisbane gave him an opportunity to see his future employer in action. A few days after their Bundaberg meeting, Wizard Stone was racing his plane against a car at Rockhampton's Callaghan Park racecourse when the Blériot plunged into a nearby cricket field. Stone managed to leap out before the crash, but the plane was extensively damaged and he was forced to cancel a performance in Brisbane planned for 6 June. The event was rescheduled for 6 July, and Hinkler was no doubt among the thousands of spectators at Brisbane's Exhibition Oval that day to see what the promoter promised would be 'sensational aerial manoeuvres' from the 'greatest of American Aviators'.[2] Stone thrilled the crowd with his flying but found the Exhibition ground too tight when he attempted to land afterwards. Coming in at a steep angle, the Blériot hit the ground hard, a wheel broke off, the propeller ploughed into the earth and the plane tipped on to its back. Stone staggered out, but sustained no serious injuries.

This was Hinkler's first experience of an aircraft crash at close hand, but one which he would become used to when he later started working with Stone. 'Aviation technique had not, on those days, reached its present pitch of perfection,' he later wrote in *Eighteen Years of Flying*, 'and my American idol had more than his share of ill luck.'[3]

For the moment, Hinkler stayed at his Brisbane job, and in August accepted an invitation to exhibit his second glider (described in the *Brisbane Courier* as 'an excellent specimen of workmanship'[4]) in the Aviation Court at the 1912 Brisbane Exhibition (the 'Ekka'), a state agricultural show. In the same week the Ekka was on, Wizard Stone came to Brisbane again, pitting his Blériot in a race against a Cadillac at Eagle Farm Racecourse. After almost two hours delay while the aircraft had starting problems, the car and plane unexpectedly went in opposite directions around the track. Although it was more a demonstration than a race, the crowd reckoned the admission price was worth it. There seems little doubt that Hinkler would have again been amongst the estimated 10,000 spectators. However, his days as a plumber's assistant were numbered. Two months later, he resigned from his Brisbane job, and headed to Melbourne to join Stone as a mechanic.

In those days there was hardly a dedicated airstrip in the country, so Stone had arranged to use the Melbourne Cricket Ground for his demonstration flights. The field that had already been a sporting venue for fifty years, and was to become an iconic site in Australian sport, was not a place of glory for Wizard Stone on this occasion. It was not 'Up there, Cazaly', in the manner of the football star who would later delight the fans, but a series of minor crashes as the American pilot struggled to keep his machine aloft.

Hinkler was kept busy continually rebuilding the plane. Rather than finding this dispiriting, the mechanic revelled in the challenge. 'The experience I gained then, with no specialised equipment, was of immense value to me,' he recalled later. 'How happy I was to find, in stripping the disabled Blériot, that my earlier ideas of construction in building my gliders had not been a serious departure from text-book rules.'[5] The experience forged a self-belief in Hinkler regarding his abilities as a mechanic and engineer that he took with him wherever he went. That self-belief and his strong determination to succeed were put to the test during his next trip with Arthur Burr Stone, to New Zealand, beginning in April 1913.

Their first engagement was at Auckland's Domain, where 11,000 people had paid to see Wizard's exploits, with reportedly a further 30,000 watching from outside the grounds. Paying customers and freeloaders alike were none too pleased when the aircraft made a forced landing after 400 yards and couldn't be repaired in time for another flight that day. The crowd rioted, and troops were called in to control the aggrieved mob.

Despite the hubbub, Hinkler wrote to his mother that he was 'having a lovely time', although he did have to sleep in the tent with the plane. He was learning a lot, he said, 'especially my way about the world'. Frances Hinkler was still not keen on his choice of career, and Bert assured her that Stone was the one doing all the flying. But her eldest son's ambition was clear: 'Hope Papa is still doing well and is pleased with my progress even though I'm not quite an aviator yet.'[6] He began to save towards his goal.

Undeterred by the experience at the Domain, Stone had found an Australian sponsor, Percy Cornwall, and a race was set up between Cornwall's racing car and the Blériot monoplane at Auckland's Alexandra Park Racecourse. In preparation for the big event, Cornwall wanted to know how fast he could take the bends on the track, and headed off on a practice run, Hinkler beside him with stopwatch in hand. Down the straight they roared, and into the first turn. As they rounded the bend at high speed, a tyre burst – the car skidded across the track and ploughed into the outside fence, scattering the rails. Hinkler was pulled from the wreck unconscious and rushed to hospital.

His left arm was almost severed at the shoulder, and there was talk of amputation. Good surgery and his own determination saved the limb, however, and just over a month later he rejoined Stone at Napier, on the east coast of New Zealand's North Island. Hinkler told his mother he was 'all strong and only for the mark on my arm would hardly feel anything had happened'. And his ambitions had only hardened: 'I am sure even after all my experience with Stone that I was on the right track with proper ideas and if I had enough money, I could have turned out an aeroplane as successful as any of the present day.'[7]

He was also keener than ever to qualify for his pilot's licence. Getting his mother on side was part of the plan. In the same letter from Napier, on 1 June, he hoped that 'your opinion has altered and you think aeroplanes can be handled in a safe way'.

What happened next was unlikely to have reassured her. Stone crashed the plane into a bank of willows at Napier, breaking his collarbone. Planned visits to Hastings and Wanganui were cancelled. This time there was no wizardry for pilot or mechanic, and they headed back to Australia, carrying a loss of £600 and damage to both aircraft and pilot.

Back in Sydney, Hinkler declared himself 'stoney-broke' but hopeful of four weeks' back pay. There was talk of rebuilding the Blériot and touring Western Australia, but Hinkler decided that the prospects of such a venture were slim, and he and Wizard agreed to part company. In a letter to his parents he made a half-hearted suggestion that he could come home for the cane crushing if needed – 'but I hardly fancy it'.[8]

He did make a brief visit to Bundaberg, but his mind was elsewhere, and he returned to Sydney to take up a job in the second half of 1913 at William E. Hart's new aeroplane works at Penrith. 'I was happy enough at work,' he later recalled, 'and never abandoned the hope that somebody would finance my desire to build an aeroplane of new type embodying the principles I had worked out in my glider, and others born of experience with the Blériot and Stone.'[9] It was a dream he never let go.

* * *

By this time, ten years after the Kitty Hawk lift-off, more than 2000 people across the world had some claim to calling themselves aviators. Planes could travel at over 125 miles an hour over distances exceeding 600 miles, and climb to 20,000 feet. Despite the numerous accidents, injuries and deaths, the appeal of flying was too compelling to resist, especially for those who, like Bert Hinkler, had already had a taste of it.

Much of the aviation development in the early years of the twentieth century took place in Europe, particularly in Germany, as well as in France, where pilots such as Louis Blériot, Gabriel Voisin and brothers Gaston and René Caudron thrilled the world with their spectacular feats. In 1913, Frenchman Roland Garros flew nonstop across the Mediterranean. English aviation gradually began to make a name for itself through the emergence of manufacturing companies such as Avro, Handley Page, Sopwith and Bristol – names that soon gained international renown. As a result, Britain became a magnet for Hinkler.

He didn't have enough money for the fare on a passenger liner, so he and Charlie Laffan, who'd helped Bert launch his gliders at Mon Repos Beach, decided they'd work their passage across. The first available ship, leaving in early January 1914, was a German tramp steamer, the SS *Alrich*, bound for Hamburg; if they could get that far, the two Queenslanders reasoned, it would be easy enough to make their way to England. Laffan already had experience as a fireman, but the ship's captain was reluctant to employ the short-of-stature Hinkler, until Charlie eventually convinced the skipper to take him too.

Hinkler had turned twenty-one in December. He didn't know it, but he'd now lived more than half his life. Even as he shovelled coal into the *Alrich*'s furnace, there were smouldering embers of ambition and discontent across Europe that would soon flare into the conflagration of World War I, a development that was to have immediate and significant consequences for the birdman from Bundaberg.

CHAPTER 3

Disturbing the air, Huns and other insects

After arriving in Hamburg a few weeks into 1914, Hinkler and Laffan made their way to the fishing port of Grimsby, on the north-east coast of England, reportedly with £2 between them. While Hinkler headed to London, Laffan was supposed to wait for him in Liverpool, but Charlie stayed in the Old Dart less than three days before boarding a ship back to Australia.

In London, Hinkler soon ferreted out a flying school, but his hopes of a quick route to his pilot's licence were dashed when he learnt the application fee: a steep £75. In dire need of funds, he secured a job with Sopwith Aviation at Kingston-upon-Thames in Surrey, to the south-west of the capital. The company had been founded in June 1912 by Tommy (later Sir Thomas) Sopwith, who was only a few years older than Hinkler, but a lot richer. Hinkler later explained how he'd gone about gaining employment at the Canbury Park Road site: 'I prowled around the drome at Kingston, sticky-beaking into this, that and the other, until at last

Tom Sopwith realised that it would be less trouble to find me a job in the factory than to hunt me off the premises day after day.'[1]

Hinkler earnestly told his parents that he'd be learning a trade he could use in Australia, even if he didn't learn to fly. 'It was only a position on the bench,' he admitted later, 'but I was among airmen and aeroplanes – that was sufficient.'[2] For the moment at least. Dreams of becoming a pilot and building his own plane were still bubbling in his head.

And it wasn't all work. Hinkler went to watch the Grand National steeplechase at Liverpool's Aintree Racecourse, where he was impressed by the size of the crowd – 'I don't know how many Bundabergs it takes to equal it,' he enthused in a letter home on 29 March. He was entertained too by the acts at the music halls, where 'the turns are about the same as Australia, but the theatres are fitted up properly nice and of course much larger'. In the same letter, he told his parents there hadn't been any more snow since his arrival in London, but he'd noticed it seemed to rain 'whenever it liked, not like in the land of the kangaroo where it gets hot and thunders for a day or two ahead'.[3]

Johnny Laffan, brother of Charlie, was on hand now to provide some company for Hinkler, having departed from Australia a week later than the other two. After a trip with Johnny to the seaside town of Brighton in Sussex, Hinkler told his mother that there was nothing much happening in the place while they were there, but he'd heard it was a different story in summer.

That particular summer, however, the threat of war overshadowed the pleasures of Brighton's grand ballroom and the attractions of holiday destinations across Europe. The assassination of Archduke Franz Ferdinand of Austria and his wife in Sarajevo in June 1914 was the trigger for a spate of military incursions that led to Britain declaring war on Germany and Austria-Hungary on 4 August.

Hinkler saw his chance, and in early September joined the Royal Naval Air Service (RNAS) in Britain as volunteer number 318, destined, he wrote later, 'to get far more flying experience than I had ever thought possible'.[4] His official service record listed him as 5 feet 3½ inches (1.61 metres) tall, with dark brown hair and grey eyes, and a scar on his left shoulder, the latter a legacy of his car crash in Auckland the year before.

The Royal Naval Air Service, previously the Naval Wing of the Royal Flying Corps (RFC), was formed in July 1914 with a fleet of seventy-eight aircraft. With the support of the First Lord of the Admiralty, Winston Churchill, the RNAS developed an offensive capability for the navy, while the Military Wing of the RFC concentrated on a reconnaissance role for the army. During the war, the Central Flying School at Upavon, Wiltshire, trained pilots and other aviation personnel from both the navy and the army.

As much as he enjoyed the training, Hinkler was surprised at being lined up and marched into class like a schoolboy. During his time at Upavon, he added a poignant note at the end of a letter, written to his mother in October 1914: 'Love to all and tell Pop he has not written me a line all the time I've been away, so I expect he doesn't care much.'[5] From the evidence available, it's difficult to comment on the nature of the relationship between John Hinkler and his eldest son. It is revealing that the correspondence between Bert and his family was mainly between him and his mother, Frances, and occasionally with his sisters, Mayme and Queenie.

* * *

Hinkler was initially classed as a leading mechanic/erector, and by the spring of 1915, he was training as an observer at Whitley Bay, in the north-eastern county of Northumberland. This involved accompanying a pilot in a two-seater plane and sketching the positions of trenches and other fortifications, which he found tricky even when not under battle conditions: 'Fair dincum it's fairly difficult at first, sketching from 5000 ft or so, but I am gradually acquiring this new art, and am beginning to fancy myself quite expert already.'[6]

They were long days – rising at 4.30 am for a morning patrol flight, followed by a full day's activities and an evening patrol. By the time the aircraft were fuelled, cleaned down and housed, it was close to 8 pm. Hinkler was an enthusiastic trainee, however, and in August was promoted to Petty Officer Mechanic.

Reminders of the fragility of their aircraft and their lives were never far away. One misty day, Hinkler and the pilot were returning to their base after a two-hour training flight when the motor failed, and the plane rapidly lost height. The pilot managed to put the aircraft into a glide towards the airstrip, but as he came in through a layer of fog to land, a high hedge loomed in front of them, and he was forced to quickly lift the nose. The plane immediately lost flying speed and plunged towards the ground.

Helpless in the front cockpit, Hinkler could do nothing but wait for the impact. 'Oh, those few moments were terrible,' he recalled in another letter home, 'and when the crash did come, the sudden stoppage was awful.' The undercarriage was ripped away, and the plane's nose buried itself in the earth. Hinkler was thrown forward, as bits of broken propeller and wood flew in all directions. Fortunately, both he and the pilot escaped with nothing more than a few scratches.

Hinkler saw the incident as simply an occupational hazard. 'Still of course in these days of war and strife, that is only a mere detail,' his letter continued, 'and will not hinder yours truly in the least from his ambition in the art of aviation.' He must have realised then how his mother might react to his account of the crash, judging by the addition of what he no doubt hoped was a reassurance: 'Now, please Mum, don't worry over the events I have chronicled this time, or I'll be sorry I have written too much about trifles. As I said at the beginning of this, all is well so that's good enough for anything.'[7]

It's hard to imagine that his words were enough to placate an anxious mother. By this time, his brother Jack, aged eighteen years and one month, had joined the Australian Army, so Frances Hinkler had two boys in the services to worry about.

* * *

On completion of his initial training, Hinkler was posted to the RNAS depot at White City, west London. In the early months of 1916 he was kept busy with squad drill and learning about air warfare. When he had a half day's leave, he sometimes visited Charles Grey, the former editor of the penny weekly aviation paper, *The Aero,* that Hinkler had subscribed to as a boy. Grey was now editor of *The Aeroplane* magazine, and Hinkler talked to him about ideas he had for inventions that might support the war effort.

One of his inventions was a dual control mechanism that allowed the gunner to take control of a plane if the pilot was put out of action. This notion impressed the authorities sufficiently for them to give Hinkler access to workshops and materials, making him 'as happy as a dog with two tails'[8] and bringing back memories of his days under the mulberry tree in the backyard at Bundaberg.

Although he didn't expect to get much for his invention, being an RNAS serviceman, neither did he plan to give it away for a pittance. 'Rest assured,' he wrote to his mother, 'your noble son has an eye to business as well as a heart for aviation.'[9] Even before the war ended, Hinkler applied for patents for the dual-control mechanism, in Canada as well as the United States, but he doesn't seem to have ever made money from it.

He also devised a lightweight improvement of an attachment to carry a plane's bomb-dropping equipment, a design that was passed on to the Admiralty, and Hinkler claimed he subsequently saw the same principle used throughout the service.

More bizarre was his idea for helping pilots unable to find their way back to their airfield after night-time skirmishes with Zeppelins – the inflated airships the Germans propelled silently across the Channel to bomb British cities in the middle years of the war. In March, Hinkler had explained his concept in yet another letter to the family:

> By my procedure the observer leaves the aeroplane per parachute, and on the way down fires special illuminated lights, which lighten up the country for miles, and so he can pick out the nearest and most suitable open field, and on reaching earth, he makes for it with all possible speed, and by the aid of a number of torches, which we have in use, he lights them and dots them round the border of the field, and the pilot is able to judge and land in the middle. Now isn't that some stunt?

To Hinkler's surprise, this particular 'stunt' had not been taken up, and he lamented to his mother: 'As I have often told you before, such progressive improvements when worked out by those in such a humble position as myself, generally receive no encouragement whatsoever.'[10]

* * *

In June 1916, Hinkler graduated from the RNAS air gunnery school at White City, and did so well he was recommended as a gunnery instructor, once he'd had more experience. This would have meant staying at the depot, however, and he was keen to complete his airborne gunnery practice at the Royal Naval Air Station at Eastchurch in Kent, because he knew that meant a greater chance of being sent to the war zone.

Shortly afterwards, he completed all the requirements, and to his delight was posted as a gunner (or, more correctly, gunlayer) to No. 3 Wing RNAS, based at Luxeuil-les-Bains near the town of Nancy in north-east France, not far from the German border. No. 3 Wing had been set up in June 1916 as part of a Franco–British force tasked with attacking industrial complexes around Essen and Dusseldorf in the western part of Germany. Some two years after he'd enlisted, Bert Hinkler was finally at war.

He was assigned as a gunner in a Sopwith 1½ Strutter, so-called because of the combination of long and short wooden struts supporting the biplane's upper wings. No. 3 Wing flew the aircraft in two configurations – as single-seater bombers and two-seater fighters. A special mounting allowed Hinkler and his fellow gunners to rapidly swivel and elevate the Lewis light machine gun fitted in the rear cockpit, and the 1½ Strutter design gave the gunlayer a wide field of fire. The front cockpit of the newer

Strutters was equipped with a Vickers machine gun, synchronised to enable the pilot to fire through the propeller, a development pioneered by the Germans.

Between July 1916 and April 1917, No. 3 Wing RNAS launched 18 raids into Germany and German-occupied territory. The laconic accounts of the action which Hinkler sent to his family are at odds with the mayhem happening around him as colleagues were killed, injured or captured through enemy action in the air, collisions and pilot error. In January 1917, by which time his unit had moved north to Ochey, closer to the town of Nancy and to the German border, he wrote to Queenie about a raid on the Saar Valley on the French–German border: 'We had a fine time, and so to speak the air seemed full of aircraft and exploding shells of aircraft. I must say Germany was well represented even on our side of the lines, too.' He told the thirteen-year-old how cold it was flying at 10,000 feet and higher, and added, 'One of our chaps had both hands frostbitten and perhaps you may not know, but the frostbitten part swells up the size of watermelons.'[11]

On 4 March, Hinkler was the gunlayer in a Strutter piloted by Flight Sub-lieutenant Charlie Pattison in a raid on German blast furnaces at Brebach in the Saar Valley. On arrival over the target, five enemy aircraft attacked their plane, and in the short skirmish that followed, Hinkler was sure he had downed one of them, but the 'kill' was unconfirmed. Their own fighter plane escaped unscathed, but as they headed back to Ochey after the raid, a German plane dogged them all the way and only fled when Pattison turned to engage it as they reached the Allied lines. As Hinkler had indicated earlier to Queenie, flying at high altitudes could also be a problem – in another raid on Brebach two weeks later, he and Pattison had to return to base early when the plane's oil pump froze.

Around this time, the work of No. 3 Wing began to wind down – crews were gradually transferred to Dunkerque to bolster the numbers in the Royal Flying Corps on the Western Front, and March saw the arrival at Ochey of twin-engined Handley Page bombers, heralding a new approach to strategic bombing. Hinkler stayed with the wing long enough, however, to take part in a raid on 14 April 1917 on the German city of Freiburg, an action initiated by the British Government in retaliation for the Germans' sinking of Allied hospital ships and their ill-treatment of Allied prisoners of war. The raid was launched from No. 3 Wing's previous base at Luxeuil-les-Bains in two waves, Flight A in the morning – which lost two planes to enemy fire – and Flight B, including Hinkler and Pattison's fighter, in the afternoon. The crews carried explanatory leaflets about the reason for the raid, which they were ordered to drop to the residents of Freiburg, along with the bombs.

Five miles north-west of Freiburg, Pattison sighted a fast-moving enemy plane attacking one of the other fighters in Flight B, and went to his colleague's aid. As they drew close, Hinkler let fly with the Lewis gun, and shells stuttered all along the fuselage of the German plane. The enemy fighter turned away towards the ground in a spinning nosedive that could have only one consequence. Hinkler and Pattison's elation over their success was cut short on the way back to base, however, when the Strutter's engine cut out seven miles from the Allied lines. Pattison managed to glide for two miles, which took them across the border, and they landed safely in a field in the area of the Vosges Mountains in the eastern tip of France.

In a subsequent letter to his parents, Hinkler said he'd been recommended for the French Croix de Guerre for his part in the Freiburg raid, but since No. 3 Wing had been disbanded immediately afterwards, he supposed the award was a 'washout'. He was right.

In any event, the 'success' of the raid was a moot point. According to the German War Office, the bombing of Freiburg was aimed at municipal buildings, and killed one soldier and ten civilians, and wounded twenty-seven other civilians, including children. The British Government faced hostile questioning in its own parliament about the raid, and the Germans protested in the American press.

With the dispersal of No. 3 Wing, Hinkler was posted to a Handley Page bomber squadron at the RNAS base at Dunkerque. Powered by two Rolls Royce engines, the Handley Page O/100 biplane was Britain's first heavy bomber, with a 100-foot wingspan, and a crew of three to five. It carried a bomb load to match its size. In a letter to Frances Hinkler for her 51st birthday in August 1917, her eldest son sent his good wishes and gave her an account of a night raid over Belgium in one of the big bombers: 'Around Ostende, Bruges and Ghent, the searchlights there are so enormous that it's impossible to count them, and they are tremendously powerful too. Naturally, the guns work in conjunction with the lights and when they get on to you, up come the shells.' As if this description wouldn't be alarming enough for his intended reader, he continued: 'They also have a[n] idea which . . . consists of a train of magnesium lights on a line. We call them "Bubbly", these strings of lights, about 20 or 30 or so at a time. If a machine gets caught in them, they are supposed to set it on fire, but luckily none has yet taken effect.'[12]

In just one fortnight in August 1917 Hinkler took part in eleven raids. No doubt Frances Hinkler was relieved that none of the 'Bubbly' lights managed to set fire to Bert's plane, but her heart must have stood still as she read his letters.

Frances missed her eldest son very much, and in one letter asked whether he could come home for a visit. 'Getting leave to Australia is impossible,' he replied. 'If I had started life on a different plane and joined the Service with a commission, there's no telling what strings you can pull. But as it is, on the lower deck you're not supposed to have nerves, brains or anything requiring talent. Simply, so to speak, one horse in a team,' he added bitterly.[13]

After three years in the RNAS, Hinkler was frustrated in the bomber squadron with his slow progress towards becoming an aviator, when an opportunity came out of the blue to fly in a two-seater again. Flight Sub-lieutenant Charles Beverly Sproatt, one of numerous Canadian officers in the RNAS, had complained to the commanding officer of No. 5 Naval Squadron at their Petite-Synthe base in western France about the lack of competent air gunners. The CO said there were some RNAS aircrew waiting at nearby coastal Dunkerque for transport back to England, and suggested Sproatt go over and check them out. The Canadian wasn't too impressed with what he saw, except for Petty Officer Hinkler, although he didn't know why. After checking Hinkler's record, Sproatt called him in.

'I asked him if he wanted to become a gunlayer if I trained him,' Sproatt recalled later, 'and I added I would crucify him if he ever let me down.'[14]

Given his experience to that time, Hinkler might have been taken aback by the Canadian's tone, but he knew it meant more time in the cockpit, even if it was not as the pilot, and he quickly accepted the invitation. Practising next day at the firing range with a Lewis gun, Hinkler struggled with jammed cartridges, and by the time he'd finished his hands were raw. Next morning, Sproatt noticed the Australian take something out of his pocket when a gun jammed, and use it to clear the cartridge. Overnight, the enterprising gunlayer had fashioned a steel extractor to deal with the jams, and Sproatt immediately arranged for the armourers to make more of the devices, for all the gunners.

For the rest of the year Hinkler joined Sproatt at No. 5 Naval Squadron as a gunlayer in one of the recently arrived Airco DH.4s, two-seater bombers designed by Geoffrey de Havilland for daylight raids. The DH.4 had similar armaments to the 1½ Strutter – a Vickers machine gun up front for the pilot, and a Lewis gun on what was known as a Scarff ring mounting in the rear cockpit. Hinkler proved himself an asset in the new team, and even invented a platform and harness that enabled him to continue firing the Lewis gun while the aircraft was upside down.

He still had his heart set on qualifying for his pilot's licence, though, and sometimes Sproatt let him have unofficial practice in the two-seater on the way home after a raid. Bert's wrote excitedly to his mother about the experience:

> On the way back I take a turn at flying the bus! Of course, flying is not a hard job, but it's practice, so as to do all movements of the control to a nicety . . . Well, even the first time I wasn't so bad, and my pilot complimented me, and now I'm going very strong and I'm beginning to fancy myself, dinkum.[15]

On 15 September, just after Hinkler had been awarded his Good Conduct Badge, 1st class, he and Sproatt in their DH.4 made a direct hit on a German light cruiser, which was subsequently confirmed as having exploded and sunk. In October, Hinkler was promoted to the rank of warrant officer, and a month later was awarded the Distinguished Service Medal. Sproatt received the Distinguished Service Cross for his part in the sinking.

Despite the medal and the opportunity to fly, Hinkler had given up hope of qualifying for a pilot's licence in the RNAS, and was thinking of trying for a civilian aviator's ticket when he was next in London on leave. If he qualified in England as a pilot, he told his mother, he might join the Australian Flying Corps after the war.

His chance to obtain the licence he hungered for came unexpectedly. Before Sub-lieutenant Sproatt returned to Canada on leave at the end of 1917, he recommended Hinkler for pilot training. After interviewing Hinkler and examining his air log, the Air Board accepted the recommendation and sent him for training immediately. By 1 January 1918, he was at the Royal Naval College at Greenwich, south-east of London, having been reclassified as a probationary flying officer in the RNAS.

Hinkler wrote to thank Sproatt for recommending him. Recalling the unsanctioned practice he'd had on the way back from raids over enemy territory, Hinkler gleefully told his benefactor, 'I am now in a favourable position to wobble the joystick, officially, in a plane of my own.'[16]

After further training, Hinkler was ready for the series of tests he had to pass to qualify for a pilot's licence. The former gunlayer had to satisfy the examiners that he could make forced landings, take pictures of a target with a gun camera, fly in formation for three hours, climb to 10,000 feet, do a spin, a loop and a roll, and fly in cloud. His plane for the test was a Sopwith Camel, a single-seat biplane made by the same aviation company that had employed him when he first arrived in England. The aircraft's name came from the hump in front of the pilot's cockpit which housed twin Vickers machine guns. Although notoriously difficult for novice pilots, the Camel was an instant success from the time it was introduced to the Western Front in mid 1917. Hinkler would hardly have been classed as a novice, despite his lack of hours in control of a plane, and he had no trouble passing the tests. Finally, in July 1918, he was a qualified pilot. Shortly afterwards, he wrote to his parents:

> I think if I remember rightly, my parting words with my dear Pater were to the effect that when I next put foot in Woodbine Villa . . . I should only [do so] as a real dincum Pilot. Now I have part of that assertion possible, I only wait the opportunity to complete it. I shall be terribly disappointed if I do not have a machine to fly back to Bundy on, as I am quite ready to give you an air show overhead before I land. And I think, after all, this [is] the only way to return to justify my hopes – and yours.[17]

His words are an indication of the strong family ties and obligations Hinkler still felt. It had been six years since he'd left home as a raw youth, virtually penniless, but full of enthusiasm and optimism, chafing for an opportunity in aviation. Now he was a 'real' pilot, following the trail left by his pre-war heroes of flight, his aviation experience unexpectedly broadened by the outbreak of war. Now that he was qualified, he had already begun to test himself and his plane, as he told his parents in the same letter:

> I climbed to about 4000 feet and tried what is known as a 'roll'. That is, while flying along level you suddenly roll the machine over sideways till you are upside down and then round straight again. My first try, oh lor, the machine spun round nearly twice before I realized what was happening. But before long I could manage the manoeuvre quite good, so good that I must have done it over a dozen times.[18]

When he landed, the instructor and his fellow pupils thanked him for the demonstration.

Despite his latent skill, Hinkler had to complete training at No. 2 School of Aerial Fighting and Gunnery at Marske, Yorkshire, before he was fully accredited. In April, the RNAS had been merged with the army's Royal Flying Corps to form the Royal Air Force, and in August 1918 Hinkler was granted a temporary commission as an RAF second lieutenant. Once again he was ready to go to war, but this time as a pilot.

* * *

While Bert Hinkler was enjoying his *Boy's Own* adventures in the Royal Naval Air Service, younger brother Jack was not doing so well. After signing up with the army, and training in Australia, he arrived in England in October 1916 and was shipped across to the 52nd Battalion in northern France a week before Christmas. The 52nd Battalion, part of the 4th Australian Division, had been formed in Egypt in March 1916 from experienced Australian soldiers and new recruits, and arrived in France in June that year. Three months later, the battalion lost half its fighting strength in the battle for Mouquet Farm in north-east France, and when Jack arrived among the reinforcements, the remaining troops were struggling through the bleak winter of 1916–17, alternating between front line duty, and training and labouring behind the lines. There are stories of water that winter being delivered to the troops as blocks of ice, of diggers waking after a few hours sleep to find their eyelids frozen shut, and ice forming around the rim of a boiling cup of tea after it was carried twenty paces. During those miserable months more than 20,000 Australians were evacuated with exhaustion, frostbite, or trench foot caused by standing for long periods in ankle-deep water.

Like many of his mates, Jack Hinkler suffered bouts of severe illness over the two years he spent on the Western Front. In 1917, the 52nd Battalion was involved in several major battles – at Noreuil in the northern tip of France in April, in the Ypres area of west Belgium from the middle of the year, and in the repulse of a concerted German offensive against the Allies in October. The battalion had significant victories in April 1918 in battles fought around the northern French towns of Dernancourt and Villers-Bretonneux, but with debilitating troop losses.

Jack was fortunate to escape the enemy's bullets and shrapnel, but his war record shows he was ill in hospital in France in January, June and October 1917. Each time he returned to the battalion.

In March the following year he was diagnosed with trench fever, an illness spread by fleas, which sent the troops reeling and caused their legs to buckle under them. Shipped to England for treatment, Jack was back on the Western Front by August 1918, only to become affected by one of the most insidious weapons of World War I – mustard gas, resulting in his return to an English hospital that October. With the declaration of the Armistice a month later, he wasn't posted back to the front, and in March 1919 was on a ship to Australia.

While his experiences in France were particularly unfortunate for Jack, they did have an unexpected and longstanding benefit for his older brother. The details are sketchy, but it seems Bert went to see Jacky (as he often referred to him in his letters) during one of the latter's hospital stays in 1917, as any good brother would. And working in the hospital was an English nurse by the name of Hannah Jarvis – or 'Nance', as she preferred to be called. Born in Sheffield, Yorkshire, the brown-haired, brown-eyed Nance was around thirty-six years old at the time, twelve years older (and a couple of inches taller) than Hinkler.

Neither of these differences seemed to matter, however, because in December 1917, banns of marriage were read in St Giles' Church, Camberwell, in south London. The two had apparently fallen in love and decided to wed after a brief courtship – a phenomenon not unknown in wartime, when life could be short and the future uncertain. Yet there was a serious glitch. Nance and Hinkler wanted to be married in the Church of England, but it was forbidden at that time for the clergy to perform marriages for anyone who was divorced and whose spouse was still alive, as this was considered adultery. Nance Jarvis was not only divorced – or perhaps no more than separated from her husband – but she had a daughter, Maida.

There may also have been legal impediments, hinted at in later correspondence between Hinkler and Nance. In any event, there was no wedding, but the relationship continued.

* * *

In the northern summer of 1918, newly commissioned Second Lieutenant Hinkler was sent to join No. 28 Royal Air Force Squadron in Italy. At the outbreak of hostilities, Italy had been a member of the alliance with Germany and Austria-Hungary, but was persuaded to join the war in 1915 on the side of the Triple Entente – Britain, France and Russia. 28 Squadron had arrived in Italy late in 1917 as part of an expeditionary force to bolster the Italian troops, who had been continually pushed back by Austro–Hungarian forces.

Equipped with Sopwith Camels, the squadron's initial role was to provide bomber escorts but as the tide of war turned against the enemy, the fighter threat disappeared, and 28 Squadron transformed itself into a fighter-bomber role. The motto of the squadron is *Quicquid agas age* ('Whatsoever you may do, do'), a maxim Hinkler might have taken for himself. When he arrived, the squadron was short of Camels, and the newcomer was apparently allocated a less-powerful Sopwith Pup. He reportedly managed to keep up with his faster-flying colleagues, however, by carefully retuning the engine and polishing the plane's exterior. If this story is true, the allocation of that aircraft may have only been for initial training, however, since he clocked up only 10 hours in the Pup.

By this time the Austro-Hungarian forces were in full flight, and in three months over the summer of 1918, No. 28 Squadron downed 53 enemy planes. That autumn, in a postcard to one of his sisters (the remnant insufficient to identify whether it was Mayme or Queenie), Hinkler described his role in the air:

> [T]he birds of prey have been rather busy. The last couple of days we have been disturbing the air, Huns, and other insects, practically from daybreak till dusk . . . This blessed war is making me a cold-blooded murderer – well that's how I feel since the last few days. We go over low, flying at about 100 feet, bombing and machine-gunning the enemy's transport and

> whatever of him we can find. Most of the roads back of his lines are crowded as he is moving back, retreating as fast as he can go. And it is our bloody duty to shoot him down not only in tens but hundreds.

It seems the elation Hinkler had felt in the raids over France and Belgium had given way to fatigue with the war. He could see the end was in sight, however, telling his sister in the same postcard how he felt coming back from one of the raids: 'I nearly went crazy with a peculiar joyful feeling. Flying just over the tips of the small trees over our newly regained ground . . . I waved to the troops still advancing, and they waved and cheered back. The war was going along splendid.'[19]

Not long afterwards, on 11 November, World War I was over. It had given Hinkler one of his most sought-after goals – his pilot's licence – and also brought him considerable flying experience as well as opportunities to use his inventive brain. During his war service, he took part in 122 flights over enemy territory, including 36 bombing raids, and as a gunner, shot down four enemy planes. Despite the misgivings he voiced to his sister when he was in Italy, he later described his time in the RNAS and RAF as 'the wonderful experiences of a Great Service', and one of the proposed chapter titles in his unfinished memoirs is 'Wartime Experiences (many excellent)'.[20]

Those experiences convinced Hinkler more than ever that there was a great future for aviation, a future in which he could play a part. Since he'd joined the RNAS in September 1914, he'd discovered that not only did he have outstanding aeronautical and mechanical skills and an innate understanding of flying, but that as a pilot he enjoyed his time in the air so much that he hardly wanted to come down. A month before the Armistice, in response to a query from May about his flying, he told her it was going 'absolutely glorious' and of the 'infinite joy' he felt when playing hide and seek among the clouds with another pilot. He was also looking ahead. 'Sometime in the future, wars finished, home again etc., etc., when the sky contains such glorious clouds floating about, I must take you around,' he wrote. 'Shooting past, just skimming over the top, and then banking over to the vertical, rounding some monstrous cloud pillar; and then diving right thru the middle. Oh, it's fine sport, and I'm sure you'll find no little enjoyment.'[21]

Hinkler was in love with flying.

* * *

28 Squadron would not finally go home until February, but at war's end Hinkler was keen to secure his aviation future as soon as possible. He wasn't the only one, of course. On both sides of the brutal conflict, the realisation that aircraft brought a new, mobile dimension to battle had seen a rapid increase in the number of pilots trained to fly the flimsy machines. While the death rate among wartime pilots was high, the declaration of the armistice meant the demobilisation of hundreds of them. Some, such as Henri Biard, a wartime flying instructor who later became a friend of Hinkler, had already seen what was coming. 'We realised quite well that peace-time would produce a glut of flyers,' Biard wrote in 1934, 'made ready before their time for a non-airminded world, and that there would certainly only be flying jobs in civilian life for a meagre margin of us at most.'[22]

Bert Hinkler decided he didn't want to be part of the 'meagre margin'. Less than a fortnight after the Armistice, he applied with his CO's support for a commission in the Australian Flying Corps, as he'd promised his mother. From its small-scale beginnings in 1914 at the Central Flying School, Point Cook, with two instructors and five aircraft, the AFC had expanded considerably during the war. It had seen action in 1915 in Persia (now Iran) and the following year a squadron was sent to the Middle East, with a further three squadrons formed to fight on the Western Front from late 1917. At the end of the war, it was less than two and a half years from being rebranded as the Royal Australian Air Force.

Hinkler reasoned that with his four years of training and operational duties in the RNAS and the RAF, the Australian Flying Corps would welcome him with open arms. In his letter of application, he mentioned his early gliders, summarised his rise through the ranks since the war began, and explained that he'd had 150 hours experience as an observer, and 100 hours as a pilot. In addition to the time he'd spent in a Sopwith Camel with 28 Squadron, he said he'd also flown three other types of plane while under instruction – a DH.6, an Avro [presumably the wartime 504 trainer], and a Sopwith Pup. When the reply came, no doubt he eagerly ripped open the envelope. His jaw would have dropped, however, when he learnt that only graduates of the Royal Military College of Australia could join the AFC. Service in the RAF didn't count.

Initially he wasn't sure what else to do. He had just turned twenty-six, and knew he was about to be spat out of the war machine, along with the hundreds of thousands of other soldiers, sailors and aircrew who'd survived. What's more, he would be back to where he'd been when he first arrived in London – unemployed and underfunded. Except that this time he had his pilot's ticket and some flying experience.

Convinced his immediate aviation future lay in England, Hinkler decided not to return to Australia by ship with the many thousands of his countrymen who'd been fighting in Europe, brother Jack among them. Not that he didn't want to get back to Australia. It had been close to seven years since he'd left Woodbine Villa, and when he'd qualified as a pilot six months earlier, he'd told his parents he'd be very disappointed if he didn't have a machine 'to fly back to Bundy on'. That chance came out of the blue.

CHAPTER 4

'Get a room ready and air my pyjamas'

When Hinkler opened his copy of *Flight* magazine for 27 March 1919, he might have sat bolt upright and shouted, 'Yes!' For there on page 406 was the report of an announcement by the Australian Prime Minister, William (Billy) Hughes, in Paris for the post-war peace talks, that the Australian Government would offer a £10,000 prize to the first aircrew to fly from England to Australia. The feat had never before been achieved in the short history of aviation, and what's more, the prize was open only to Australians.

This was beyond anything Hinkler had dreamed of. Not only would such an opportunity mean he could honour his promise of returning to Australia by plane, but the government would reward him generously for doing so if he was the first to make the crossing. Even before the announcement, he'd been talking to his previous employer, Sopwith Aviation, about the possibility of using one of their Camels for such a venture. He'd tested out with the company some of his notions about what might be required for a long-distance flight, such as increasing the engine size and fuel capacity. 'Up till then, no one had projected any such flight,' he explained to the Brisbane *Daily Mail* a decade later. 'For a long distance flight – any flight – aeroplanes were looked on as rather dangerous things to monkey with.'[1]

Sopwith didn't think the Camel was up to long-distance flights, however, and suggested an alternative: the Dove, a new civilian aircraft with a top speed of 100 miles an hour, developed from the successful wartime Pup. The Dove was a two-seater, but Sopwith were so taken with the idea of pioneering long-distance flying that they sacrificed the passenger seat in Hinkler's plane for extra fuel tanks. When he took delivery in late April 1919, he described it in a letter to his parents as a 'grand little machine, single seater, 80 horsepower and capacity for ten hours continuous flight'.[2]

Hinkler had already worked out a schedule for a flight to Australia: pre-dawn rises and flying by compass in stages of at least 1000 miles a day, with afternoon landings to avoid becoming lost at night, and to give him time to check the engine thoroughly. By that schedule he'd be in Darwin in eight days, Bundaberg in ten and Sydney on the eleventh day. What a whirlwind trip that would be in a little plane – but since no one had ever tried it, there was no benchmark.

Earlier, he'd sought financial support for his proposed trip from the Queensland Agent-General in London. No doubt inundated with all sorts of requests from the masses of demobilised Queensland servicemen (and a small number of women) looking for opportunities in a world still recovering from the devastation of war, the Agent-General gave Hinkler his good wishes, but no money. The pilot shared his disgust in a letter to his parents:

'Oh, Queensland is a fine country to belong to, but if you want a hand, try somewhere else.'[3]

So when the £10,000 prize was announced, Hinkler thought his troubles were over. He knew other Australian wartime pilots would be interested, but he had a plane and a plan, and was ready to go. With British civilian pilot's licence number 48 in his pocket, Hinkler tried out the Dove over south-east England, found it 'satisfactory in every way', and prepared for a departure on Wednesday, 6 May 1919. 'We filled out Form Z211 or whatever it was,' he recalled later, 'and waited for the word "Go".'

His one concern was that he wouldn't actually own the plane, since Sopwith had requested guarantees he felt he was not in a position to give. And he certainly didn't have the money to buy the Dove outright, either. 'I thought and thought, lying awake, going over the chances of persuading people to back me.'[4]

* * *

The wartime exploitation of aviation for purely military purposes had meant that long-distance flying had been neglected, and post-war financial incentives were seen as a way of opening up international routes. Before the war, London's *Daily Mail* had offered £1000 for the first person to fly across the English Channel, a prize won in 1909 by Louis Blériot, Hinkler's boyhood hero. Ten years later, the *Daily Mail* restated its pre-war offer of £10,000 for the first successful non-stop flight across the Atlantic Ocean, in either direction. The Australian Government's promise of a similar reward for an England–Australia flight came shortly after the *Mail*'s announcement, and the South African government made another £10,000 challenge, this time for the first successful passage by air from London to the Cape of Good Hope.

Some young men who'd learnt to fly in wartime adopted other aerial pursuits, taking advantage of the cheap planes to try to earn a living as barnstormers. Reflecting an increase in crowd-pleasing sensationalism since the pre-war antics of Wizard Stone and others, these flyers travelled across the country performing various daredevil stunts, which often featured a crew-member wing-walking or hanging by his teeth from a trapeze dangling below the aircraft. 'Aerialists' played tennis or shot at targets while standing on the wing, or jumped from one plane to another in mid-air. Usually operating from a local field for a day or two before moving on, the pilots also offered joy flights to anyone looking for a quick thrill. In America, the barnstorming 'season' extended from early spring until after the harvest and the autumn county fairs. The phenomenon was short-lived – by the later 1920s, after numerous crashes, deaths and injuries, legislation was introduced in the US and elsewhere to control the barnstormers' antics and protect their adventurous passengers. Not many made good money from the venture.

* * *

Hinkler's plan for an early-May departure turned out to be optimistic. The idea for the air race had come from Australian government ministers, who had proposed it to Hughes while he was in France. When the Australian Prime Minister received a positive response to the notion from the British authorities, who would have to oversee the preliminary arrangements, he publicly announced the offer. But the Australian Government had yet to finalise the details. So, around the date Hinkler had planned to leave for Australia, representatives of the Australian High Commission in London, the British Air Ministry and the

Royal Aero Club established a preliminary set of conditions: the competition was open only to Australians in British-made seaplanes, flying-boats or aeroplanes, and the flight had to be completed within 720 hours (that is, thirty days) of take-off, and before 31 December 1920. The organisers announced that the full set of conditions would follow shortly.

Hinkler was not impressed by the delay – 'd___ rotten' is how he described it to his parents on 7 May, the closest he ever came to swearing in his letters home. Adding that he was 'just about fed up',[5] Bert explained that the reason for his having not written to them for a while was that he'd been expecting to land in front of the family home on Gavan Street before any letter had time to arrive.

Tired of waiting, he proposed to the Sopwith executives that he head off to Australia anyway, but they insisted he had to fly as part of the competition because of the publicity it would generate for the company. Hinkler's thinking at the time came to be a hallmark of his later flights: 'The publicity value of a secret flight in a Dove, had it been successful, would have made all the other machines look like also-rans.'[6] Despite his frustration at the administrative delay, he fancied his chances for the prize, ending his letter to Frances and John Hinkler with a special request: 'Oh, say, will you get a room ready and air my pyjamas.'[7]

The subsequent additional stipulations for the England–Australia race stated that competitors had to take off from either Hounslow Heath Aerodrome, west of London, or Calshot Seaplane Station, on the Hampshire coast; there would be checkpoints at Alexandria in Egypt and at Singapore; and the finishing point would be 'in the neighbourhood of'[8] Port Darwin, in the Northern Territory. Furthermore, the Royal Aero Club would administer the rules and oversee all flights for the prize, at a cost of £100 per entry.

In addition, the authorities were worried about the possible lack of infrastructure for an England–Australia flight, and duly commissioned surveys of various landing grounds en route. The total distance via Africa and Asia was around 10,000 miles, and the number of 'hops' would be determined by the amount of fuel carried. Pilots would have to find their way to numerous landing sites along the way, in areas that were foreign to them in more ways than one. Up to that time, nothing had been organised along the route, not even fuel stocks, particularly between India and Australia.

Finding the scattered airstrips wasn't a concern for Hinkler. While waiting for the final authorisation of his race entry, he'd designed a 'Navigation Board' – a device with three arms and two protractors that would enable him to calculate the corrections he needed to make for wind direction and strength in order to stay on track. A London firm was so impressed, they made up a prototype for him to take on the flight, although he never mentioned using the device on any of his subsequent flights.

In mid June, while the surveys of landing fields were under way, Captain John Alcock and Lieutenant Arthur Whitten Brown picked up the *Daily Mail* prize for the Atlantic crossing, flying from Newfoundland to Ireland in sixteen hours. It was the world's first significant long-distance flight, and the involvement of newspapers ensured the public became excited about such ventures.

Finalising the England-to-Australia route took longer than expected, and in the meantime, the Australian Government decided to amend the conditions. All competing aircraft now had to have a minimum flying capacity of 500 miles and carry a competent navigator; entrants had to provide proof that they had arranged for spare parts and fuel to be available at marked landing places; and no start was to take place before 8 September 1919.

By August, when Hinkler was formally demobbed from the RAF, there were four other entries for the England–Australia competition alongside his own. As frustrated as he was by the decision to delay the start date, Hinkler was also wary of the motives of the Australian Prime Minister. 'I . . . learned where you got that cock-and-bull story of all the competitors getting full pay and being sent to a School of Aeronautics for navigation etc,' he told his parents. 'Take it from me, Hughes with his big, Welsh noisy mouth is feeding you unsuspecting people the cheapest sort of claptrap possible. He has already got more than his share of advertisement out of the belated flight.'[9]

Hinkler waited impatiently for 8 September to roll around. His plane was ready, his schedule was fixed, and his fuel supplies were organised.

The go-ahead never came. The Royal Aero Club became concerned about Hinkler's plan to make the flight solo, and in a small, single-engined plane. Although the rules said that the mandatory navigator could also be the pilot, all the other entries had at least two crew-members, and the other single-engined planes had more power than the Dove. The club decided the venture was too risky for Hinkler and his aircraft, particularly the final stage across the Timor Sea, and so rejected his entry. After waiting months for a start, Bert Hinkler was out of the race.

As if to make the rejection complete, Sopwith withdrew its offer of a plane, re-converted the Dove to its traditional two-seater form, and sold it to a waiting customer. Sopwith Aviation was among those aircraft manufacturers struggling for survival in the post-war transition to a mainly civilian market. The company tried to adapt its designs, without much success, so turned to working with another firm to produce motorcycles, and also diversified into car and engine manufacturing. The attempts at diversification were not enough to keep the company in the black, however, especially when it seemed His Majesty's Government was likely to demand payment of excess war-profits duty. Less than two years after the end of World War I, and just eight since its first factory opened on Canbury Park Road in Kingston-upon-Thames, Tommy Sopwith's eponymous aviation company closed its doors for good.

So, two-thirds of the way through 1919, Hinkler had no job, little money, and his big chance to fly home to Australia with the promise of a $10,000 prize had evaporated. Despite these obstacles, he was anxious to assure his parents that he was determined to fly to Australia *sometime*. 'Much as I want to return and renew my nearest and dearest home-ties (and at present I feel sort of being in exile), I feel most uncomfortable to return in the simple orthodox way, after such an impression has been circulated thru the very unimportant fact of having made an entry for the flight.' At the end of the letter, he made another plaintive reference to his father: 'Tell me how Papa is doing these days. I am afraid he will, after all, be very disappointed over his eldest son. I suppose he will write me a line or two one of these days. I do hope so.'[10]

Not that it would've been any consolation to Hinkler, but another Australian entrant, Charles Kingsford Smith, who had registered as a co-pilot in a converted Blackburn Kangaroo, was replaced in his team, apparently because executives at Blackburn Aircraft were concerned about Smithy's reputation for barnstorming, ignoring regulations, and possibly even stretching things a little with insurance claims for air crashes.

* * *

Whether Hinkler would have succeeded on a flight to Australia in the Dove is speculation, but the race didn't turn out well for the majority of the six teams whose entries were accepted. The first to take off, on 21 October 1919, were Captain George Matthews and his mechanic, Sergeant Thomas Kay, in their specially designed Sopwith Wallaby. Although the prize conditions stipulated that the flight had to be completed within thirty days, on 2 December, fifty-three days after departure, Matthews and Kay were still waltzing around Vienna while their aircraft was being repaired. They never did reach Australia on that flight. But at least they were alive.

Another pair was not so fortunate. Lieutenant Roger Douglas, MC, with Lieutenant J.S.L. Ross as navigator, left London's Hounslow Heath aerodrome late in the morning of 13 November. Their single-engined Alliance P.2 Seabird had a 450-horsepower motor – considerably more powerful than the unit Hinkler would have used in his Sopwith Dove. Within minutes of take-off, Douglas and Ross were in trouble. As it headed south towards the Channel, the Alliance failed to gain height, and before it had cleared suburban London, the plane suddenly came out of the clouds in a spin and nose-dived into the ground. Douglas died on impact, and Ross a few minutes later. A subsequent inquiry found that the controls and engine were in good order, and returned a verdict of accidental death.

In the Blackburn Kangaroo team, Smithy was replaced by the distinguished Captain Hubert Wilkins, MC and Bar, who joined Lieutenants Val Rendle, Reg Williams and Garnsey Potts. Leaving England on 21 November, they were forced to land in France for repairs. They carried on until engine problems forced them down again, this time on the island of Crete, where they reportedly crashed into the fence of a mental hospital. No one was injured, but the damage was enough to persuade them to abandon their flight to Australia.

The team that left next covered about the same distance as those in the Kangaroo, but with tragic results. Captain Cedric Howell and air mechanic Henry Fraser departed from Hounslow in their Martinsyde on 5 December, bound for Melbourne. Four days later, after an overnight stop in Taranto, Italy, they set off for Athens; four days after that, the Lloyd shipping company representative on the Greek island of Corfu sent a telegram: 'Information just received British aircraft wrecked off St. George's Bay, Corfu, December 10. No hope of survivors.'[11] Howell died in the plane; Fraser's body was never found.

Only two of the original six teams reached Australia. Lieutenants Ray Parer and John McIntosh took off on 8 January 1920 in a de Havilland DH.9, and eventually reached their destination 206 days later. Not only were they outside the time limit, but the prize had already been won. Two brothers from South Australia, Keith and Ross Smith, with Wally Shiers and Jim Bennett as mechanics, left England in a twin-engined Vickers Vimy bomber on 12 November 1919. When they flew triumphantly into Port Darwin on 10 December, after battling blinding monsoon rains, thunderstorms, strong cross-winds and boggy airstrips, they were two days inside the limit. The Australian Government not only awarded the four-man team the £10,000 prize, but the two Smith brothers received knighthoods.

* * *

Fed up with the treatment he'd received since being discharged from the Royal Air Force, Hinkler considered leaving Britain. He regarded the country as a major centre of aviation development, but post-war he was less enamoured of it as a place to live, describing it as 'a country of strikes and high prices'.[12] He bought a motorbike to avoid the high public transport costs in London, which, he noted, were about double their pre-war levels.

These were not the only changes Hinkler came back to. After the war, entrepreneurs in London embraced the lighter mood of the nation by opening new venues for dancing and jazz. The inner city took on a more modern feel. On the outskirts, new estates sprang up to cater for those seeking a less closed-in lifestyle, followed by electric railways to enable them to commute to their jobs in the city, where a new generation of financial and industrial companies – firms like ICI and British Petroleum – were beginning to establish their power bases. The wireless radio became the technological marvel of the decade. Light industry, increasingly electric-powered and automated, also began to move to outer London, and the opening of the King George V docks in 1921 ensured the city continued as an important centre of world trade. By this time, inner London had close to four-and-a-half million residents, with another three million in the surrounding areas.

For Hinkler, the aviator, London was not the place to be, however. He came up with the idea of setting up a photographic business in Halifax, Nova Scotia, with a Canadian he'd met in the RAF. The venture would be based around a miniature camera that Hinkler had invented during the long wait for the England–Australia flight competition to be finalised. The trigger for this invention had been an unsuccessful request to borrow a camera from a company in England, which he'd thought would be good publicity for them when he flew to Australia – 'but, no, I was turned down there as well'.[13] The camera used movie film, and Hinkler enlarged the tiny negatives with a specially developed processing box, which he said enabled him to print photographs more quickly and easily than through any existing method. He claimed the camera could produce photos for less than a penny each, and that it was possible to take out the exposed portion of film without exposing the rest.

Hinkler and Nance Jarvis were probably living together at this time, having maintained their relationship, but there is no record of what she thought of his proposal to relocate to Canada, or if Bert even considered her to be part of it. However, whether because of Nance or for some other reason, Hinkler decided against the move. He now had to compete with the masses of other demobilised wartime pilots looking for a flying job in England, and he knew it wouldn't be easy.

CHAPTER 5

A pretty battered old Baby

If he was to find an aviation job in England, Hinkler needed to convince a prospective employer that he had more to offer than the standard combination of a pilot's licence and flying experience. Armed with a letter of introduction from his friend Charles Grey, editor of *The Aeroplane*, Hinkler went to see Roy Chadwick, the newly appointed chief designer with a major aircraft firm, A.V. Roe and Company, at Hamble, near the Hampshire port of Southampton. He also took with him the miniature camera he'd invented.

The designer, just a few months younger than his visitor, was immediately intrigued. Chadwick later recalled of this initial meeting:

> It was apparent even during our first talk that Hinkler was an outstanding personality. He had done a lot of flying in the Great War, but in addition he had a very fertile and inventive brain . . . I was so impressed with our talk, and Hinkler's

> obviously detailed knowledge of aircraft construction and engine installations, which was exceptional in a war-time pilot, that I persuaded our Board to engage him as a Test Pilot.[1]

This was a coup for Hinkler, and a big boost to his confidence after the rejection of his entry in the air race. Alliott Verdon Roe claimed to be the first Englishman to make a powered flight (in 1908) and had formed the company in Lancashire with his brother Humphrey in 1910. The Avro brand quickly became famous, especially in World War I through the Avro 504 biplane, which became the training aircraft for British pilots, and was also used by the Australian Flying Corps. Roy Chadwick is considered one of the greatest aviation designers of the twentieth century, responsible for such iconic planes as the Avro Lancaster bomber and later the Avro Vulcan, with its radical delta-shaped wings.

Still unmarried, Hinkler and Nance moved into a two-storey apartment in a suburb of Southampton, close to the Avro works, and the first of several rented properties over the next few years. Nance wasn't in paid employment, but she was a keen gardener, dressmaker and tennis player. Where her daughter, Maida, was at this time is not clear, because there is no mention of her in accounts of the couple's life in Southampton. By this time Nancy was almost forty years old, and there was no suggestion that she and Bert would produce offspring.

Once he'd settled into his new job, Hinkler told Chadwick of his ambition to fly to Australia. The designer later said that although most of the aviators pioneering long-distance air routes were financially supported in various ways, Hinkler wanted to make the flight on his own, without being obliged to anyone in any way.

The Australian still favoured a single-engined plane for the journey. He particularly liked the Avro 534, a new single-seater biplane designed by Roy Chadwick and intended for the civilian recreational market. With wire bracing and a canvas-covered wooden frame, the 534 was built around a modified 35-horsepower motor manufactured by the Green Engine Company. Initially known as the Avro Popular, the prototype crashed due to pilot error, but the engine and other parts salvaged from the wreck contributed to the building of a second one, which came to be called the Avro Baby. In June 1919, carrying British registration G-EACQ, the reconstructed plane and its pilot managed to win the handicap section of the Aerial Derby at Hendon. The route comprised two circuits around outer London, each of about 100 miles, beginning and ending at Hendon aerodrome.

The following January, a mid-winter mishap by Chadwick led to Hinkler acquiring the Avro Baby for himself. Chadwick was flying G-EACQ over Hamble when he blacked out momentarily in the freezing air, and lost control of the plane, which dropped suddenly into a clump of trees in a walled garden below. The pilot escaped without serious injury, but the biplane's nose splintered back as far as the cockpit, and the top wings collapsed on to the lower ones. Once again the aircraft was rebuilt, using the engine and parts of the airframe. During the reconstruction, Hinkler suggested modifications to increase the Avro Baby's range. By the time the rebuild was finished, he had convinced himself that this was plane that could take him to Australia.

He negotiated with Alliott Roe to buy the plane for a nominal sum, convincing his employer of the publicity value of a successful flight to Australia. 'A pretty battered old Baby it was,' Hinkler later told Brisbane's *Daily Mail*, 'dissipated beyond its years.'[2] Just as teenagers become excited about their cars, however, Hinkler must have been delighted to own his first aeroplane. And with his experience, he didn't need P-plates.

Designed for owner–pilots willing and able to do their own maintenance, the Avro Baby could be spun, looped and rolled with ease, had exceptional stability, and was claimed to be cheaper to buy and easier to maintain than a motor car of the time. The *Illustrated London News* described it as 'a type of pigmy aeroplane, costing £500'.[3] It had a top speed of 90 miles an hour, cruised at 60–70, and 25 gallons of petrol would fill its tank. The Baby still had an open cockpit, whereas more expensive designs were closing them in.

Hinkler fitted the Avro with a bigger fuel tank and the various gadgets he'd designed for long-distance flying, and carefully checked the engine and fuel consumption. By April 1920 he was ready to go. Then more delays: a mechanic starting the plane ripped a piece off the propeller, which had to be patched, and an engine part malfunctioned and had to be overhauled. Hinkler was beside himself: 'I began to think I would get a start in the year 1960, with my beard trailing in the wind as I took off.'[4]

The problems were not only mechanical. The Air Ministry had banned flying between Palestine and India because of anti-British feeling among Arabs in the Middle East, who, it was claimed, were likely to execute anybody who fell into their hands. But Hinkler reckoned he'd waited long enough, and decided to make a start for Australia.

* * *

Apparently with A.V. Roe and Company's blessing, on 31 May 1920, just before dawn on a hard, cold morning, Hinkler lifted the little white Avro Baby into the air from Croydon Aerodrome, London's first official public airport. Croydon had been open just two months by this point and had a road through the middle of it, where an official with a red flag (later replaced by a gate) halted road traffic while planes took off. Although no reporter was present to observe the take-off, a hallmark also of Hinkler's later long-distance flights, he had kept the press informed. As a result, on 2 June the Rockhampton *Morning Bulletin* reported Hinkler's departure two days earlier and that he was en route to Australia. It added that he did not expect to get beyond Europe for the moment, however, because of unrest in the Middle East. The *Bulletin* suggested Hinkler's biggest challenge was crossing large stretches of water in the single-engined Avro, 'but he is a bit of a sport and believes he will reach Australia eventually'.[5]

The flight did not start well. Once across the Channel, the Queenslander found himself in cloud so thick he couldn't identify any landmarks in France. 'It was compass or *fini*,' as he later put it.[6] Forced to fly low to the ground, Hinkler hedge-hopped until he saw the Eiffel Tower – then knew he was over Paris.

Regaining his bearings, he headed south-east into better weather. Soon the Alps lay dead ahead, almost completely covered in thick cloud. He could see ugly black peaks poking through, and decided to take the Avro up to 10,000 feet, which put a lot of pressure on the 35-horsepower engine.

He checked his instruments. The oil pressure was down – a leak! He knew it would be another hour before he cleared the Italian side of the Alps. The best thing to do was to drop the engine back, to conserve oil, and hope to reach a landing ground. But that would mean losing height, dropping into the cloud, and he would have no idea how close he was to the peaks below . . .

He decided to push on at the same height and speed, hoping that there was enough oil to get him through. Anxiously he nursed the Avro above the cloudbank, knowing there was no chance of setting down safely if the plane lost power. His eyes stayed glued to the oil pressure gauge and the altimeter. The minutes ticked by.

Suddenly the country opened up before him like a patchwork quilt, and he found himself in clear skies over north-west Italy. He spotted the city of Turin ahead, and no doubt his shoulders relaxed.

A short while later he nestled the Avro down on the city's airstrip. He'd been in the air for nine-and-a-half hours and had covered some 700 miles, doing a very economical 30 miles to the gallon, and had fuel to spare. The Italian airport staff laughed at how little petrol he needed to refill his tank.

The oil leak had been caused by a faulty valve, and the setback forced him to rethink his schedule. Hinkler was reluctant to abandon the trip to Australia, but commonsense told him that the combination of a need to ensure his engine was in perfect order and the unstable political situation in the Middle East meant it would be foolish to go on. He decided to return to England.

He took almost a week to fly back, first heading to Rome, his original day-one destination, then hopping through towns in Italy and France. Even that had its moments. While heading from Rome to Nice, he found himself in what he described as a 'blue bowl': blue sky above, blue sea beneath, and a blue haze all around that limited visibility to a few miles.[7] He had no idea where he was, and had only a small-scale map to guide him. Next minute, one of the valves cut out completely, and he was forced to fly the plane on only three cylinders. Unable to escape the blue haze, and with the Mediterranean somewhere below, he decided to head north, and eventually crossed the Italian coast near Genoa.

Following the coast westwards, he recognised Monte Carlo from photographs he'd seen in *The Aeroplane*. From there, Hinkler continued to follow the coast, his engine's three remaining cylinders sufficient to carry him on to Nice, from where he eventually flew back to Hamble. Soon afterwards, he called at the Green Engine Company to discuss the valve problem.

Outwardly, the trip was hardly a success. On his long-awaited flight to Australia, Hinkler didn't even reach Rome. It was his first long-distance flight in the tiny Avro, and the difficulties he faced over the Alps may have shown him the immensity of the task he had set himself, and the limitations of his plane.

There was subsequent speculation about whether Bert Hinkler seriously planned to go to Australia on this occasion. Certainly, he didn't seem very well prepared for the trip – 'I would hate to tell you what my finances were,' he admitted years later.[8] From the newspaper reports of his take-off, it seems he also knew in advance of the British ban on flying over parts of the Middle East, so that shouldn't have been a surprise to him when he reached Rome. Afterwards he assured his parents that he had set off 'in the direction of' Australia, but hadn't alerted them beforehand because he wanted to surprise them.[9]

* * *

The apparent anticlimax turned out to be anything but. Hinkler might not have reached his homeland, but when the English aviation world heard of his London-to-Turin flight, they fell over themselves with superlatives. The editor of *Flight* magazine declared that, on the face of it, a nonstop flight over that distance in such a small plane, *and* over the Alps, seemed an impossibility, but he acknowledged that with extra fuel and a following wind it could be done. The editor ranked Hinkler's flight 'among the finest in the history of aviation', adding: 'One scarcely knows which to admire most, the machine, the engine, or the pluck, determination, and endurance of the pilot.'[10] The year before, the Smith brothers, while on their way to Australia and knighthoods, had taken two days to reach Rome in their Vickers Vimy – which had twenty times the horsepower and fuel capacity of the Avro 534.

Ranking the flight among the finest in aviation history was some claim, considering the developments that had taken place in the seventeen years since Orville and Wilbur Wright had launched the Flyer. But it came from a respected authority, and soon the feat was widely recognised. So much so that, with this single flight, Hinkler truly arrived on the British aviation scene. The Royal Aero Club awarded him the Britannia Trophy, its annual award for the most meritorious performance by a British aviator. In July 1920, the plane went on display on the Avro stand at an aviation show at London's Olympia exhibition hall; and late that same month, Hinkler flew it in an air race in England, the fifth Aerial Derby.

Introduced in Europe before World War I, air races were a popular form of public entertainment, as well as an opportunity for manufacturers to show off their products. Pilots competed against each other in time trials and navigation competitions around courses sometimes as restricted as a car racing circuit and occasionally across several countries. In England, bookmakers took bets on the results. On this occasion at Hendon, only nine of the fourteen starters finished the race, with the winner coming in at odds of 100 to 6. Hinkler was second favourite at 15 to 2, and his 'battered old Baby' came in second on handicap behind a brand-new Avro Baby – the official entry from A.V. Roe and Company. Several bookies betting on the event decamped before the (un)lucky punters could collect their winnings.

Funds, as always, were very much on Hinkler's mind. 'Aviation is, of course, by no means a poor man's hobby,' he'd written to his parents early in July, 'and while as you know, I'll never give in to your objections to flying, still, before long, if something serious doesn't happen, I'm afraid I shall have to try and forget about such a glorious pursuit.'[11] Given his single-minded quest for a career in aviation since boyhood, the likelihood that John and Frances Hinkler's eldest child would give up at this point, at the age of twenty-seven, must have been remote. After all, he was working at an aircraft company as a test pilot, he had a plane of his own, and he'd had his first taste of long-distance success.

Over the next few months, Hinkler consolidated his position at A.V. Roe. After the aviation show, Captain Harold Hamersley, the company's chief test pilot, asked him to take the latest Baby – the Avro 543, a two-seater variant of the Avro 534, with a 60-horsepower Cirrus 1 engine – for its initial test flight. All went well, and shortly afterwards, Roy Chadwick persuaded Hinkler to take him up on a second flight, which the designer used to help settle any nerves he had about flying again, after his earlier crash. The flight was so successful that the two stayed in the air longer than usual for a test flight, and between them took the new aircraft up to 11,000 feet – a considerable achievement for a small plane not long off the assembly line.

Hinkler became a regular visitor to the Chadwick family home, and impressed the designer's teenage sister, May, who later recalled: 'He was a man whom you did not meet without realizing that here was someone special – mainly because he was so direct . . . He was a most natural man, with no "side" or affectation. He did not smile a great deal, and yet he had a quiet charm.'[12] Over the years that Hinkler worked at A.V. Roe and Company, he and Nance became close friends with Roy Chadwick and his wife, Mary.

Even while he was extending his skills at Hamble, Hinkler's ambition was still to fly to Australia. He hoped his camera invention might raise the necessary funds, but business was not brisk. It brought in some money, but he admitted that selling a commercial product was unlikely to make his fortune.

The very next year, he finally did return to Bundaberg, but not exactly in the way he'd hoped.

CHAPTER 6

A black future or glorious prospects?

As Hinkler strode up the gangplank of the Blue Funnel liner *Ascanius* in Glasgow on a raw January day in 1921, he should have been in high spirits. He was leaving the sharp iciness of a British winter to visit the sunny, temperate shores of his native Australia, having decided that the only way in the short term to fulfil his pledge to see his parents was to travel by ship.

His promise that he would perform some aerial stunts over the family home and roll his plane up to the front door wasn't forgotten, either. A.V. Roe and Company had given him leave to make the trip, and G-EACQ was packed into two crates in the ship's hold, to be reassembled once he reached Sydney. He also had in his mind a vague plan to make a separate, spectacular flight in his homeland that might bring him publicity and perhaps garner support for a solo England–Australia effort.

Another reason for Hinkler's return to the country of his birth was to apply for an Imperial Service Grant – a war gratuity of £50 per year of service, payable to Australians who'd served in any of the British services, provided they returned home by mid 1920. However, there were exceptions for Australians who'd been overseas before the outbreak of war, and Hinkler hoped the authorities would consider what he regarded as his special circumstances.

Instead of being excited and optimistic about the opportunities and possibilities ahead, however, Hinkler was anxious, concerned about his relationship with Nance and uncertain about his future. As the tugs nudged the *Ascanius* along the River Clyde towards the open sea, one can imagine him standing on the deck against the rail, his gloved hands in his jacket pockets and his shoulders shrugged against the cold, staring unseeingly at the passing docks.

When he'd said goodbye to Nance, she was in bed, suffering from an illness of which one of the apparent side effects was her hair falling out. That wasn't the only reason she wasn't with him. The former nurse had made it clear on several occasions that she didn't want to go to 'bally Orstrayler',[1] whereas he still entertained the possibility of moving back to Australia if he could find employment there.

The *Ascanius* would take seven weeks to reach Sydney, and Hinkler wrote to Nance almost every day, telling her how much he loved her and asking after her health. Keen to show how much he would enjoy a more settled life with her, Bert suggested that on his return they could perhaps sing duets or learn the latest dances together. He groped for ideas that might please her: 'I must take up something to practise. Something that will give us pleasure and [be] of some benefit to us. The fiddle perhaps? Or the piano?'[2] Hinkler also encouraged Nance to socialise with people in their district, but hoped she didn't go to the Tuesday-night social occasions at the nearby village of Hamble.

'It seems – as I suppose with all one-horse villages – to be a bed of scandal,' he wrote.[3]

As the steamship headed down the west coast of Africa, three weeks out from Glasgow, Hinkler knew there was only one more port of call before the long trip eastwards across the Indian Ocean. 'If I don't receive news at Capetown from my Beloved about her health,' he told her on 18 February, 'I will have been living – nay – existing in ignorance for over a month and a half, or about seven weeks, or about 42 days, or about 1030 hours or about 61,800 minutes, or about 3,708,000 seconds . . .'[4]

At the end of a day spent sightseeing in Cape Town and taking photos with his miniature camera, he returned expectantly to the ship and checked through the mail. There was nothing from Nance. He immediately dashed off a letter.

'Say Nance, can you realize my extreme disappointment today when after searching the plentiful mail in the rack I was to find I drew a blank,' he lamented. 'No, nothing at all. I still exist in ignorance of my Beloved's condition.'[5] All he could do, he added, was head for the bar and drown his sorrows.

Hinkler's anxiety about Nance's health turned out to be a mask for a much greater worry. As the *Ascanius* ploughed eastwards towards Australia, five weeks after he'd left Glasgow, he finally put into words something that must have been gnawing away at him throughout the voyage: 'Sweetheart, do you know how I felt when you asked me a certain question which cut me like a knife to bleed the heart? Painfully, you asked me on the morning of Friday Jan 28th 1921 whether I intended to come back to you.'

Adding to the poignancy, the question had come during their final moments together, just a day before the ship's departure. 'Here am I loving my Sweetheart with all my life, every fibre of my body vibrating to hers,' his letter continued, 'and thinking that she loved me just as warmly in return, to have such a query thrown in my face, so to speak.'[6] Hinkler went on at length, assuring her of his love, and insisting that he didn't understand why she had lost confidence in their relationship.

Nance Jarvis was forty years old, and the couple had been together for just over three years. In response to her question about whether he would be coming back to her, Hinkler had a proposition:

> Sweetheart my Own, I am going to make your happiness complete by making, as soon as I return, very special arrangements for a certain day. The reason that it has been postponed so far, my Love, you and I, my Darling, understand each other there, but now I want to have your happiness complete, and to seal our love I promise you after my return, it's on the top of our wonderful future program.[7]

Nance might well have considered this an obliquely worded proposal of marriage. Although they couldn't be married in the Church of England, it would have been possible to have had a civil ceremony in a government registry office, assuming that Nance was free to marry by this time.

It would be another week before the *Ascanius* touched port again and he could post the letter. The next day, he wrote again from the ship to reassure her of the strength of their relationship: 'How peculiar and wonderful the heart singles out just one and will not be satisfied or even consoled by any other.'[8]

At the same time, another important question was weighing on Hinkler's mind. Namely, what to do with the rest of his life.

He had the test pilot job to go back to, but he hankered to do something for himself, preferably in a business that would make use of his abilities as a mechanic and pilot. At the back of his mind, he still clung to the notion of building his own plane. The main problem, as ever, was that setting up in business required financial support, and that was an area he struggled with for most of his life.

Being on the *Ascanius* for weeks on end gave Hinkler time to consider various possibilities, and the range of suggestions he sent to Nance indicates just how uncertain about his future he was during this period. A week into the voyage he'd written: 'I've been thinking that for our happiness, pleasure and benefit that, if I am able to pull as much out of Aviation as possible for the coming year or so, and then fix up a large homestead near one of the large towns in Australia, with a good field adjoining and a small 2-seater bus [plane], we ought to be able to maintain ourselves very comfortable.'[9] In another letter he promised he'd teach her to swim once they were living in Sydney. He seems to have forgotten then that Nance had told him she didn't want to go to 'bally Orstrayler', and none of his later proposals accord with the life of domesticity in England he suggested in earlier letters to her.

The longer that Hinkler was at sea, the more diverse became the job options he considered, and the further they were from aviation. After the ship left Cape Town, he met a mining executive who enthused about the industrial opportunities available in South Africa and invited him to visit the mines on his way back. Hinkler interpreted this as a job offer and wrote excitedly to Nance about the possibility. A few days later, he fell into conversation with an Australian farmer and became captivated by a completely different venture – setting up a pig farm and bacon factory.

Sea voyages are traditionally times for relaxing, clearing the head and seeing things in greater perspective, away from the hustle and bustle of everyday life; in Bert Hinkler's case, he seems to have become more and more confused about what he should do. 'Perhaps it must be the effect of this rotten voyage, but at times I feel absolutely miserable, and afraid of the future; it all seems so black,' he confided to Nance as the ship neared Australia. 'And then at other times when I think of the various possibilities, I feel really excited at the glorious prospects.'[10]

It was in these two minds that Hinkler scuttled down the gang-plank when the SS *Ascanius* arrived in Sydney on Friday, 18 March, glad to be out of the small cabin he'd shared with two other men on the voyage. A news reporter later commented that Hinkler's record-creating London to Turin flight and his second place in the 1920 Aerial Derby should have brought Australia's leading newspapermen scurrying down to the wharf as soon as they spotted his name on the ship's passenger list. He was not yet a big enough news story, however, although it was something he was working on.

* * *

The next few days were busy ones. He met up with his friend, Edward Hart, editor of the Australian aviation magazine, *Aircraft*, and made contact with Harry Broadsmith, who'd come out from England to set up an Avro agency in Australia. Broadsmith's firm, the Australian Aircraft and Engineering Company, had a display at the Royal Easter Show, which had just begun, and Hinkler did not need much persuasion to exhibit the Baby at the company's stand, just inside the main entrance gates.

The Queenslander was delighted to find that many people in Australia were aware of his record-breaking flight to Turin.

For some years, in fact, newspapers across the nation, and particularly in Bundaberg, had been reporting on the wartime exploits of Herbert Hinkler, DSM, and his activities since. This was thanks mostly to his mother, who acted like his press agent in Australia, sending copies of his letters to the *Brisbane Courier* (later the *Courier-Mail*) and other newspapers for publication.

* * *

Hinkler was still unsure where he should head on his proposed long-distance flight. During the voyage, he'd considered Brisbane to Melbourne; another possibility was Sydney to Adelaide, from there to Hobart, and then back to Sydney. 'If you don't mind having a look at the map of Australia,' he'd written to Nance from the ship, 'you'll see that makes a triangular course, and of course connecting up the capitals would get into the limelight more . . .'[11] While he pondered, he made time to submit his delayed application on 23 March for an Imperial Service Grant. He had served, he wrote, for four years and 345 days, and his repatriation had been deferred to enable him to undertake further training in aircraft construction with A.V. Roe and Company. By this time it had been seven years since he'd last been in Australia, and just over 18 months since his demobilisation. The Department of Defence clerk took the completed form from him, glanced through it, and told Bert he didn't like his chances.

By the time the Easter Show was over, Hinkler had decided which way he would go. Not to Brisbane or Melbourne, nor the triangular route via Adelaide – but straight to Bundaberg.

He set off in the Avro Baby from Sydney early on Monday, 11 April, from an airstrip deserted except for a sleepy night-watchman, and without alerting the media. Tracking initially to north-western New South Wales, he was forced to drop from 6000 to 3000 feet over Glen Innes to avoid a heavy cloud build-up, but the weather was clear as he crossed the Queensland border in airspace that had probably never seen a plane. Hinkler was struck by the extent of the rugged border ranges and the forests stretching ahead of him. It was a far cry from the 'green and shaded lanes'[12] of England he was used to flying over, and he suddenly felt very lonely.

After pushing north-east for a couple of hours against a light breeze, his mood lightened significantly when he saw the distinctive patchwork of red soil and green canefields around Bundaberg, and the two bridges across the Burnett River, like giant staples linking the north and south of the town. As he circled, he could see a crowd of enthusiastic locals who'd assembled for the occasion, no doubt alerted by his mother. John Hinkler had been having a drink downtown when he heard the noise of the plane, and had scurried across the bridge to be on hand to welcome his son. Now in his mid sixties, Papa Hinkler had not been in good health, and whatever impression his eldest son had received from his father's lack of letters, both would be very pleased to see each other.

Hinkler landed on the foundry green in North Bundaberg, close to his old workplace, and only a stone's throw from Woodbine Villa. But he didn't stop there. He nudged the Avro across the edge of the field, and with a stream of excited citizens trailing behind, bumped the plane gently along Gavan Street, until he saw the white picket fence and the pointed iron roof of the house where he'd grown up. He switched off the motor and clambered out, to be met by his joyful family.

Frances Hinkler later told a reporter, 'When he left home as a lad in 1913 . . . he made a promise to himself that he would fly to my home. He said, "Look here, Mum and Pop, the next time you see me is when I come flying home." I said, "What do you want to go flying home from England for? Couldn't you bring the 'plane to Sydney and fly from there? As long as you fly in Australia I am satisfied." Well, that is what he did.'[13]

Since leaving Sydney that morning, Hinkler had been in the air for nine hours, about the same time as his London–Turin flight, and he and the Avro Baby had covered 700 miles, which was a new national record. He sent a telegram to the Vacuum Oil Company in Sydney, one of his sponsors: '700 miles of perfect lubrication effected by one gallon of Mobiloil, BB.'[14] As he'd hoped, the flight received wide newspaper coverage in Australia. He told a bemused reporter that he'd made the flight 'to save the rail fare',[15] and that the trip had cost him only £3 10s for 20 gallons of petrol and a small amount for oil. It was this sort of laconic remark, along with his tenacity and aviation skills, that came to endear Bert Hinkler to the Australian public.

* * *

At the time of Hinkler's flight to Bundaberg, Australian domestic aviation was in its infancy. As in Britain, World War I had shown many of those serving in the armed forces the potential of aircraft, and some military-trained pilots returned to Australia eager to establish civil aviation. Although the planes that were available were mostly unsuited for the purpose because of their high operating costs and limited space for passengers, by 1919 there was enough private interest in flying to sustain branches of the Australian Aero Club in six states. The club was initiated in 1914 by the small group of young officers at the newly established Central Flying School at Point Cook, who wanted to promote the cause of aviation and also affiliate with the influential Royal

Aero Club in Britain. The outbreak of war interrupted the club's development, but when peace returned, so did the enthusiasm for promoting aviation.

Following his championing of the England–Australia air race, Prime Minister Billy Hughes declared himself a 'fanatic' in his belief in aviation. Under Hughes's stewardship, Australia was an inaugural signatory to an international convention for regulating aerial navigation, designed to protect national airspace and ensure pilots were licensed; the agreement had the added benefit of controlling the sometimes reckless activities of freelancers like the barnstormers. In 1920 the Australian Government set up a Civil Aviation Branch within the Department of Defence and earmarked £100,000 for the encouragement of civil aviation. The following year, when Hinkler returned home with the Avro Baby, was also the year that Sydney and Melbourne airports opened for business.

Early in 1922, the first domestic air route was established in Western Australia, from Geraldton to Derby, operated by Western Australia Airways, with Charles Kingsford Smith as one of its pilots. Later that year, the Queensland and Northern Territory Aerial Service (Qantas), headquartered in Longreach, central Queensland, inaugurated its domestic outback service. Over the next few years, regular services commenced in most states, and by the 1930s international airlines were beginning to join the dots across much of the globe.

For most Australians in 1921, however, the sight of an aeroplane was a rare event, and over the next couple of weeks Hinkler gave a lot of his time to the people of Bundaberg and the neighbouring towns, thanks to an arrangement with the *Bundaberg Mail* newspaper. Armed with copies of the *Mail*, bundles of advertising leaflets and a few items of personal mail, Hinkler flew in and out of Bundy in the Avro, delighting residents in the surrounding area with overhead stunts, while throwing out handfuls of publicity dodgers. He'd then swoop down to deliver the local paper, attend a school fete or civic reception, and hand over letters of greeting from the mayor of one town to another. In return he received much adulation, and usually a cheque for his efforts.

When Hinkler performed a few stunts over the mill town of Bingera en route to Mount Perry, the thrilled locals had a whip-round and persuaded him via telegram to land at Bingera on the way back, to pick up his cheque. They earmarked £5 of the £50 payment as a special gift for Nance. He also swooped low over the property near Mount Perry where Charlie Laffan lived, his boyhood friend and shipmate on the voyage to England eight years earlier. On another occasion, he happily rolled up to his old school at North Bundaberg for an evening euchre tournament and dance.

There was always a crowd to greet Hinkler when he returned to town after his local flights, since the *Bundaberg Mail* kept track of his movements via phone and telegram. One evening, as residents lined the banks of the slow-flowing Burnett to watch him come in, he decided to give them a demonstration they'd never forget.

Instead of tracing his usual curve down to the foundry green, he swooped the little white Avro down over the river and began to follow it along, almost skimming the surface. Next moment, to a collective gasp from the crowd, he zoomed under the traffic bridge and then under the railway bridge. The onlookers hardly had time to catch their breath before he turned the agile plane around and, only metres above the water, repeated the feat from the other direction. This time the crowd found its voice and broke into a sustained cheering that washed up and down the riverbanks like a wave. Hinkler had let the larrikin in him break out, but it was also a calculated risk by a skilful pilot.

No doubt to his mother's delight, he considered using Bundaberg as a base for an aviation charter and mail delivery service – prompting one excited reporter to quote the poet Tennyson, suggesting that Hinkler 'saw the heavens fill with commerce, argosies of magic sails, pilots of the purple twilight, dropping down with costly bales'.[16] The Bundaberg Racing Club held a special meeting to discuss Hinkler's request to use the racecourse as an airstrip, but despite their support, nothing ever came of the idea, and the sugar town's celebrated flyer didn't drop down with a single bale.

After almost two weeks of being based in his hometown, Hinkler flew south to Gympie, swooping low over the house where his grandmother lived. When he landed at the racecourse there, he reached into a small cage beside him and produced a magpie, jokingly claiming he'd caught it on the way. There to greet him were his mother, Frances, her aunt, Mrs J. Bonney, and Bert's aunt from Melbourne, Mrs Beatrice Bonney.

At the official reception, he announced he'd be leaving the following Monday to return to Sydney, and thence to England. A.V. Roe had reminded him that he was due back in time to fly one of its new aircraft in the sixth Aerial Derby, in July.

* * *

Hinkler left Gympie on 25 April, the date that would become recognised nationally from 1927 as Anzac Day. He then spent a few days in Brisbane, preparing the aircraft – re-designated G-AUCQ by the Australian authorities – for the flight to Sydney, where he was to be guest of honour at an Aero Club dinner. Two weeks before, he'd flown cross-country to Bundaberg, up over the New England tableland and the border ranges; on the return trip, he decided to follow the New South Wales coast, where today the Pacific Highway snakes along. Just as he was about to head off, a heavy shower delayed him for half an hour. It was nothing compared to what was to come.

Forty minutes after take-off, Hinkler ran headlong into weather along the north coast that was almost cyclonic in its intensity. Rain squalls pushed the Avro downwards, so that sometimes it nearly touched the waves, and water ricocheted off the propeller with such force that it chopped into the plane's fabric. Struggling with the controls, Hinkler forged southwards, but by the time he reached the Central Coast, the rain was sluicing into the open cockpit, and he could see hardly a plane's length in front of him.

As darkness closed in, he decided the only option was to put the Avro down on a beach before he was forced to land on the wind-whipped waves. With the rain and wind beating relentlessly against the tiny craft, he managed to wrestle it down onto a stretch of sand, which fortunately stayed firm under the wheels. He taxied to the end of the beach, which, although he didn't know it at the time, was Anna Bay, just north of Newcastle.

Even at ground level, wind gusts threatened to tip the plane over, forcing the diminutive airman to jump out and drag it to a more sheltered nook. For a while he stayed there, holding the flimsy aircraft down, and considering his next move.

By now, darkness had settled – he'd have to go for help. Hardly had Hinkler left the beach, when he heard a sound behind him, and looked round to see that the plane had been pushed onto its nose by the wind and was balanced there precariously.

Before he could move, another gust flipped it upside down like a lightweight wrestler being slammed onto his back by a more powerful opponent. Unable to right the plane by himself, Hinkler stabilised it as best he could and set off again.

Today Anna Bay is an up-market area, the beaches fronted by million-dollar homes; in 1921 it was deserted. Hinkler plunged inland through the pitch-blackness and rain for 10 miles or more before he found an inhabited farmhouse. After convincing the occupants that he really was a pilot who had force-landed his aircraft on the beach, he rang the Aero Club in Sydney, where the members continued their dinner without him.

Following a change of clothes and a meal, Hinkler went back with the farmer to the beach and secured the plane. In the morning, they hitched five horses to the Avro – a combination that must've made a strange sight as it moved slowly along the coast to Stockton (now a suburb of Newcastle). A lorry took over from the horses to tow the plane at a similarly solemn pace through the streets of Stockton. Hinkler followed anxiously behind, wearing a weather-beaten straw hat and his storm-battered clothes from the day before. Adding to the spectacle was a cluster of bare-legged urchins running alongside the bedraggled procession, delighted by this unexpected piece of entertainment. Fortunately, there was very little damage to the aircraft, which was dismantled in Stockton for shipment to Sydney.

When the Avro Baby arrived in the state capital, Hinkler decided not to take it back to England. Instead, he sold the plane to Harry Broadsmith, the Avro agent from Australian Aircraft and Engineering, who had persuaded Hinkler to exhibit the Baby at the Royal Easter Show just a few weeks earlier. Perhaps Hinkler's recent experience in the rainstorms along the coast confirmed what he'd suspected when he flew to Turin on 31 May the previous year – that the 'battered Baby' was not suitable for the sort of long-distance flying needed for a journey from England to Australia.

Despite the earlier publicity, only his mother and his friend Edward Hart were there to see Hinkler off when he boarded the ship for England. On his five-week visit, he'd pioneered the Sydney-to-Bundaberg route, delighted his parents, thrilled the local residents and citizens of nearby towns, barnstormed under two bridges, and triggered headlines in Australian newspapers. He hadn't, however, made the spectacular point-to-point flight he'd contemplated; he hadn't found a commercial venture that would allow him and Nance to 'maintain themselves very comfortable'; and he no longer owned a plane. So he was no closer to making a longer-term future for himself.

But he still had a job with A.V. Roe and Company. And, in answer to the plaintive question she'd asked him before he left England, he was going back to Nance.

CHAPTER 7

The restless years: test pilot and air racer

Hinkler's return to England in mid 1921 heralded the beginning of a period in his life when he had the opportunity to settle into a more established existence, taking advantage of his permanent job in aviation, and consolidating his relationship with Nance Jarvis. However, his ambition and circumstances combined to make this a restless but often exciting time for him.

Once back at Hamble in Hampshire, he put the Avro 534C, or 'Racing Baby', through its paces in preparation for the upcoming Aerial Derby. 'It is really hot stuff,' Hinkler enthused of Roy Chadwick's new creation.[1] Not hot enough, it turned out. On 16 July, on the first of two laps around the 100-mile circuit from Hendon, the engine suffered magneto failure and Hinkler was forced to land in a field next to a hospital on the south-eastern outskirts of London. 'It's rather hard luck after hurrying back so quickly,' he said stoically.[2]

Harder luck befell another Australian pilot, Harry Hawker, who died when his Nieuport Goshawk crashed during practice for the same event. Born in Melbourne, three years earlier than Hinkler, Hawker had several things in common with the Queenslander: he trained as a mechanic before setting off in 1911 for an aviation career in England, his introduction to the industry came through Thomas Sopwith, and he was relatively short in height.

Hawker's career accelerated much more rapidly than Hinkler's, however. The Victorian quickly gained a pilot's licence, and even before World War I, he'd begun work as a test pilot and designer with Sopwith Aviation, where he soon achieved height and distance records. Like Hinkler, he applied to join the RNAS, but was held back to continue his important work as an aircraft designer. Among other machines, he created the Sopwith Tabloid, a revolutionary short-winged biplane with remarkable speed and manoeuvrability.

Described as Australia's first 'apostle of flight', Hawker took a Tabloid to Australia for several months in 1914, giving rides to such notables as the Governor-General and the Defence Minister, as well as indulging in some barnstorming. Later he was made a Member of the British Empire for his contribution to the development of biplanes for the Allied war effort. Post-war, he tried for the *Daily Mail*'s trans-Atlantic prize, and raced cars and speedboats. When Sopwith Aviation collapsed in 1920, Hawker joined with Thomas Sopwith and others to set up H.G. Hawker Engineering, predecessor of the famous Hawker Siddeley aircraft manufacturing company. It was a starburst career, brought to an untimely end at the age of thirty-two.

In his short life, Harry Hawker achieved what Hinkler, as he approached his thirtieth year, was still aiming for: designing and building aeroplanes and developing a business to support his endeavours. It's hard to imagine that Hinkler didn't yearn to emulate the other pilot's success. But Hawker was a mile-a-minute man, always looking for the next challenge, ever ready to respond to a publicity opportunity. Charles Kingsford Smith was of a similar mould. Bert Hinkler's approach, on the other hand, was more measured, and despite his public affability, as time went on he became increasingly secretive, preferring media attention after he'd made his flights, rather than creating expectations in advance.

Following his London-to-Turin breakthrough, another factor Hinkler considered was the possibility of press scrutiny regarding his relationship with Nance. 'If we go flipping around together, our dials are sure to wander into the papers, and it would be fatal to take such chances,' he'd told her by letter while on the *Ascanius* voyage, presumably referring to some aspect of Nance's lawful marriage. 'If all's clear, of course I want you to come out in the limelight, as I'm so proud of my wonderful wifie, that I want her to take her full share . . .'[3] As Hinkler's aviation profile grew, Nance gradually did come into the limelight – Hannah Jarvis became known publicly as Mrs Nance (or Nancy) Hinkler – but she never became his legal 'wifie', whatever he'd intended by that offer of 'very special arrangements for a certain day' in another letter from the *Ascanius*.

Nevertheless, despite the refusal of the Anglican Church to marry them, Nance and Hinkler were regular worshippers at Holyrood Church in Southampton.

Not long after Hinkler's return to England, Harold Hamersley left A.V. Roe and Company, and Hinkler was offered the position of chief test pilot, which he gladly accepted. As a result, he was on hand to test-fly two remarkable machines that Chadwick had designed: the Avro Aldershot heavy bomber and the Avro Bison fleet spotter.

Designated as Avro type number 549, the Aldershot was at that time the world's largest single-engined aircraft, and the first Avro plane with a metal fuselage. It had a huge, 680-horsepower motor, and carried a crew of four: two pilots side by side, a rear gunner, and a bomb aimer/radio operator in a compartment behind the pilots. The plane was so high off the ground that the crew had to climb into the cockpit via special ladders fitted to the fuselage. Hinkler found the bomber a 'lively brute' to fly, which he proved by allegedly lifting it off the ground within six seconds of opening the throttle. The Avro 549 was a far cry from the little planes he usually flew, and he described the experience as 'the joy of my life'.[4]

There was just one hitch: Hinkler was too short to see over the front cowling of the cockpit, so a tailor in the company's fabric shop made two cushions for him to sit on. From then on, whenever he flew the Aldershot or the Bison, he could be seen carrying his two cushions through the factory and out to the waiting plane.

The Avro 555, or Bison, was similar in shape to the Aldershot, but smaller. Hinkler reportedly turned up to test-fly one at the RAF's Flying Training School at Sealand, in north Wales, wearing a bowler hat and an overcoat too long for him. On other occasions he was known to don a straw boater, an affectation he'd first adopted as a young man in Bundaberg.

In addition to the prototypes, Hinkler flight-tested aircraft coming off the production line, before they were delivered to British and international customers. He also helped with follow-up service, and it was on one such occasion that the rumour arose of his involvement in espionage.

It was 1922. The Treaty of Versailles, negotiated among the nations who'd participated in World War I, was not long concluded, and Russia's Communist revolution was only five years old. The political air across the world was thick with intrigue, and countries were constantly suspicious of each other's motives and actions. Seemingly innocent international visits were routinely construed as covers for clandestine operations.

Against this political background, Hinkler's employer sold an Avro Baby to a buyer in Russia. To ensure safe delivery, Hinkler was to accompany the Russian pilot, Ye Gwaita, in another Avro 534. The full escort detail was vetoed, however, when it was discovered that Hinkler couldn't fly the company Baby out of the country because of insurance restrictions, so his watchdog mission ended at Lympne Aerodrome in Kent.

Soon afterwards, Gwaita was forced down in Holland by bad weather, necessitating repairs, and Hinkler was dispatched to provide support. He picked up the relevant spare parts, caught a commercial KLM flight from Croydon to Rotterdam, then took a train to the plane's location at Tilburg, in the country's south. The aircraft had tipped over on soft ground during landing, slightly damaging the rudder, but with his mechanic's skills, Hinkler quickly completed the repairs. Next day, he flew the Avro to a military airfield 10 miles away, and filled it with fuel and oil, before watching Gwaita take off safely in the direction of Germany, en route to Russia. Hinkler then retraced his route to England.

This event might've been seen as nothing more than an example of good after-sales service, if it weren't for the politically uncertain times. For conspiracy theorists, Hinkler's rendezvousing in Holland with a Russian pilot was too good an opportunity to resist, leading to speculation in the press that he'd been spying for Britain. A later visit to Latvia fanned similar flames. There doesn't seem to be any evidence to support such a notion. Indeed, Hinkler's subsequent interactions with the British Air Ministry as a private pilot suggest that his dealings with that agency were often tenuous, and hardly based on any special relationship developed through earlier, clandestine activities.

* * *

Roy Chadwick and Avro were also developing new versions of the company's highly successful Avro 504, a two-seater biplane that had been produced in the thousands as a fighter and then trainer in World War I, particularly as the 504K, and continued to be popular with civilians and air forces across the world into the 1930s. During 1922, Hinkler was kept busy testing various features being considered for these production models, one of which was an oleo undercarriage, with oil-damped, rubber shock absorbers. Hinkler claimed it was almost impossible to make a faulty landing with the so-called 'indestructible' undercarriage, and proceeded to demonstrate this to an Air Ministry official – by stalling his Avro 504 at around 15 feet as he was bringing it in to land, causing the plane to pancake into the ground. The undercarriage flattened out beneath it . . . then dramatically stood up of its own accord, pushing the aircraft up with it.

Moments later, Hinkler took the plane up again and flew it horizontally into the sloping bank at the edge of the airfield, undercarriage first . . . Normally, this would have wrecked the landing gear, not to mention probably breaking the pilot's neck.

But the plane merely bounced along the ground a short distance before coming to a stop.

After overcoming his shock at what he was sure would be two appalling crashes, the official was so convinced of the worth of this new technology that the undercarriage system became mandatory at flying schools throughout Britain. Hinkler enjoyed the demonstrations immensely. 'They were the sort of thing I used to dream of, and during my qualifying period I'd almost have sold my soul for,' he enthused to his friend Edward Hart, editor of Australia's *Aircraft* magazine.[5]

In September that year, Hinkler had just taken off from Hamble in an Avro Baby 534C, registered as G-EAXL, in preparation for the first King's Cup Air Race the next day, when the engine failed. He was over the tidal estuary of Southampton Water, and turned the Avro sharply in an attempt to reach the shore, but the plane was too low, and splashed into the sea. Rescue came quickly, and Hinkler suffered only cuts to his face, but the aircraft was lost. Nor was a replacement machine available. 'He goes into these races heart and soul,' the editor of *Flight* commented, 'and his disappointment at being unable to start in the race was shared by many'.[6]

Three months later came the sort of experience he loved. Avro installed an even bigger motor in the Aldershot bomber – a monster of a unit that developed 1000 horsepower – and again Hinkler was the first to try it out in the air. During a demonstration for Air Ministry officials, he engaged in some startling acrobatics given the size of the plane, and zoomed it across the aerodrome at head height at a speed of 140 miles an hour.

Newspaper reports of the time compared the thrust produced by the 1-ton Napier Cub engine to the power of a railway locomotive almost ten times its size. Hinkler wanted his parents to make the same comparison. 'Next time the "Brisbane Mail" comes in,' he suggested in a letter to them, 'go along and have a look at the engine, then try to imagine the power I had at my command on the occasion of these flights.'[7]

Despite his apparent enjoyment of this work, Hinkler had other ambitions. In late 1922, Edward Hart sounded out on his behalf Lieutenant-Colonel Horace Brinsmead, Controller of Civil Aviation in Australia, about the idea of a trans-Tasman aerial service. The Australian Government was keen to foster aviation, and Brinsmead apparently supported the notion, although, at that time, no one had even flown across the Tasman Sea, let alone set up a regular service between Australia and New Zealand.

On Hinkler's calculations, the outward journey would follow an arc to the south of Sydney and Auckland, and the return trip an arc to the north, to take advantage of the prevailing winds. He thought a small payload could be counterbalanced by passengers' willingness to pay a premium for the time saved. 'From a passenger's point of view, travelling by night while he sleeps, will not experience any loss of time for travel,' Hinkler reasoned in a letter to Hart the following March, 'so that really you don't only lessen the four days boat journey by a percentage: you simply wipe it out completely.' He was sure there would be people willing to pay for such a service, and while he conceded that potential passengers might need to be 'educated up to it',[8] carrying mail could cover the operation's costs in the meantime.

Hinkler was quite passionate about the idea, but nothing came of it. It wasn't until five years later that an aeroplane crossed the Tasman – with Kingsford Smith, Charles Ulm, Harold Litchfield and Tom McWilliam on board.

In 1923, A.V. Roe and Company designed and built small-engined monoplanes known as ultralights, specifically for the *Daily Mail* Light Aircraft Trials at Lympne, Kent, held in October. The first plane Hinkler flew in the trials had engine problems, but he had more success flying laps around the 12.5-mile circuit in another ultralight. In fact, one member of the Avro team suggested that the only way to coax him down for lunch might be to place some bread, cheese and beer on the tarmac as bait. Hinkler eventually completed eighty laps.

Although Nance had made it clear that she didn't want to live in Australia, that didn't prevent Hinkler from considering another possible business there – namely, skywriting. Major John Savage had perfected the art of skywriting in England after World War I, using a plane and white smoke to form letters against a clear sky. His first commercial demonstration was in June 1922 during the famous Derby Stakes at Epsom Downs Racecourse, when a plane traced *Daily Mail* in the sky, to the cheers of the crowd below.

Savage subsequently set up skywriting businesses in other countries, including France and the United States, and Hinkler became interested in developing an Australian operation. He discussed it with Savage over a period of months in 1923–24 and was confident that the venture would go ahead. 'He is sending me out as his representative, in charge of operations,' the Queenslander told Hart, 'and as suggested by me, and Savage has agreed, if available, to enlist your assistance in the department in which we feel you are well qualified – managing the business end.'[9] Despite Hinkler's enthusiasm, again, nothing came of the proposal. Savage did eventually set up an Australian skywriting operation but Hinkler was not involved, although the major later again offered him a role in the business.

By 1924, in response to strong orders from the RAF, Aldershot bombers were rolling off the assembly line at Hamble, while the company's Manchester plant was building Bison spotter planes. Hinkler was kept busy testing the new aircraft, and as the tempo of work increased, he took on a deputy chief test pilot, who would be based up north. Meanwhile, Hinkler continued his work in Hampshire, flying aircraft as diverse as a transport plane built for the RAF for its Cairo–Baghdad desert air route, and a three-seater seaplane designed for Oxford University's Arctic Circle expedition, which sat on floats designed for use on snow and water.

Early the following year, Hinkler test-flew the largest Avro ever built, the twin-engined 557. Christened the 'Ava', this was a torpedo bomber close to 20 feet high, with rounded biplane wings that spanned almost 100 feet. Two pilots sat together in its open cockpit, and there were nose, ventral and dorsal gun turrets. Hinkler would have needed his two cushions to fly the wooden protoype, and again when he flew the metal version two years later.

* * *

At the same time as he was conducting an intensive program of test flights for A.V. Roe and Company and exploring business opportunities outside the firm, Hinkler had lost none of his enthusiasm for the idea of flying to Australia. Yet despite the stability of his employment, he was not able to build up a big enough nest egg or raise sufficient funds from other sources to help him buy an aircraft and support the flight. Four years after his post-war Australian visit, he did head overseas again, but this time to the United States, when he was chosen as a reserve member of Britain's 1925 Schneider Cup air-racing team.

The prestigious Coupe d'Aviation Maritime Jacques Schneider, commonly known as the Schneider Cup, was a prize offered by a Frenchman of that name – a financier, balloonist, and speedboat and aircraft enthusiast (and one-time French Under-Secretary of State for Aviation) – to the winner of an international seaplane race held over a triangular course. Schneider's intention was to promote the development of seaplanes for commerce and transportation, but over the eleven occasions that the race was run from 1913 onwards, it gradually became a test of speed, with an increase from 45 miles an hour in the first year to 340 miles an hour by 1931, the last year the event was held. During this period, only Britain, France, Italy and the United States ever competed, and not all of them took part every time.

For the 1925 event, the British team had three new planes, each specifically designed for the race and fitted with the powerful Napier Lion twelve-cylinder engine: a pair of Gloster-Napier IIIs, and the more radical Supermarine-Napier S4. The two Gloster IIIs were streamlined wooden biplanes sitting on duralumin floats; the Supermarine S4 was a contemporary-design cantilever monoplane mounted on twin wooden floats. Earlier in the year, Henri Biard, chief test pilot for the de Havilland Aircraft Company, had set a new world speed record in the S4 of almost 227 miles an hour, and would pilot the plane in the upcoming race. Hubert Broad, his counterpart at Supermarine Aviation, would be in control of one of the Gloster IIIs, with the other held in reserve. Hinkler would be on standby.

Flying the sleek machines required outstanding skill, nerve, and lightning-fast reflexes. Both of the British entries had crashed during pre-race trials for the previous year's competition, which had been cancelled when only the United States was ready to start, but there was quiet confidence about their latest challenge. 'It would be dangerous to be over-confident,' the editor of *Flight* wrote, 'but this much may, at any rate, be said, that the British challengers should this year have a sporting chance in the race, which, after all is said and done, is all that one has any right to expect.'[10]

The Schneider Cup race comprised individual time trials over seven laps of a triangular course at nearby Chesapeake Bay, and was preceded by test flights to ensure navigability and watertightness. For the navigability trial, each pilot had to take off from the starting line, take the aircraft into the air, land on the water again and taxi between two buoys at a speed of over 12 miles an hour; then take off, land, taxi half a mile between a second set of buoys; and finally, take off for a third time, land, and taxi over the finishing line.

The British team got off to a good start on Friday 20 October when Broad successfully completed his tests in one of the Gloster IIIs. But disaster struck just after Henri Biard – who'd slipped on the ship's deck during the Atlantic crossing and was nursing an injured wrist – took off in the Supermarine. Despite his experience, Biard almost immediately lost control of the machine as it banked, and the monoplane fell 200 feet into the bay. Fortunately he was not badly hurt, but the S4's floats and undercarriage were smashed. The mishap might have been caused by pilot error, or it might have been Biard's first experience of the then little-known phenomenon of wing flutter. Given the S4's futuristic design and recent speed record, the British team and spectators alike were disappointed at its early demise.

Biard's misfortune was Hinkler's opportunity. He would take over in the reserve Gloster. The race regulations specified that the navigability trials be completed on a day in advance of undertaking the circuits around the course, but darkness fell before Hinkler could take off. The race itself was due to be held the next day, and, as the organisers, the American contest committee met to discuss if the rules allowed Hinkler to complete the tests the following morning, and then take part in the race in the afternoon. With the Italian team's agreement, they decided he could go ahead.

Next day, Saturday, Hinkler was at the bay at daybreak, eager to get under way. The weather was just as determined to stop him. A storm that had originated in the Gulf of Mexico was gathering intensity and wreaking increasing havoc as it swirled northwards up the US east coast. Blinding rain almost obscured Chesapeake Bay, and pelting winds whipped its normally placid waters into a frenzy. By Sunday evening, the winds were close to hurricane force, and crews anxiously secured their planes. The US Navy lost seventeen of its seaplanes in Baltimore that night, torn from their moorings and broken up by the waves.

On Monday morning, although the skies were still the colour of lead, the wind had moderated, and Hinkler was keen to attempt a take-off. He knew that to complete all the requirements by the 2.30 pm deadline, including the six-hour watertightness test, he would have to finish the navigability tests by 7 am. To add to his worries, the Italian team now expressed concern about the two-day delay and were reconsidering their agreement that the regulations could be bent. They protested informally to the contest committee, who decided to proceed with the trials and worry about the validity of the protest later.

As soon as it was light enough to see the course markers, Hinkler in the reserve Gloster-Napier was winched down the ramp and into the water. Near the shore, the water was protected from the winds, and he took off smoothly. As he headed out to the starting line, about a mile away, he could see the boats below carrying the official observers were rolling heavily in the swell. He circled around and came down for the first of the three required touchdowns. On the shore, the British team watched anxiously. Hinkler knew they were depending on him as the back-up pilot, and he didn't want to disappoint them.

Although the wind was blowing strongly and unpredictably as he brought the biplane in across the green corrugated surface of the bay, it touched down smoothly, skimming across the tossing waves. Just as it seemed he was down safely, the Gloster hit a patch of rough water that grabbed viciously at the metal floats. One of the struts collapsed, and the plane dipped to one side, like a person whose leg has folded under. The fuselage sank down but was stopped from going under by the cross-braces between the floats. For a few moments Hinkler sat forlornly in his cockpit, too dejected to move. Minutes later, a boat came alongside and picked him up, and he didn't even get his feet wet. A gig from one of the American navy tenders towed the Gloster-Napier back to the wharf. It was out of the race, and so was its pilot.

It would've been a fairytale ending if the remaining British entry had gone on to win, but the American team triumphed, with army lieutenant Jimmy Doolittle (later a wartime hero) flying a specially built Curtiss racer around the course at speeds in excess of 230 miles an hour. Broad came in second in the other Gloster III, well behind Doolittle.

Despite the loss, the British team enjoyed their time in America, where their hosts spared no effort in making sure they had a good time, and they attended a reception in their honour given by the British Consul in New York. On the team's voyage home to England, the larrikin in Hinkler emerged briefly when he uncharacteristically joined his teammates in playing a prank on a fellow passenger. They'd decided to bring a pompous man down a peg by taking his only pair of shoes from his cabin when he retired for the night, and tacking them to the masthead. Hinkler's part was to distract the man and steal the boots. Amongst much hilarity, when the passenger disembarked the next morning, he was forced to walk down the gangplank in his socks.

CHAPTER 8

A plane with potential

When Hinkler returned to England after the Schneider Cup meet, it was back to domesticity – house-hunting with Nance. After several years renting various properties in the Southampton area, and buying a modest property in Havelock Road, which they lived in for a while, Bert and Nance decided they wanted a larger place of their own, with some space around it. One newspaper claimed that just before Hinkler headed off to the US, he and Nance inspected a house by plane. In this account, Hinkler piloted his partner in an Avro Baby to view a house for sale at Birchington, near Margate on Britain's south-east coast. Unable to find a landing ground close by, they allegedly undertook the inspection from the air, repeatedly circling low over the property, and peering through the windows.

Whatever the truth of that story, Hinkler often took Nance flying with him on his days off, if he wasn't competing in air races. Although he had sold the Avro Baby in Australia on his trip there in 1921, he had access to various aircraft over the years he worked at A. V. Roe and Company. 'We would think nothing of flying 100 miles to drop in on a friend for afternoon tea,' he later recalled, 'and our week-ends were generally spent knocking about different parts of the English atmosphere.'[1] They were not alone in the air – recreational flying blossomed in Britain after the war, as private owners took advantage of the chance to buy cheap war surplus planes and later upgraded to more reliable and better-equipped small aircraft specifically designed for the 'sporting' market.

Unable to find a ready-built home that suited their purposes, Mr and Mrs Hinkler, as they were known, eventually purchased land in a new private subdivision, Thornhill Park, just east of Southampton, near Sholing, and signed a contract with a builder, H.W. Small, from nearby Bitterne. Blessed with long-standing oak trees, their piece of land was extensive enough for them to be able to build a substantial residence and also have room for a shed.

The new house was distinctly different from the modest North Bundaberg cottage where Hinkler had grown up. It was an imposing four bedroom, double-storey, cavity brick residence, with two chimneys, a slate roof with gables, large white-trimmed bay windows, and a generous upper level verandah on two sides, accessed through French doors. A concrete-like veneer known as 'pebble dashing', a common external insulation for English houses, decorated the top half. By this time Hinkler had acquired a small car produced by the Riley company at Coventry (motto: 'As old as the industry, as modern as the hour'), and when they moved into their new home late in 1925 he garaged the two-door Riley underneath the verandah.

Their purchase was assisted by building grants, and land would have been cheaper in regional areas than in London. For some reason, the house was in Nance's name only, an arrangement for which she would later be grateful. Although English women's magazines, concerned about women's increasing independence, promoted marriage as 'the best job of all' throughout the 1920s, through choice or circumstance Bert and Nance remained unwed.

Although it was of English design and construction, the new house retained a link with Hinkler's birthplace. On a plaque beside the front door they engraved the name 'Mon Repos', from the French meaning 'my rest' – and after the Bundaberg beach, of course, where Hinkler had successfully experimented with his gliders as a teenager. It was a reminder of both what he had achieved back then and of what he had promised himself and his parents – to fly home. Despite the expansion of aviation in the first half of the decade and the post-war evolution of new aircraft, the England to Australia route had not been attempted since McIntosh and Parer's flight in 1920 and Hinkler's truncated effort the following year.

* * *

Meanwhile, Hinkler hadn't given up another connection with Australia – the application for an Imperial Service Grant he'd made a few days after he arrived in Sydney with the Avro Baby in 1921. He heard nothing during the five weeks he was in Australia, but just a few days after his ship left Sydney on the return voyage, his mother received a package from the Office of Navy Accounts, Melbourne addressed to him at the family home in North Bundaberg. Frances Hinkler returned it, telling them he'd gone to England and giving them his current Southampton address. Nothing more happened, so in December that year Hinkler sent in a new claim. This time he gave his English address.

Navy Accounts then wrote to him to explain they couldn't consider his claim until he returned to Australia. He replied that wasn't fair because he'd made the claim when he was in Sydney. The Navy responded not to Hinkler, but to his mother, asking her to advise her son that, when he settled permanently in Australia, he would be entitled to a gratuity of £153, 5s and 9d. Frances asked hopefully if the cheque could be sent to her for onforwarding to Bert: 'I want to help him on with his experiments, with the money, so that he may be able to come back to Queensland, and it needs a little money to make money.'[2] She pleaded that she wanted 'to help the lad' by getting the money due to him. The 'lad' by this time had just turned thirty. The Navy Accounts Office declined the request.

From this time, Hinkler, his mother and members of her family engaged in an ongoing battle with the Navy Accounts Office for payment of the gratuity to Bert, despite the fact that he remained in England. He continued to plead commitments in England were keeping him there, but implied that he would return to Australia as soon as possible. Navy Accounts was unmoved, but agreed to extend the deadline for his return to 30 June 1924.

Frances Hinkler took up the fight, writing to tell a government minister it would be 'very hard luck' to do her son out of his grant after all his years of service, and complaining to her local state member of parliament, George Barber about the decision. Barber shot off a letter to the local federal member, Frank Forde, about the stipulation that Bert turn up by 30 June to qualify. 'This seems an outrageous action if true,' Barber wrote, 'and my vocabulary of nautical remarks would be exhausted if they were mean enough to rob Hinkler.'[3] At the same time, Hinkler's aunt in Melbourne, Beatrice Bonney, contacted *her* local member about the matter. The pressure worked – the Secretary of the Naval Board, George Macandie, wrote to tell Bert Hinkler that the Defence Minister had extended the cut-off date to 25 February 1925, but if he was not back in Australia by then, no further extension was possible.

Just as the deadline was about to expire, Francis Hinkler summoned Bonney family members in Tasmania to the fray. On their behalf, the Honourable L. Atkinson, a federal MP from that state, wrote to the Secretary of the Naval Board that 'Major' Hinkler still had commitments in England so would not be able to return to Australia for two years. Atkinson proposed, however, that since Hinkler's mother was in ill health, his father had been an invalid for some years, and his brother was gassed in the war, all or part of the grant should be paid to Mrs Frances Hinkler.

This suggestion initially outraged Macandie, but he eventually advised Atkinson that the payment could not be made to Hinkler's mother, and that he had nevertheless a new deadline for the pilot's return to Australia, 28 February 1926, as a final concession.

Come 1926, Hinkler was still in England, and therefore did not receive the gratuity. After five years of serve and counter-serve, and despite an elastic deadline for Bert to be back in Australia, the government's patience had run out. The saga was apparently over.

* * *

Hinkler had now not seen his family in Bundaberg for five years. His father was 70 years old and in poor health, and his eldest son was continually on the lookout for some means of flying home. For the moment, however, Bert's focus was on testing Roy Chadwick's latest creations. These included the final version of

Avro's stalwart, the 504, which had been produced in a number of different guises since the war; a medium-sized tubular steel torpedo carrier, developed as a private venture; a single-seat fighter plane; an autogiro (a sort of mini-helicopter); and a new two-seater biplane. It was this last craft that would eventually help Hinkler fulfil his dream of flying to Australia. Yet the dream nearly came to a premature end one day in spring 1926.

Hinkler had just taken off from Hamble for a test flight in the new torpedo carrier, known as the 571, or 'Buffalo', when one wing dropped, and continued to drop. He moved the joystick, but to no avail.

Instantly he realised that the controls for the ailerons – the hinged flight control surfaces attached to the trailing edges of the wings – had been crossed, so that every response was the opposite to the one intended. He immediately pushed the stick in the opposite direction, and the aircraft levelled out. By carefully controlling the stick, he was able to circle the plane back to the airfield and land safely. Only that instantaneous understanding of the situation and the sharpness of his response saved the Buffalo from plummeting into the ground. Ironically, the potential for tragedy that day was underlined at Avro some twenty years later, when two other test pilots and Chadwick himself died in crashes resulting from crossed aileron controls.

A different sort of flying technique was required for the autogiro. This hybrid aircraft incorporated an unpowered overhead rotor for lift, and a standard aeroplane engine at the front to provide pull. A forerunner of the helicopter, the autogiro had been developed in Spain in the early 1920s by Don Juan de la Cierva, and A.V. Roe and Company became involved in the co-construction of two of these machines in 1926 for the British

Air Ministry. Because of the specialised nature of the autogiro, Cierva employed his own pilot at Hamble to test the machines, but it was hard to keep Hinkler away from such a challenge. Before long, he was test-flying one of the strange new machines, which were based on an Avro standard aircraft with stub wings. 'Tho it flies,' Hinkler wrote to his parents, 'it is by no means an aeroplane.'[4]

Hinkler's skill and versatility was a source of wonder to Chadwick during this period:

> I flew with him on many occasions, both on test flights and cross-country flights, and one always felt the greatest confidence due to his masterly handling of the aeroplane. When he was flying, Bert Hinkler concentrated on the job in a way I have not seen with any other pilot. For example, when on a cross-country flight, he would be incessantly glancing at his compass, then his map, then looking out first on one side and then the other, and I am sure that he knew his position exactly and all the time.[5]

Nevertheless, there were times when Hinkler found the going tough. In July 1925, for example, while competing in the King's Cup, a round-Britain race, he was coming in to land in heavy fog at one of the designated touchdown points, Newcastle Aerodrome, when another plane suddenly appeared through the mist in front of him, landing in the opposite direction. Fortunately, the other pilot was able to lift his aircraft, missing Hinkler's plane by metres – but the Australian's machine hit the ground hard, damaging the undercarriage. The fog was so widespread across northern Britain that midsummer day that ten out of the fourteen competitors were forced out, and one of the remaining four only just escaped disaster when a wheel of his aircraft clipped a mountain top in Scotland. Hinkler was later delayed by a leaking petrol tank, which he overcame by applying a thick coating of soap around the leak. He eventually came in last of the four survivors, rolling to a stop a few metres behind the third place-getter and just seventeen minutes inside the time limit for the first complete circuit. Knowing he was well behind time, he withdrew from the race at that point.

Hinkler was always up for a challenge, however, and in the latter part of 1926, became involved in a scheme to land a plane on a mountaintop in Britain. The idea had been cheerfully proposed to John Leeming, Chairman of the Lancashire Aero Club, by the Director of Civil Aviation, Sir Sefton Brancker, as a means of promoting light aviation. Sir Sefton said that officially the government couldn't organise such a venture, but that he'd ensure there was full co-operation when it was needed. After initial reluctance from the managing director, A.V. Roe and Company agreed to lend Leeming an Avro Gosport, a two-seater biplane which carried a new experimental 100-horsepower radial engine, the Alpha. The Gosport was also fitted with one of the latest oleo rubber-damped undercarriages, designed for robust landings – Hinkler had tested the prototype for Avro four years earlier.

Mount Snowdon in Wales was originally proposed as a possible landing site, until it was discovered that the summit consisted of jagged rocks. An alternative site was found – Helvellyn, a peak 3118 feet above sea level in the picturesque Lake District of north-west England. A.V. Roe and Company began to work on fine-tuning the machine and its engine, and, as the company's chief test pilot, Bert Hinkler was brought in to test-fly the plane. With difficulty, and a guide, Leeming climbed the peak for a close-up reconnaissance, and an advance party subsequently cleared sufficient boulders from the lightly sloping site to make a track wide enough for an aircraft to land on the rocky surface.

Over the days that followed, the plane and its engine were made ready, but it was now early December, and the weather deteriorated, with the threat of snow increasing. Hinkler and Leeming practised landings in the dual-controlled Gosport while they waited for better flying conditions, and Hinkler challenged his fellow pilot to see which of them could touch down closest to a sheet of newspaper the Australian had pegged out on the aerodrome. Like Chadwick, Leeming was impressed by the test pilot's ability:

> He did not seem to 'fly' the machine, but rather to be actually part of it. Just as the legs of a trained athlete obey his brain, so the wings of an aeroplane answered Hinkler's instinctive control. He was a master one could not hope to copy, but to fly with him as I did gave an insight into the ways of the pilot who was undoubtedly a genius.[6]

For the landing attempt itself, Leeming would pilot the Gosport, and Hinkler would follow in a plane chartered by the *Manchester Guardian*, with a photographer on board to capture the event. After a false start on 15 December, when violent weather buffeted the planes, they tried again six days later. Hinkler's aircraft suffered an engine problem, however, and it was decided he would accompany Leeming in the Gosport for the attack on the summit, without the photographer. The second attempt too was abandoned when gale force winds near Helvellyn almost brought the aircraft to a stand-still in the sky.

After refuelling at the Lancaster aerodrome to return to their base at nearby Woodford, they were just taking off, the plane only 20 feet into the air, when the Alpha engine spluttered and died. Leeming later claimed that if he'd been flying the machine, the Avro would have crashed. At the first cough of the engine, however, Hinkler pushed the aircraft's nose down and swung the biplane around in a sharp vertical turn. The left wingtip brushed the grass and then the pilot flattened the plane out and skimmed it across the aerodrome a foot or so above the surface. Moments later, he touched down and pulled the Gosport up unscathed, close to a bordering hedge. After the two pilots cleared sediment from the carburettor, which was the cause of their near-miss, darkness was moving in, so they tied the aircraft down and went to find overnight accommodation.

That evening they discovered that both of them had come away without their wallets, but were saved embarrassment at a nearby hotel when the local garage owner bailed them out next morning and also helped service the plane's engine. After promising to forward the obliging garage man a cheque for the loan and expenses, they took off into fair skies, determined to make the summit this time. As they climbed steadily through three thousand feet, following Lake Windermere, one of the jewels of the Lake District, the engine coughed, ran smoothly for a few minutes, and then spluttered again. After their experience with the take-off the day before, they quickly decided to put the plane down. Below, the pattern of hills and valleys that make the area so attractive offered little in the way of a possible landing ground. 'That one there,' Hinkler shouted from the front seat. The field he was pointing to was so tiny, with tall trees on two sides and the lake in front, that Leeming knew he had no chance of setting the Gosport down on it, Oleo undercarriage notwithstanding.

Hinkler took the controls. 'Leave it to me,' he said.[7] He put the plane into a long steady glide down to about a thousand feet, then wriggled the aircraft back and forth in a series of sharp S turns until it was 10 feet above the lake, but continually heading in the direction of the grassy patch he'd spotted earlier. Moments later a slight bump announced the arrival of the Avro on terra firma, and Hinkler again brought it to a stop undamaged. They discovered they'd landed in the grounds of a children's hospital, and a nurse rushed up to tell them that, with only three days until Christmas, as the plane came overhead the excited young patients were convinced Santa Claus was arriving.

After cleaning the petrol filter, the two pilots took off again, Leeming happy to have Hinkler at the controls. An approaching storm front threatened to put a dampener on the rest of the day, but they could now see Helvellyn, jutting above the surrounding hills in the grey winter air, and the opportunity seemed too good to miss. Leeming took over just before the plane encountered a series of severe bumps, one of which bounced them both sharply into the air, but their safety belts pulled them back. The cushions that Hinkler habitually used to give him more height, however, shot out from under him and over the side.

When they circled the Helvellyn summit minutes later, the bumps had subsided and Leeming prepared to land. Below, they could see a figure crouched behind a cairn of stones, seemingly awaiting their arrival. With the plane pushing against a strong steady wind, Leeming was able to drop the machine down closer to the summit than originally hoped for, and run it up a steep slope to a stop. With the engine still running, Hinkler held the plane in position while his fellow pilot jumped out and chocked the wheels with rocks. The person they'd seen earlier was Eric Dodds, Professor of Greek at Birmingham University, who was in the district on vacation, and he readily agreed to sign a note as a witness to the landing. There was momentary consternation when none of them could locate a writing implement, but Professor Dodds eventually found a pencil stub, and certified on the back of an old receipt that John Leeming and Bert Hinkler had landed on Helvellyn summit on 22 December 1926. The pilots took a few photos with a pocket Kodak camera as further proof.

A few minutes later they prepared for take-off. In front, the plane was only thirty yards from the edge of the precipice, but they were afraid that if they rolled it backwards to gain a longer run-up, they wouldn't be able to stop it. So they decided to run the engine at full bore, and try to lift the Gosport into the air before it dropped over the edge of a thousand-foot cliff. After saying goodbye to Dodds, they strapped themselves in, pulled their goggles over their eyes, and Leeming opened the throttle. The plane shot forward, but with five yards to go, it had still not lifted into the air. Next moment the nose dropped sharply into space and then the biplane lifted smoothly into the sky, away from the long sharp ridge hikers know as Striding Edge. Sir Sefton Brancker would be happy.

Earlier that day, while they were preparing the plane, Bert was whistling the tune of 'Brown Eyes', a popular song of the time. Leeming later wrote, 'I hear that tune sometimes, and it never fails to bring back a picture of those days before Helvellyn – and Bert Hinkler: Bert, the best pilot I ever knew, the cheeriest of sportsmen, who went his way quietly getting on with his job, unassuming and unafraid.'[8]

Although the Helvellyn landing provided the sorts of aviation challenges Hinkler revelled in and showed his remarkable skills, it was merely a diversion for him, however. For his future plans, it was Chadwick's new two-seater touring plane, the Avro Avian, that now captured his attention.

That September, the *Daily Mail* – a promoter of British aviation events for almost twenty years by this point – sponsored the third staging of the Lympne Light Aircraft Trials. Avro's chief designer had specifically developed the Avian for the two-seater category. Designated type 581, the new aircraft was a single-engined biplane, with a wooden fuselage and two open cockpits, and a large wing area that enabled it to carry larger loads – and hence earn more points in the competition. Hinkler liked the 581 from the first time he flew it. Although the plane was eliminated in the Lympne trials because of an engine problem, it was sufficiently repaired for Hinkler to win a six-lap race (and £200) on the final day.

Back at Hamble, the Avian was fitted with a larger, 85-horsepower Cirrus engine, and the wingspan shortened, and after some racing success, Avro decided to redevelop it into a more advanced model. Hinkler reckoned he could see potential in the prototype, and late in 1926 he acquired the 581 from Avro. According to author Peter Clegg, Hinkler was given the plane, but a history of the aircraft company claims he paid his employers £750 for it. Gift or purchase, it now belonged to Hinkler. This was the aircraft he had sought for so long, and he had but one aim: to fly it to Australia in record time.

Hinkler's ambition to leave as soon as possible was no doubt spurred by a flight from England to Australia that year by Alan Cobham, the first time the distance had been conquered by air since the Smith brothers in 1919 and McIntosh and Parer soon after. On 30 June 1926, Cobham and a mechanic, Arthur Elliot, took off for Australia from the River Medway in Kent in a de Havilland DH.50J biplane fitted with floats and powered by a 385-horsepower Armstrong Siddeley Jaguar engine. Younger than Hinkler by two years, Cobham had joined Geoffrey de Havilland's new aircraft company as a test pilot in 1921, and five years later had established himself as a long-distance flyer, including a 12,000-mile round trip from England through Europe to the Middle East and north Africa, and back through Spain, and a return flight from London to the Cape of Good Hope.

As the de Havilland flew over Iraq on the 1926 flight to Australia, an apparently disgruntled Bedouin in the desert below took a potshot at it, and the bullet struck Elliott, killing him instantly. After landing at nearby Basra, Cobham later continued with a mechanic co-opted from the nearby RAF base, Sergeant R.W. Ward, and arrived in Melbourne on 15 August, after stopping over in Darwin to swap the floats for wheels. The flight did not break the Smith brothers' record, but Cobham and his companion received an enthusiastic welcome in Australia. Despite the rigours of the outward trip, the pair then flew back to Britain in the DH.50J, with a representative of the Armstrong Siddeley company also on board. Cobham majestically landed the de Havilland seaplane on the Thames River on 1 October 1926 beside the Houses of Parliament. A short while later he was knighted for his pioneering efforts with long-distance flying.

After the success of Cobham's return flight, Hinkler's prospects of reaching Australia must have looked slim by comparison. He was planning to fly alone, the Avro's Cirrus II engine developed only 85 horsepower, less than a quarter of the thrust Cobham had at his disposal in the DH.50J, and the plane was not equipped with floats, so he would have to hope he was always able to find a suitable landing ground on the 10,000-mile journey across deserts, mountains and oceans. Furthermore, although wireless transmission to and from aircraft was now increasingly common, for some reason – possibly the extra weight and also his independent set of mind – Hinkler decided not to install a radio in his plane. He would be on his own in more ways than one.

CHAPTER 9

'My plans are unsettled'

If Hinkler had any reservations about what he was about to attempt, he kept them to himself. In February 1927, he told the British Air Ministry he expected to make a start for Australia within a month or so. His projected route was over France and Italy, across Greece, Iraq, and Persia, and then on to India and Burma, over Siam and the Federated Malay States, and finally to the Dutch East Indies, his stepping-off point to Australia. He asked the authorities to obtain the necessary permissions to fly over foreign territories. Rumours circulated in Britain and Australia that his departure was imminent, and at the end of February, *Flight* magazine forecast that he would be leaving for his homeland within two weeks, 'accompanied by a mechanic and small luggage'.[1]

Decked in silver livery except for a jungle green strip along the top of the fuselage, Hinkler's Avro Avian had its British registration, G-EBOV, imprinted in chunky black letters along both sides of the fuselage, and repeated beneath the lower wings.

The letter G (identifying it as British registered) sat prominently on the rudder, and the words *Avian Cirrus*, angled across each side of the cockpit in italics, spelt out the machine's twin heritage.

Additions Hinkler had made to the plane included a self-starting device so that he wouldn't have to rely on another person being available to kick the engine over, and a folding wide-track undercarriage, which not only relieved the load on the aircraft's tail when the wings were folded for storage, but also brought the engine lower, to give him easier access for maintenance purposes. Because of the modifications, it had its own designation – Avro Avian 581E. Chadwick helped Hinkler fine-tune the undercarriage design, and decided it was such an effective modification that he included it as standard on the Avian Mark II.

Despite the modifications to the 581E and other preparations, Hinkler failed to leave for Australia within the period he'd specified to the ministry, however, and by April he still wasn't ready to go. The problem wasn't technical or bureaucratic – it was Hinkler's financial state. He simply didn't have enough money – he reckoned he needed about £2000 – to pay for the trip.

The Australian pilot had tried various sources around London – to no avail.

'The response was as good as if I'd been trying to sell rotten fruit,' he later reported.[2]

British newspapers scoffed at his idea that they pay him £1 if he should beat the Smith brothers' England–Australia record of twenty-eight days by one day, with the amount doubling for each further day. Editors were growing increasingly tired of supporting long-distance flights with poorly prepared pilots and aircraft, ventures that often ended a few hundred miles from their departure point. Hinkler reportedly could also have taken out a policy with Lloyds Insurance that would've paid him more than £2000 if he bridged the distance within sixteen days, but he claimed he didn't have the £150 for the premium.

The delay to his schedule meant that the approvals he'd received after his initial request to the Air Ministry to fly through foreign air spaces had lapsed, but the problem didn't end there. Typically, such requests were handled by the Civil Aviation Branch of the ministry, who then asked the Foreign Office to approach the countries concerned. As with all such arrangements, Hinkler had been required to pay a deposit before the telegrams were sent, with the balance to be settled when the full cost was known. The telegrams had already been dispatched to embassies and consulates along his proposed route, and Civil Aviation therefore sent him an invoice for the balance – which the Australian repeatedly avoided paying by pleading a lack of funds. Irritating the ministry staff even further, at one point he suggested he could pay off the cost at £5 a time, at his discretion.

Unsurprisingly, given his other distractions, Hinkler found the strain of working full-time at Avro too much. In March, after more than seven years at Hamble, he resigned from his position as chief test pilot and agreed terms to instead work for the firm in a freelance capacity.

For the next couple of months, Hinkler carried on modifying the plane, and the newspapers continued to predict his imminent departure. He wrote to his parents in July, four months after he'd hoped to leave England, telling them that his plans were 'unsettled' and he couldn't look even a month ahead. 'I have not prepared my start for home and beauty yet,' he said. 'The blessed papers have made too big a story all too soon and sort of queered my pitch. But when all is quiet I'll just come toddling along.'[3] He assured his parents he and Nance were well, and that they were thriving at Mon Repos after 18 months in their new residence. To cater for Nance's keen interest in gardening, they established a glasshouse attached to the building.

Also in July, in his new role as a freelancer, Hinkler flew the newly completed Avian Mark II prototype in the 1927 King's Cup Air Race, but was forced to withdraw when the carburettor cracked. A month later, he took off from Croydon Aerodrome in his own Avian on a long-distance flight that would give him a chance to test out the plane for his Australian trip. He flew to Riga, the capital of Latvia, on behalf of another client – William Beardmore and Company, a Scottish-based aircraft manufacturer which also operated one of the biggest shipyards of the early twentieth century, on Clydeside. Like Sopwith Aviation, the company struggled to survive after World War I, and had only reopened its aviation section in 1924.

Beardmores had sold several aircraft to the Latvian Government, and Hinkler's flight was part of the after-sales follow-up. He added extra fuel capacity and a supplementary oiling system to G-EBOV for the trip, both modifications to his own design, and both of which would be useful on his proposed trip to Australia.

Latvia lies on the western edge of what is today known as the Russian Federation – but in August 1927 went by the rather more austere title of the Union of Soviet Socialist Republics. For much of the flight across Northern Europe, Hinkler flew at 4000 feet in brilliant sunshine, until low-lying cloud and fog forced him down to a height of just 100 feet for two hours. As he passed over the Baltic Sea port of Swinemünde, in the north of Germany (now Świnoujście, part of Poland), the weather cleared enough for him to see summer bathers on the beaches below. He made sure to keep away from the politically sensitive airspace close to the Polish border. 'Low black clouds were gathering fast,' he later recalled in an article he wrote for *Airways* magazine, 'as if Nature was lending her aid to guard the secrets of Poland.'[4]

As he neared Latvia, Hinkler discovered that his map didn't show his destination, Riga, a large seaport, situated on the southern shore of its eponymous, horseshoe-shaped gulf. He wasn't surprised, because he was navigating from his *Times Atlas*, with a scale of 50 miles to the inch. The atlas was a constant companion on his long-distance flights, and sometimes, it seems, the only chart he carried. Besides, he reckoned he knew roughly where Riga was, and landed in the city ten-and-a-half hours after he'd set out from London, having completed a total distance of around 1200 miles. It was by far the longest nonstop flight ever undertaken up to that time in a light aeroplane, but it would not be recognised as a world record because (typically) Hinkler hadn't told the press he was going, and no one had officially observed the start.

Glad to stretch his legs, the long-distance flyer had hardly jumped down from the cockpit before the local military guard appeared, all wearing helmets left over from World War I – some French, some German. Unfortunately for Hinkler, they spoke only Lettish, so he was unable to tell them why he was there. Just as the situation was becoming tense, local representatives of Beardmores arrived and eventually convinced the sceptical soldiers that Hinkler had just flown across from London.

The next day, after he had concluded his business for Beardmores, he gave Latvian Air Service officers a display of flying in G-EBOV. The locals were particularly impressed by the self-starting modification and the folding undercarriage, and Hinkler had to refuse numerous requests from the officers to take the plane for a spin. That evening he was a guest of the air force at what he described as a 'somewhat hectic dinner', where he was respectfully presented with the badge of the Latvian Air Service, a golden eagle suspended from a red swastika. He also drank vodka for the first time. 'I now fully understand,' he said later, 'the frequency of Russian revolutions.'[5]

On the return flight to England a few days later, via Berlin, Hinkler travelled across more than a dozen European countries. He was pleased with the way the Avro had performed. Nevertheless, he made more modifications at Hamble, fitting wings designed by Chadwick for the Mark II, along with an all-metal propeller. The undercarriage was also strengthened to make it more robust for any possible emergency landings on his way to Australia.

Ironically, in September 1927 Hinkler flight-tested a further modification of the Avian, the Mark III, which had been fitted with long-range fuel tanks specifically for an attempt on the England–Australia record by one Captain Bill Lancaster. The British-born Lancaster had been in the Australian Flying Corps in the Middle East and had flown with the RAF in India and, like Hinkler, was attracted by the idea of tackling the long journey to Australia for the first time in a light aircraft. Also like Hinkler, Lancaster originally planned to fly solo. However, a young Australian woman living in London, Jessie ('Chubbie') Miller, persuaded him to take her as a passenger, on the proviso she would pay half the costs. When Lancaster took the Mark III up for a pre-delivery flight at A.V. Roe and Company's newly acquired premises at Woodford, Cheshire, on 7 October, he was impressed by how well the plane performed. Hinkler knew that it would, of course. A week later, the test pilot was there to farewell Lancaster and Miller when they took off from Croydon aerodrome, bound for Port Darwin, Australia in the new plane, now christened *Red Rose*.

Hinkler could only wish them the best. His own plane was ready to go, but he was still working on garnering financial support. The agony of the delay was exacerbated by the news from Bundaberg that his father had died on 13 September, aged 72. The official cause of death was old age. Frances and John had been married for 35 years, and Bert had arrived in their lives near the end of their first year together. Since he'd left home 15 years before, they'd seen their eldest son in Bundaberg only twice – for a week or so in August 1913 after his New Zealand adventures with Wizard Stone, and for two exciting weeks in April 1921, when he'd landed on the foundry green the first day, and taxied up Gavan Street to the front door of Woodbine Villa.

Hinkler's frustration at having continually to postpone his departure was matched by that of A.V. Roe and Company. They had been waiting to see Hinkler's Avian break the record, and were ever hopeful of a take-off. In his ongoing dealings with the Air Ministry over non-payment for telegrams, Hinkler had indicated that Avro would pay, but after he'd personally visited the ministry in October, an official wrote a file note: 'I gathered that at the moment Mr Hinkler is dissatisfied with the A.V. Roe Co. concerning the arrangements for the proposed flight, and on telephoning Mr [John] Lord [an Avro executive], I learned the company are equally dissatisfied with Mr Hinkler.'[6]

Harald Penrose, a long-time employee of Woodland Aviation, and their chief test pilot from 1931, reckoned Hinkler always had problems working at Avro. He claimed that Hinkler's 'forcefulness of opinion on technics prevented him becoming an established test pilot, even though he acted in that capacity with A.V. Roe

Ltd for some years'.[7] Hinkler's friend Charles Grey, editor of *The Aeroplane* and the man responsible for introducing him to Roy Chadwick, also said the Queenslander was sometimes forthright in his technical opinions in a way that ruffled feathers. However, in his book on early test pilots at Avro, Peter Clegg is adamant that Hinkler made a positive and welcome contribution to the development of the company's aircraft:

> [Hinkler] had such an appreciation of the qualities of flying, and the ability of each aircraft he tested, that his engineering background could enable him to translate the deficiencies through to Roy Chadwick . . . in a simple and constructive way, and usually accompanied by his own suggestions for the aircraft's general improvement. His own suggestions, too, were more often than not acted upon in detail, and certainly no better working relationship existed than between Bert and Roy.[8]

Despite the limitations claimed by Penrose, Avro continued to employ Hinkler in a freelance role into early 1928, when he flew many of their new models. Nevertheless, the company would've been glad to see him take off in G-EBOV for his long-promised flight to Australia. As it happened, his next international trip was not to his homeland, nor was it even in the Avian.

* * *

Before Hinkler's Riga flight, 1927 had already been marked as a year of a rare and spectacular aviation success amid a host of failed international flights. In May, following in the footsteps of 1919 *Daily Mail* prize winners Alcock and Brown, a 25-year-old American pilot named Charles Lindbergh made the first nonstop solo crossing of the Atlantic, this time from New York to Paris. Sponsored by a syndicate, and in a quest for the long-coveted Orteig prize, Lindbergh set off from Long Island in his purpose-built Ryan monoplane, *Spirit of St. Louis* – which featured a single, 237-horsepower motor, fed by a 450-gallon fuel tank – and was greeted in Paris thirty-three hours later by huge and hysterical crowds. As well as collecting New York hotelier Raymond Orteig's $25,000, the young mail pilot and US Army Air Corps reservist was later awarded the Medal of Honor for his feat. Lindbergh's achievement not only went down in the annals of long-distance flying, but it established him as the most celebrated American aviator of all time.

Yet there was a spate of less stellar attempts to cross the Atlantic that year, many of which resulted in loss of life; by October 1927, nineteen aviators had died in trans-oceanic flights over the previous ten months. The editor of *Flight* magazine referred disparagingly to the British pilots' affliction as an 'Atlantitis',[9] and opined that no useful purpose could be served by attempting to repeat what others had already accomplished. Why not look to the East, he suggested, and try to beat distance records in that direction? There were calls in Britain for the Secretary of State for Air to be given discretionary powers to veto any trans-Atlantic flight that was considered unsafe, but senior Air Ministry officials and aviators opposed the idea. Despite such activity in local civil aviation, the current climate wasn't the time to be looking for backers for long-distance flights in any direction, as Hinkler knew only too well. 'It looked as if a suicide club had been formed in air circles,' he later observed.[10]

In November, *Flight's* editor wrote 'with unfeigned pleasure'[11] about a proposed flight to the East, to Karachi and beyond.

Providing the source of this pressman's delight was none other than Australian pilot Bert Hinkler, although this time not through any planned solo venture. An experienced long-distance flyer, Captain Robert McIntosh, had invited Hinkler to join him in trying to beat the England-to-India record, in a bright blue Dutch-built Fokker VII monoplane, *Princess Xenia*. By accepting the challenge, the Queenslander once again deferred his attempt to fly solo to the country of his birth.

From Hinkler's point of view, this India flight was an opportunity to raise interest from backers for his long-hoped-for Australian odyssey. Although the editor of *Flight* was miffed that McIntosh and Hinkler were using a foreign machine (while adding approvingly that at least 'the Bristol "Jupiter" engine is very British'[12]), he was confident that these two experienced flyers could do the job. *Aircraft* magazine's British correspondent, Major Frederic Robertson, felt the same way. Both men were wrong.

Hinkler and McIntosh didn't favour the conventional route to India, via Iraq and the Persian Gulf, preferring instead 'the Great Circle': through Central Europe and south-east Russia to Afghanistan, and then into India above the Khyber Pass. They made the choice despite a warning about the possible consequences of a forced landing in Russia or Afghanistan, or of crashing into the so-called Frontier hills of India, where the local Pathans might be hostile to what Major Robertson termed 'mysterious airmen arriving from the direction of Russia, in a machine which did not show the rings of the RAF'.[13]

Setting off from the grassy strip of the Royal Air Force base at Upavon, on Salisbury Plain, on 15 November 1927, Hinkler and McIntosh ran into foul weather almost immediately. 'We were as blind as bats,' Hinkler admitted. 'We saw nothing for the fog and snow . . . We passed a sleepless 25 hours, with snow continuously falling.'[14] The Fokker's airspeed indicator froze completely, and at one point the plane tumbled several thousand feet before they were able to bring it under control. On the first night, the two pilots found themselves encircled by mountains, and for hours flew up and down a valley until morning dawned and they could see a way out. One of them later told a reporter that 'the 12 hours of flying through utter darkness and continuous sleet and snowstorms was the most terrifying experience either of us had ever had'.[15]

Princess Xenia carried sufficient fuel for almost fifty hours, but apparently the pair landed the next day at a town in Eastern Galicia, an area with a complicated and an often bloody political history; it now lies in the Ukraine, although back then its annexation by Poland had recently been officially recognised (by all bar the Ukrainians). Two days passed before Hinkler and McIntosh were able to take off again, only for the Fokker to be forced down once more, after progressing just 75 miles from their previous point. They made a perfect landing in the snow at another small town, and had almost come to a standstill when the left-side undercarriage collapsed. The plane fell forward onto its nose, throwing the two men forward. Neither pilot was hurt, but the propeller and wing tip were damaged. So that was it, the end of their attempt to reach India.

A newspaper report described the trip as a 'glorious failure',[16] but McIntosh and Hinkler were greeted with rousing cheers by Nance and a horde of admirers at London's Liverpool Street Station on their return, without the plane. The two pilots were not publicly forthcoming about their excursion – possibly because they had something to hide. One account tells of them both being arrested after the second landing in Poland, then released, then arrested again in the morning when they couldn't pay a farmer for overnight accommodation. In that same account, McIntosh and Hinkler tricked the police into letting them move the aircraft, ostensibly to protect it from the weather, then took off without warning (allegedly 'chuckling at the success of their ruse'[17]) and flew to a Polish city, where they sought help from the British Consul. The culmination of their failed attempt was reportedly the later repair of the Fokker by the Polish Air Force as 'an act of grace',[18] after which McIntosh returned to Poland and flew the plane back to England. Whatever the actual circumstances on their short-lived attempt to fly to India, the failure of the venture meant that it did not generate the financial support for his Australian flight which Hinkler had hoped for. His experience with the flight did help him confirm which way he should go, however. And despite the good relationship he had with McIntosh, he still wanted to fly solo.

In Australia, doubts were expressed about the wisdom of Hinkler's proposed flight, with one newspaper claiming the consensus of technical experts was that they applauded the effort but felt the plane was too small for the proposed journey, particularly because so much was over water. The New South Wales branch of the Australian Aero Club issued a 'manifesto', declaring itself opposed to ocean-flying 'stunts', which, they said, could put back the course of aviation.

Hinkler was undisturbed by the naysayers. He had a point to prove about what he saw as the golden future of light aviation, and belief in himself and his plane. Although he had not publicly indicated his schedule, except to say that he wanted to beat the Smith brothers' record of 28 days, he still had in mind the timetable he had hatched for the Avro Baby seven years before – daylight hops of around 1000 miles a day. Civil Aviation officials believed him – on one occasion, when they sought approval for him to fly over the Malay States, they told government officials to expect him at Penang between eleven and sixteen days from his London departure, a time that would have him arriving in Australia just a few days later, well inside the record. A *Times* article predicted that if Hinkler was able to maintain a cruising speed of 90 miles an hour in the Avian, he would have to remain aloft for nine hours at a stretch in order to cover 700 miles in a day. 'If he should be able to maintain that figure, which seems unlikely,' the *Times* opined, 'he would reach Australia in 17 days.'[19]

In the meantime, it had become obvious that Lancaster and Miller would not bother the record keepers in their attempt to reach Australia. After their mid-October departure from London, they had overnight stops in Paris, Marseilles, Pisa, Rome and Naples, covering nothing like the distances Hinkler had in mind. On the island of Malta the two flyers were persuaded to stay for the weekend. Then wet weather delayed them for five days in Baghdad, and when the pair finally reached Basra in Iraq on 10 November, they were grounded for 16 days while they waited for a replacement magneto for the *Red Rose*'s engine to be sent from England, and by a cholera scare. By Christmas they'd reached Rangoon, where they spent a week waiting for a replacement piston, and on 6 January 1928 they arrived in Singapore. Already their trip had taken close to three months.

Back in England, Hinkler was still chafing at the bit to leave on his solo odyssey. By the new year, he and A.V. Roe and Company had patched up their differences, and John Lord told Air Ministry officials he was ready to come to an amicable arrangement with the pilot about the telegram costs, 'especially in view of the fact that he is considering now carrying out his long awaited flight'.[20]

By this time Hinkler had scraped together enough money to warrant a start. He also had in-kind support: Castrol oil from the company owned by Sir Charles Wakefield – an aviation benefactor of the time – and Shell aviation spirit from the Imperial Oil Company, along with other mostly engine-related products. As required by the ministry, he had arranged in advance for fuel stocks at aerodromes where he was likely to land along the way. Hinkler told the authorities that he had now decided on a definite date for his departure for Australia: 7 February 1928.

In response, ministry officials pointed out that the approvals obtained earlier from foreign powers to fly over their airspace had now lapsed and that new permissions would have to be sought. Although John Lord had ensured that the 1927 telegram costs were met, this time the civil servants refused point-blank to send any cables in advance without a deposit from Hinkler. Apparently not wanting to approach Lord again, Hinkler demurred. It was a stalemate. Three days before the proposed departure date, Sir Philip Sassoon, the Secretary of the Air Council – the ministry's governing body – wrote to the would-be record breaker:

> As regards Iraq, Persia and the Dutch East Indies, the Council are not prepared to send cables on your behalf without a deposit of £20 to cover the cost involved, and I am to make it clear to you that if you proceed on your flight without first having obtained the necessary permits, the [Air] Council can take no responsibility for sponsoring your flight, cannot make provision for Royal Air Force facilities in Palestine and Iraq

to be available for you, and can accept no responsibility for flights over foreign territory.[21]

What Sir Philip didn't say was that the ministry was also considering refusing him access to fuel at British bases.

For Hinkler, bureaucratic demands and ripples of concern about the wisdom of the flight were minor irritations after the years of waiting. Nance signed for receipt of the Air Ministry letter on his behalf, but the only stipulation he agreed to was that, since the Egyptian authorities required fifteen days' notice of flying over their territory, he would stay outside the 3-mile border limit of that country.

Since he'd left home mid-way through 1912, Bert Hinkler had been determined to make his parents proud of him. Despite his solid war record, and regardless of the recognition he'd received as a test pilot and an air racer, flying back to Bundaberg was an important personal goal. At least his mother would still be there to welcome him. Now the stars were aligned, and he would be denied no longer. This was something he was going to do by himself, and in a sense, for himself. Almost without exception, his achievements to this time had been as an employee or as a member of a team. This flight would be in his own plane, with his own modifications, and on his own terms. He was ready, finally, to fly 10,000 miles – to Australia.

CHAPTER 10

On the trail that leads us home

Hinkler reached out and quelled the alarm. It was 4.30 am on Tuesday, 7 February 1928. He'd stayed in London overnight, and had hoped to see the cheerful glow of the descending moon, but it was screened by a curtain of grey cloud, and the road outside was darkly wet under the streetlamps. As he went off to prepare for the day, he was suddenly, unexpectedly, overcome by anxiety.

Nance was still asleep. Her car had broken down on the way up from Mon Repos the night before and he'd waited anxiously until she arrived later by train, cheerful and confident, but disappointed that she couldn't go with him. He'd bluntly told her that she would just get in the way. 'My common sense revolted against the idea of a woman with me,' Hinkler later wrote, 'because she can be of no assistance and can only hamper.'[1] He acknowledged that taking his partner might give him more publicity, but said he wasn't looking for publicity.

Now, at the point of departure, he was having second thoughts about the flight, overwhelmed by the scale and audacity of what he was about to do. He paced the floor, his mind awhirl with the circumstances that had brought him to this point and with the uncertainties ahead. He had chosen to make this flight alone, with minimal personal and financial support, in a single-engined plane with an open cockpit, and now it seemed as if the burden of that decision had settled on his shoulders like a sack of the coal he'd shovelled into a ship's furnace on his way to England fourteen years before. There were so many unknowns in the hostile and sometimes uninhabited environments he would have to cross, that any error or misjudgement on his part, any defect with the aircraft or its motor, or any severe weather event would almost certainly mean disaster, and possibly death.

Hinkler's sudden drop in self-confidence would probably have amazed those who knew him in England, since the plucky Australian's willingness to take on seemingly any challenge and his strong belief in his own abilities and opinions were already legendary. On that cold February morning, it took him an hour to talk himself around. 'Hang it. I'll go,' he decided at last. 'I've waited ten years for this. Not another hour!'[2]

He woke Nance, and they set off together for the Croydon Aerodrome hangar. As the slate-grey light of dawn pushed through, the rain that had been threatening held off. The temperature was not much above zero, however, and Hinkler had made a triple-decker attempt to keep out the cold – a woollen sweater pulled over a lounge suit and a greatcoat buttoned over them both. The Avian 581E was fully fuelled and ready to go. Nance sat in the front cockpit when she flew with him, but for this flight he'd replaced her with a 46-gallon fuel tank that would help him bridge the daily distances he'd planned. Behind his own cockpit, Hinkler had stowed a rubber raft and paddle into a specially constructed metal tube, but he knew that if he went down in the sea, with no radio to call for help, a raft and paddle would be little consolation.

Lancaster and Miller had also chosen to fly without a radio when they headed off to Australia in *Red Rose* the previous October. Their attempt had come to grief on 10 January when the Avian crashed while attempting a take-off at Muntok on Bangka Island, in the Dutch East Indies, only a couple of days short of their destination, Port Darwin. They escaped with cuts and bruises, and Jessie Miller had a broken nose, but the plane was extensively damaged and eventually transported back to Singapore for repairs, which would end up taking almost two months. Although they were not the sort of circumstances any flyer would wish on a fellow pilot, the way was now clear for Bert Hinkler to take the England to Australia records for both the fastest flight and the first in a light plane. Bill Lancaster expressed the belief that Hinkler had delayed his flight to give *Red Rose* time to succeed.

Anxious to get going, Hinkler packed sandwiches, biscuits, chocolate and a flask of coffee into the cockpit, along with a blue-covered logbook to record his journey. Hidden away from the eyes of customs officials was a case of whisky to serve as gifts on arrival, although Hinkler himself mostly preferred ginger beer.

He believed that the press's continual conjecture regarding both his departure date and the wisdom of the venture had hindered his plans up till now, so he maintained the strategy he'd adopted for the Latvia flight, of not alerting the press in advance. Consequently, only Nance and A.V. Roe's general manager were there that morning to see him off, apart from two airport staff, who looked on without great interest. As part of his strategy, Hinkler had contacted the Australian Press Association and arranged to cable a report to them from each stopover. So they knew he was going, but not exactly when.

He shook hands with the Avro boss, who then moved away to let Hinkler say goodbye to his partner of the past ten years. 'I wish you all the best, Bert,' Nance said, as she gave him a hug, trying not to show her anxiety. 'Good weather and safety. It won't be long.'[3] He smiled and nodded, then turned and climbed into the plane that he had chosen to carry him to his native land. As he slipped on his fur-lined gloves, pressed in his earplugs, and tugged his flying helmet on, he thought how grey and mysterious the world looked at that time of day.

Pulling his goggles over his eyes, he sat in the cockpit while the engine warmed up, and wondered if his mother knew he was on his way to see her. With his father's recent passing, Bert knew she'd be looking forward more than ever to having her eldest son by her side. He'd told her for months he was nearly ready to go, but with all the postponements, he'd been reluctant to raise her hopes again by suggesting he had a final date for a take-off. By the time he knew he was definitely going, there was so much to finalise, not to mention dealing with officialdom, that he decided he'd explain when he arrived in Bundy. In any event, if all went well, she'd soon read about his progress in the papers.

When all was ready, Hinkler waved to Nance and the Avro manager, before taxiing the aircraft through a layer of ground fog to the top of the runway. Despite the soggy ground and the full load, the Avian picked up speed quickly and took off smoothly into the breaking dawn, its silhouette dark against the backlit clouds. It had been a joke among Croydon Aerodrome staff that the little plane had been built around Hinkler, and for a moment all that the observers below could see was the shape of his flying helmet above the cockpit. Then, with a final wave, he was on his way, taking the Avro into a steep climb over grainy London, the city's lights twinkling below through scattered cloud. 'I suppose one of those philosopher fellows would have been wondering where the end of that day would find him,' Hinkler later wrote of his first few minutes airborne. 'I was thinking that the coffee would be good-oh if the weather got much colder.'[4]

Hinkler still hadn't publicly nominated a target, but the various schedules he'd submitted to the Air Ministry, and his unsuccessful approaches to newspapers and Lloyd's insurance company, all pointed to his wanting to slash the Smith brothers' time for the flight. He was not just hungry for the record, he wanted to devour it. His intention was to fly as far as possible each day while there was daylight, planning that each stage would bring him to a designated aerodrome, preferably one where the Imperial Oil Company had arranged to leave stocks of Shell fuel and oil. He prayed peace would be maintained in Syria, so he could fly across the Middle East. Otherwise he might have to divert, which would affect his attempt on the record.

Although Hinkler didn't know that it had even been mooted, Air Ministry officials had decided the day before not to withhold fuel supplies from him at British bases.

* * *

Heading across the cloud-shrouded Channel, Hinkler could feel a side wind nudging him northwards, but he was determined to make a good start, and pushed on, heading for Rome. As the Avro bumped across the thermals, all he could think was: 'At last! At last!'[5] After his experience with McIntosh in the *Princess Xenia*, Hinkler had rejected the Great Circle route for the one the 1919–20 competition flyers had followed: south-east across Europe, then down through the Middle East and across India to the Dutch East Indies (now Indonesia), and on to northern Australia.

The *Canberra Times* later published an 'air shanty', written by Melbourne poet, William Tainsh, to celebrate the occasion. The song begins:

O, London Town is a lovesome place,
And it lies right near my heart;
But a man must go while the going's good,
And it's time for me to start.
So it's tune my 'Baby Bunting' up,
And shape her nose for Rome;
For we're off non-stop for the first long hop
On the trail that leads us home!

On this first long hop, Hinkler flew in grey cloud over most of France, but emerged thankfully into sunshine over the Rhone Valley in the south-east of the country. As he forged on, he noticed the scenery ahead wasn't getting any closer – it took a moment for him to realise that he was flying into a strong headwind. He dropped the plane down to less than 100 feet and, protected now by the hills, was able to scuttle over the mosaic of farms and cattle below, until he saw ahead the diamond points of the afternoon sun sparkling on the waters of the French Riviera.

He was in familiar territory now, but, fearful of the crags on the island of Corsica, Napoleon's birthplace, he decided to follow the Italian coast around. Visibility was about 15 miles, and below he could see the white sails of ships etching their way across the deep blue of the Ligurian Sea. But the winter sun was sinking fast, and despite his sweater and overcoat, the cold was intense in the open cockpit.

With only two more hours of daylight left, Hinkler began to wonder if he would reach Rome before dusk, and so kept his eyes peeled for an alternative landing ground. The city of Pisa was close by, but he decided to continue on towards Rome as planned. Having landed in the Italian capital before, he knew roughly the location of Centocelle, the public aerodrome, and expected that there'd be flares along the runway if he did have to come in after dark.

As the sun slid down the blackening sky, a fog stretched itself out lazily around the aircraft, and, as if in response, Hinkler's mood changed. 'I felt a little blue,' he would later tell newspaper readers throughout Australia. 'It's easy to be optimistic in the sun, but it feels a bit queer to be away up on your pat [i.e., alone] with darkness coming on, and only a guess at where and how you will land.'[7] By now, Hinkler could hardly make out the coastline below, and he couldn't see the dashboard at all. He used his pocket torch to check the dials, and was feeling so low that even its narrow yellow beam was enough to hearten him. Seeing the moving buttons of lights from cars on the roads below also cheered him – at least there were other people out there.

A wind sprang up, whining its way through the struts and bumping the Avro around. He said to himself, 'Keep her going. You'll get there and break the record.'[8] A short while later, his eyes were drawn to a peculiar ball of light in the sky behind him and, as he watched, it transformed itself into a cheerful moon. He smiled. After all, he knew the moon in England, too.

Finally he saw another glow – from the lights of the Eternal City. Better than that, there was a big red flashing light over Centocelle Aerodrome. As he flew closer, though, he realised it was actually an illuminated advertising sign. The airfield itself seemed to have disappeared. He flew round and round in the dark, then zigzagged above the city, all the while trying to locate his landing site. Like a bird that's mislaid its nest, he thought.

After half an hour, he spotted the tiny lights on top of the aerodrome's radio masts, but the runway itself was in darkness. From 1000 feet, he flashed an SOS on his little torch to indicate that he needed flares, and twice zoomed down to alert the ground staff. Nothing happened.

Hinkler decided he'd have to land in the dark. Just as the Avro's wheels touched down, flares blossomed along both sides of the strip, one so close it looked like it might set fire to the plane. As he rolled G-EBOV to a stop, there seemed to be hundreds of soldiers around the terminal building. One report claims that he landed at a military airport instead of the civilian one, and was arrested and bailed out by the British Consul. Whatever the circumstances, Hinkler was relieved to be able to complete formalities and finally tumble into a bed at 1 am. Tired as he was, he lay there for a moment thinking of the day's journey from his early morning start in London. The lights of home, and the lights of Rome, and 1200 miles in between, he thought.

He had covered the distance in almost thirteen hours, and the Avian hadn't missed a beat. It was a good start. Already, however, he'd noticed how winds could affect his schedule, and he'd experienced the feeling of being alone in the air. He'd been on long flights before by himself, but this time there were many days to go. On returning to the aerodrome the next morning, after four hours' sleep, he was disconcerted to see a second cluster of high radio masts, which he hadn't even noticed the night before during the landing. His flight to Australia had been very close to coming to an end on day one.

* * *

After sending a cable to the Australian Press Association, Hinkler had trouble getting away. The cause was not the weather conditions, nor mechanical woes, but a constant stream of visitors, who'd heard about the arrival of a small plane that was rumoured to be flying to Australia. Centocelle Aerodrome was by this time a busy commercial centre and, like today's pilots, Hinkler had to line up for take-off – except that in 1928 the 'control tower' was an official standing in the middle of the field with a red flag.

His next stop was Malta, a flyspot in the middle of the Mediterranean and just 600 miles away. It was a shorter distance than he would have preferred for a day's flying, but he did not want to risk the plane over the additional 450 miles across water to the North African coast. Also, Malta was a British naval and air base, where he was confident he'd be warmly received.

As he headed down the west coast of Italy, the rugged Apennine mountain range on his left sent up thermal currents that buffeted the little Avro. Below, the sea sparkled emerald in the sunshine as it curled up against the dark rocks, but it was sandy beaches that Hinkler was constantly on the lookout for – if anything went wrong, he'd need somewhere to land in a hurry. Not that he lacked confidence in reaching his final destination: 'I got a fine view up there,' he'd write later in his syndicated newspaper column, 'floating along towards Bundaberg.'[9]

He burst through the spume of smoke streaming from the crater of Mount Vesuvius, near Naples in southern Italy, and soon afterwards was stunned by the immensity of another volcano, Mount Etna, on the island of Sicily. Hinkler pushed the Avro 581E close to its limit across the Mediterranean and a few hours later he landed on the tiny, flat and stony isle of Malta. As he'd predicted, the RAF made him very welcome at their mess in the town of Valletta, so much so that he eventually had to beg to be allowed to get some sleep.

Again he cabled the newspapers. In his native Queensland, the *Brisbane Courier* reported that no definite announcement had yet been made about the route Hinkler was to take on the way to Bundaberg, but that fuel supplies were being arranged for Normanton, in the Gulf of Carpentaria. Interest was beginning to simmer.

* * *

Overnight rain at Valetta had made the red soil airstrip boggy and there was a strong wind blowing as he prepared for take-off next morning. The little Avro shrugged these off, though, and on Thursday, 9 February, Hinkler headed south-east towards North Africa and Italian-controlled Libya. He'd enjoyed the camaraderie of the RAF, but as he flew across the open waters on this third day, the loneliness of the long-distance pilot again consumed him: 'I was now getting out of the range of companionship. No longer would the frequent sight of villages and cities cheer me. I felt lonely and dispirited, though just as ever convinced that the little bus would not let me down.[10]

He also took the precaution of flying slightly south of his plotted line, knowing the wind would bring him back on course, thus ensuring he was always on a path where searchers would look for him if the Avro went down. Nevertheless, flying over water was part of the reason Hinkler undertook the journey to Australia. He later explained that it was a way of demonstrating how safe light aircraft were for everyday travel. 'I might have flown over land for 10 years without banging home the lesson,' he wrote. 'To risk my life, as most would view it, in traversing long sea stretches, was a dramatic exhibition of my faith.'[11] As he flew steadily on, the sky seemed more intensely blue under the glare of the Mediterranean sun, and he could feel the heat rising.

It took Hinkler six hours to reach the North African coast, at which point, being without a radio, he landed at the port city of Benghazi to ask the British authorities there to advise RAF Malta of his safe arrival. He then set off for Tobruk, flying across the Western Desert, where thirteen years later General Rommel's Afrika Korps would fight Allied troops for control of some very desolate country. 'Rivers of blood were poured out over miserable strips of land which, in normal times, not even the poorest Arab would have bothered his head over,' the German general lamented afterwards. Hinkler didn't think much of it either. Flying low along the coast of Libya, in airspace controlled by Italy's air force, the Regia Aeronautica, the Australian saw 'great gorges that ran in from the sea as though a giant's fingers had scooped out the rocks in a temper', and hills 2000 feet high that 'reached up for my under-carriage'.[13]

On this eastward course, the plane struggled against a headwind, and as the shadows lengthened, Hinkler realised that he wouldn't make Tobruk by nightfall. This was not only a blow to his schedule, but it meant he'd have to improvise a landing in the desert. At least by now the terrain had flattened out below him, compared with before. There is an Arab saying that 'the desert shows you nothing; you must find everything', and that evening Hinkler was kept busy trying to find a suitable landing spot. On several occasions when he dropped the plane down, he discovered vicious outcrops of camel thorn, which clutched at the undercarriage, forcing him to pull out of the landing. Eventually he made a bumpy touchdown on a rocky but relatively flat strip of ground.

As darkness fell, he made short work of the sandwiches and coffee that the RAF boys had given him, and looked around for somewhere to make a bed. Then he had an idea. Reaching behind his seat in the Avro's cockpit, he pulled out the tube containing the collapsible life raft, pumped up the raft, turned it over, and settled down for the night on his pneumatic mattress. He knew that if he could keep up his present rate of progress, he would accomplish the flight to Australia in under 20 days.

But sleep didn't come easily, and not just because the desert temperature had plummeted. Hinkler well knew of Cobham's experience just over 18 months earlier, when the unfortunate Elliott had died by a Bedouin bullet, and would have been aware of the general antipathy among much of the population in this part of the world to the British presence. As much as he yearned for a cigarette – although he was normally a non-smoker – he didn't dare light one for fear of drawing attention to himself. Later he wrote in a newspaper piece headed 'Alone in Desert' that at the time he'd had the thought that only heroines in moving pictures welcome the arrival of sheiks.

Twenty-four hours later, he met one, face to face.

CHAPTER 11

Desert sands and a load of anxiety

When Hinkler awoke next day, he discovered that there was a mass of thornbush ahead of the plane, which hadn't been visible at dusk when he'd landed. He also discovered that two Arabs were now heading his way, and watched them apprehensively.

In fact, they turned out to be curious more than anything else. Using hand signals, Hinkler persuaded the pair to help him clear a path for 100 yards ahead of the Avro. Concerned about taking off across sand on such a short makeshift runway, he then abandoned some of his petrol in order to lighten the load. In the event, the little Avian skipped off more quickly than he'd expected, and was soon making its way towards Tobruk, where Hinkler planned to refuel. After just half an hour, he landed at the aerodrome in fierce heat.

Alerted from Benghazi, the Regia Aeronautica in Tobruk had been preparing to send out search planes. They knew that if an aircraft had gone down in the desert, no one on board would survive long in the extreme temperatures. The Italian pilots now insisted on escorting Hinkler's plane for 50 miles east towards his day-four target, Ramleh, in Palestine, about 1000 miles from his overnight stop in the desert. He would've preferred to land before then, in Egypt, and was sorry he hadn't given the required fifteen days' notice of intention to fly over the Egyptians' territory.

Once the Italian flyers had left him, Hinkler prepared himself for a long day of lonely flying. After three full days in the cockpit, he was feeling cramped, and with only one free hand, he found it difficult to eat, not to mention juggle flimsy maps in the wind. At least the glass tube through the cork in the top of his thermos allowed him to drink easily.

He also found it a challenge to accustom himself to the pervading silence, when the only sounds for long stretches were the steady drone of the Cirrus engine and the wind whistling through the wooden struts that connected the two levels of wing. 'I used to sing and call out,' he later reported, 'just to hear the sound of my own voice, and it sounded so queer I used to fall quiet again.'[1] Sometimes when he was feeling particularly annoyed or frustrated, he relieved his feelings with what he called 'army-type' sayings. 'Twice I said "Bother!" and once I said "Dash!",' he joked.[2]

A situation that called for a bit of 'Bother!' and 'Dash!' came late that day as a small but persistent oncoming breeze guaranteed he wouldn't be reaching Ramleh before nightfall. 'Land-keeping people think nothing of a 10 miles-an-hour wind,' he'd later tell readers, 'but in an aeroplane it is just enough to take the devil out of the speed.'[3]

This was a tense time for Hinkler. As dusk closed in, he knew he'd have to make another desert landing, this time on an uncertain surface: soft sand would not only make it difficult to take off the next day, but it might tip the Avian over if the wheels caught. If that happened, and if he was unable to right it or the plane was damaged, he knew he had no way to call for help.

He picked out a likely spot, and after first swooping down to check it out, gingerly touched down. Almost immediately he was pushed back in his seat as the wheels gripped in the sand, but the plane's speed and light weight stopped it from sinking, and he managed to land without mishap. Still, he'd need harder ground for take-off the following morning. There was a likely stretch not far away . . . but how to get the Avro over there?

As if on cue, scores of Arabs appeared, attracted by the unusual sight of this silver and green biplane setting down in the desert. Hinkler was just wondering how he might ask for their help, when among them he spied a sheik, who reminded him of the silent-movie idol of the time, Rudolph Valentino. 'I asked him in the best English if it would be all right to let some thousands of his followers do a job for England,' Hinkler recalled in his newspaper account. 'After he had translated this into fingers, he gave an order, and the road gang was ready.'[4]

Within a short time, the newly recruited volunteers had jostled the aircraft into position, ready for day five, and Hinkler duly rewarded them from his dwindling supply of cigarettes. To his surprise, they didn't leave immediately: 'What excuses they gave their wives next day, I don't know, but they lit big fires and sat down with me and talked themselves to sleep.'[5] He retired to his upturned lifeboat.

During the night, he awoke with a start and found several Arabs huddled around him. They examined him and his inflatable craft, before crawling back to their fire, their curiosity apparently satisfied.

* * *

In the morning, Hinkler asked his new-found friends to build another fire, this time alongside the makeshift airstrip. Using the hard ground, and with the smoke as an indicator of wind direction, he took off without a hitch. As the plane rose, he could see the Arabs waving to him, and he circled over them – 'out of compliment to Rudolph',[6] as he later put it – before heading off to Ramleh. During the course of the 70-mile flight, he discovered that the small rocky strip where he'd landed was in fact the only safe pocket of land in the surrounding desert.

It was 11 February, his fifth day in the air, and as ever, he was keen to push on. He planned to refuel at Ramleh and give his engine a quick check after the two forced nights in the desert, before departing for Basra, 900 miles away in Iraq. He knew it was long stages like that which would help him achieve his goal of smashing the 1919 record time.

Now known as the Israeli city of Ramla, from 1920 to 1948 Ramleh was a town within Mandatory Palestine and, like Iraq, under British rule. It served as a base for both the Royal Air Force and a British Army armoured car division, and when Hinkler's Avro landed, all personnel were on parade for the usual Saturday morning inspection. After being given the order to dismiss, some of the air force men insisted that their new arrival have breakfast with them. The Queenslander was keen to move on, but acquiesced.

During the meal, the RAF officers told him of the current diphtheria scare in Palestine and asked if he had a health clearance. This was a detail that Hinkler had overlooked, so next moment he was on his way by car to the doctor in town for a medical examination. He quickly satisfied the requirements, but his departure for Basra was delayed further when he had to obtain a customs clearance at Ramleh aerodrome.

In Hinkler's description, the Palestinian customs forms were 'as big as a large-sized bedroom mirror, but not nearly so clear'.[7] By the time he'd completed the documentation, any chance of making Basra that day was diminishing fast. And in between the two locations was some pitiless country – hardly the sort of place that one would choose to force-land a plane. The RAF boys persuaded him not to make the attempt that day after all, arguing that if he was in bed early for once and suitably rested, he'd be fitter for the flight ahead. Having had only sporadic sleep over the last two nights, Hinkler agreed, since the delay also gave him a chance to thoroughly check the engine.

The early-to-bed idea quickly went by the board, however. The Ramleh station staff invited him to join them and their wives for a night of cabaret and dancing in the nearby town of Jaffa, and it wasn't until 1.30 am that he finally stumbled into bed. By his account, he was merely abiding by the RAF officers' slogan: 'What's the good of being a Royal Air Force man if you can't be Jaffish?'[8]

To Hinkler's surprise, almost all of his companions from this night out were there to bid him farewell the next morning. As he took off in G-EBOV, he wondered if anyone beyond those he'd met on the trip knew anything about his progress. He'd continued to send cables to the Australian Press Association, but he had no idea if anything had actually been published.

He needn't have worried. All the major Australian and British newspapers were reporting on his progress, in snippets and short items. There was increasing public interest in the flight, and just four days after his take-off from London, the *Sydney Morning*

Herald had published a map of his likely flight path from England to Australia.

He journeyed south-east across Palestine and over the very lands that the Biblical figures he'd learnt about in Sunday School had roamed. It surprised him how much of the country below was arid and inhospitable. Soon he was flying across the Dead Sea, and then over present-day Jordan and the sun-scorched wastes of the Assyrian desert in northern Iraq. It was so hot that even in the open cockpit of the Avro, it seemed stuffy; his bones ached with cramp, but stretching backwards only hurt his spine. He talked, sang and whistled to try to relieve the tedium, which the steady drone of the engine seemed only to accentuate. He later reflected on how lonely he'd felt: '10,000 feet above the earth, with not a sound except the propeller, a man begins to realise what solitary confinement is. I love flying, but I did not love that day.'[9]

Hinkler was relieved to finally see the Euphrates River and then the Tigris, and a few hours later the city where the two rivers join: Basra, which had an Imperial Airways base at Shaibah Aerodrome.

Formed in Britain in 1924 by a consortium of pioneering airlines, Imperial Airways initially operated flights from London into Europe, but as its name implies, the intention was that it would extend its reach to the rest of the empire. Its first foray was into India via Egypt when it set up the Cairo to Karachi route with de Havilland Hercules airliners in 1925, followed two years later by a service between Cairo and Basra. Because of the difficulty of navigating aircraft across hundreds of miles of desert that had no significant features, as well as to improve communications, a road was constructed between Damascus and

Baghdad, interspersed with a chain of emergency landing grounds. To further aid pilots, each of the airfields was marked with a giant letter of the alphabet or Roman numeral. Hinkler stayed north of the road on his way to Basra, and used the aerodrome marked 'A' as a navigation point.

As he neared Shaibah Aerodrome, the Avro passed close to the spot where Cobham's mechanic, Elliott, had died. Hinkler was a little anxious at the time, but happily reported in a later account of his desert crossing that the few Bedouins he'd seen 'showed not the slightest disposition to loose off at me anything more deadly than curiosity'.[10]

Despite the forced desert landings, it had taken Hinkler only six days to reach Basra, the legendary hometown of Sinbad the Sailor. In 1919, Ross and Keith Smith hadn't reached the city until the eighth day out from London.

That night, Hinkler once again opened his blue log book, and quickly jotted down the information required about the day's journey. Although he'd been sending the press brief summaries of the highlights of each stage, he was much more niggardly when it came to his log. Using a pen or thick pencil – whichever he could lay his hands on – he hastily scribbled the minimum information in the pre-printed columns provided for recording each day's details – date, journey from/to, name, address, nationality ('British'), place of departure, and duration of flight. He gave his address each time as 'Croydon, England'. In the column 'State of the aircraft on departure', he invariably wrote 'OK'. This was an understatement, considering the lack of trouble he'd had with the Avian on the flight so far, apart from the petrol leak.

* * *

Early next morning, Hinkler headed out over the dull grey mudflats of the Euphrates estuary towards Jask, in southern Persia (now Iran), another 900-mile goal. His earlier flying experience had been in Britain and Europe, and briefly the United States, none of which prepared him for the contrasting weather conditions he ran into on this leg of the journey.

Not long after he'd left the Euphrates behind, the air below was so clear that he could see the image of his plane reflected in the mirror-like Persian Gulf, yet ahead, he could see hardly a mile for heavy fog. Rather like London fog, he thought, except for the smell and taste. 'It was easy to feel that I was alone in the world in my little floating bus,' he wrote in an aptly titled article, 'Monotony of Flying'.[11] He ploughed on through the two dimensions until the aircraft eventually emerged into clear skies again.

There was hardly time for him to appreciate his view to the horizon before a sandstorm hit the plane – a much greater threat than the fog, because the sand could blast its way into his engine and stall it. He tightened the strap on his goggles and prepared for the worst, but his concern was short-lived. Whatever the impact of a sandstorm at ground level, he found that at a few thousand feet the effect is more like fog because the particles are so small and the sting negligible.

The sandstorm also didn't last long, and shortly afterwards he crossed the Gulf of Oman and circled the peninsula of Jask, which, he wrote later, 'looked like an unwanted tool thrown carelessly down at a farm gate'. At that time, Jask was a British concession, important as a telegraph station and stopover point for every pilot heading east, and had an appointed commissioner who, in Hinkler's words, 'plays the part of fairy godfather to everything with wings'.[12]

The aerodrome was a mile and a half from the village, and Hinkler swooped down across the roofs to alert the residents of his arrival. He was so successful that when he landed, his plane was almost overwhelmed by hundreds of 'coolies' – the term commonly used in those days by European colonial powers as a generic name for the local population. 'I thought I'd managed to alert half of Persia,' Hinkler wrote of his welcoming committee.[13]

The commissioner arrived soon afterwards, and offered him the choice of a donkey or a bicycle as a means of transportation to the village. There were no cars, because there was nowhere else to go. Hinkler chose the bike: the donkey's rudder control seemed defective, he said.

Apart from the occasional aeroplane, Jask's only contact with the outside world was a monthly steamer. Perhaps thinking of his visit to Jaffa's cabarets a couple of nights earlier, Hinkler found the place depressing. 'Jask has no amusements, except tennis out of doors and crosswords inside. I noticed no night life, no vices, no happiness. It is a missionary's paradise.'[14]

He was glad to cycle back to the airstrip early the following morning, where the local Shell representative helped him refuel. Halfway through the refuelling, he noticed petrol dripping onto the sand below. One of the Avro's tanks was leaking, at a steady and ominous rate.

There were no repair facilities at Jask, and Hinkler's next destination, Karachi, was 650 miles away. Part of the flight was across the Arabian Sea, and the only option in an emergency would be a dash north to Ormara, an isolated town on the southern coast of India where Alexander the Great once camped with his army. Although he was ahead of the Smith brothers' schedule, Hinkler could see the record slipping away like the escaping fuel.

He counted the drips from the tank 'like a doctor taking a pulse',[15] and calculated that if the rate of loss stayed steady, he could probably make it to Karachi. He decided he'd take the chance.

* * *

Hinkler initially headed east along the Persian coast towards Pakistan. Although his mind was on the fuel supply, he couldn't help noticing the holiday-makers sunning themselves on the beaches below and bobbing about on boats inshore. He was reminded of the English seaside resorts he'd visited, and realised how much alike different peoples were in that regard, even though the British sometimes imagined those in the part of the world he was flying over took their pleasure 'in some queer Arabian Nights way',[16] as he later put it.

Suitably enlightened, he flew on, his eyes flicking constantly to the fuel gauge. There was a 10-gallon petrol tank on either side of the top wing of the biplane, and these were fed from the larger tank he had installed. His practice was to change from one top tank to the other every two-and-a-half hours. Usually, if things were going well, there might still be fuel left in the first tank at the changeover. This time, however, the tank seemed to be emptying faster than the mileage accounted for. Hinkler convinced himself that the drip had transformed itself into a stream. He could see it in his mind. Would there be enough fuel to reach Karachi? He flew on, like a motorist wondering whether he'll make it to the next service station. Except that the consequences for Hinkler would be far more serious if he couldn't make the distance.

As time passed, he grew more hopeful – 200 miles completed, 300 miles, and then he was over halfway. After following the dark brown line of low rocky coastal cliffs, Hinkler angled south-east across the Arabian Sea to give himself the shortest possible distance to Karachi. The turquoise blue of the ocean where it lapped the beaches was soon replaced by dark blue swells.

One hundred and fifty miles to go. He made more calculations and kept his gaze on the fuel level. As the miles sped past, his concern gradually changed to relief, and then exhilaration. He could see he was going to make it. 'If you want to know full happiness, running over,' he subsequently wrote, 'go through a section of the sky with a load of anxiety in the cockpit, and throw it overboard at the last moment.'[17] Less than two hours later, he landed at Karachi (then in British India, today the largest city in Pakistan), near the mouth of the Indus River.

Outlasting the fuel leak was not the only cause for celebration that Tuesday, 14 February. His arrival in Karachi after just eight days set three new world records: fastest journey from England to India, longest solo flight, and longest flight in a light aeroplane. He was also three days ahead of the Smith brothers' schedule. The press, which had been dutifully reporting his cabled progress in single paragraphs, now became more excited. In London, the Australian Press Association dubbed him 'Hustling Hinkler', a nickname quickly taken up by newspapers in his home country. The Royal Aero Club cabled from London: 'Keep it up, Bert.'[18] At last he was beginning to make the mark on the world he'd been hoping for. 'Sleepy as I was, there was no one happier in all India,' he recalled.[19]

Australian newspapers began following his journey with increased optimism, stirring the nation. The words in the *Brisbane Courier* of 16 February were echoed in every state: 'The last thing Hinkler thinks of is himself; he never has a hamper; just a cake of chocolate, a couple of sandwiches, and a thermos of coffee.'[20] This image of Bert Hinkler as the diminutive pilot from Bundaberg, bravely flying solo across the world on the smell of an oily rag, became an enduring one in the minds of the public.

Of more urgency to the man himself, at Karachi he was able to draw on the expert and willing assistance of the Royal Air Force, whose mechanics found that the leak had been caused by 'panting' – that is, movement of the fuel tank walls as the tank emptied. The solution was to brace the walls. 'I am glad to say that the work we did at Karachi did the trick, for from that day to this the braces have kept down the pants,'[21] Hinkler later said wryly.

* * *

After less than three hours' sleep, he was up again with the mechanics at 3.30 am. Used engine oil kept the dust down on the sandy Karachi airstrip as he pulled the Avro into the air just before dawn and headed for Cawnpore (now Kanpur), 930 miles away in north central India. He looked down with trepidation at the dry, rocky mountains below, and was relieved when he emerged over the green and highly populated areas further east.

Hinkler's RAF colleagues in Karachi had convinced him that to stave off the fierce Indian sun in the Avian's open cockpit, he should replace his flying helmet with a topee, or pith helmet. This seemed like a good idea until about five hours into the flight, when his head began to ache because the topee prevented him from using his earplugs. The constant noise of the engine and the battering of the wind on the plane pounded through his head for hour after hour. His eyes, too, felt the strain. 'I was near as a touch conking out,' Hinkler later reported.[22]

He held on, however, and once the Jumna River came into view, he knew it wasn't long now. When he landed at the Cawnpore airstrip, which was also used as a parade ground by the occupying Essex Regiment, he quickly completed the formalities before tumbling into bed at 5 pm.

Just 70 years before, Cawnpore had been the centre of atrocities on both sides in what the British called the Indian Mutiny, and what some Indians would later call the First War of Independence. Not long after those events, following years of partial economic domination, the British Government seized control of the country, and by the time Hinkler arrived in 1928, India was firmly in the period of rule known as the British Raj.

That was to change some 20 years later, but Bert Hinkler would not be around to witness it. All he wanted at the moment was to break a record. Many newspapers were now printing almost verbatim the daily cables he sent, and public expectation of a new record began to grow, not only in Australia, but across the world.

CHAPTER 12

Sticky mud and summer storms

Hinkler recovered quickly from the unpleasant effects of wearing a topee, and with flying helmet and earplugs firmly in place once more, he continued east across India on 16 February. His target distance on this, his tenth day, was a comparatively low 630 miles to Calcutta, the former capital of British India, known in the twenty-first century as Kolkata and located near the Indian border with Bangladesh.

The plane bumped in the thermals over more mountains – a sensation that Hinkler came to know well in the tropics – before he forged a way through fog so thick that it once again reminded him of England. For the last 100 miles that day, he was astonished by the vast numbers of people below, particularly around the Ganges River. He enjoyed the colourful contrast of yellow fields and green jungles, but felt sorry for the water buffalo straining in the heat.

When he landed at Dum Dum Aerodrome, 10 miles north-east of Calcutta, he met two English pilots who operated a local aerial taxi and photography business, using an Avro Baby. Although Hinkler would be toiling away on the Avian until well after midnight, with enthusiastic assistance from these Englishmen, he at least took some time out beforehand to travel into the city. The traffic on the road made a big impression on him:

> The water buffaloes, cars of all makes, dog carts, buggies, all use the road, the pace on which is set by the slowest traffic – the buffalo. This animal whizzes along at three miles an hour; when he is especially enthusiastic he reaches four miles. Anything behind him stays there, and you have the queer spectacle of cars in first gear crawling behind a buggy, which follows a smart dog cart stuck up by a team of water buffaloes. You can accelerate nothing on that road except language.[1]

* * *

Following his stopover in Calcutta, Hinkler abandoned the easterly flight path he'd been following since his arrival in north Africa a week before, and turned south-west, in the general direction of Australia. His immediate destination, however, was Rangoon, at that time a thriving centre of commerce and the capital of Burma, another country subjected to British rule, administered as part of the Raj.

Leaving behind the muddy estuary of the Hoogli, he headed across the Bay of Bengal. The sky was hazy, made worse by jungle fires, and he took the Avro up to 7000 feet to avoid the bumps of the thermal currents. When he reached the eastern coastline of the bay, he turned south near the town of Akyab to begin following the coast of Burma down.

At this stage of his long journey to Australia, Hinkler was about to exchange the deserts and dry mountains he'd encountered in the Middle East and the Indian subcontinent for the turbulence and humidity of South-East Asia in the monsoon season. The weather would be a constant consideration. Winds could drive the Avro off course, electrical storms brought thunder and lightning that might knock the plane from the sky, and massive cloud fronts and rain squalls could cut visibility to zero and turn navigation into guesswork. Adding to the discomfort, temperatures regularly topped 30 degrees Celsius at this time of year, and the relative humidity could reach a sweaty 90 per cent. As the weather changed, Hinkler began to discard the garments he'd donned in wintry England at the beginning of his flight.

Although it was only early afternoon when he landed at Rangoon Racecourse, in the north of the city, he decided not to risk going further that day. He was mindful of the stretches of sea and jungle lying ahead on his route, terrain that would require a full day's flying to cross. Besides, by now it was obvious that he would easily break the 28-day England–Australia record if he could maintain his current pace. It had been 11 days since he'd left London; the Smith brothers had taken 16 to reach the same point. In fact, he'd already decided that if he were to make the flight again, he could save a further two days.

That evening in Rangoon (now known as Yangon), the Anglo–Dutch company Shell gave a dinner in honour of the visiting pilot. The sponsors were beginning to take advantage of the publicity value of the flight; the politicians would not be far behind.

That night, in the column in his log book that asked about the state of his aircraft, Hinkler once again scribbled 'OK'.

* * *

The next day was a Saturday, and a race day in the old colonial outpost. As always, Hinkler was keen to get away early, but first, some fifty horses had to be cleared from his path. The animals took it calmly, he said: 'Not a horse of them looked up, not a leg was waved.'[2]

With the runway clear for take-off, Hinkler then flew south from Rangoon along the coast, towards Victoria Point, 600 miles away near the border between Burma and Siam (now Thailand). He marvelled at the vast areas covered by thick green jungle, which ran right down to the water's edge, so different from the neat meadows and hedgerows of England. 'Tiny rice fields held back the tree army for a little,' he'd write in his syndicated story, 'but the efforts of man looked futile.'[3] Forced to ride the thermals at 5000 feet, he flew over hundreds of jungle-covered islands in the Andaman Sea, and probably over the area where Charles Kingsford Smith and Tommy Pethybridge would disappear in November 1935 during another attempt on the England–Australia record.

Hinkler made it safely to Victoria Point, however, which was then a settlement populated by two white rubber planters and 100 local Burmese. The area is today known as Kawthaung, the southernmost point in Myanmar, and until recently, under the country's military administration, western visitors were not encouraged. In 1928 there were no such barriers, and the planters were expecting him. The airstrip was a clearing in the forest, and he was allocated a spreading tree as his hangar. No sooner was the Avro under its branches than an intense storm hit, the resulting downpour cutting visibility to 100 yards. Hinkler was glad he was not in the air.

With the help of one of the planters, he checked the engine with a torch while the storm raged around them. The torchlight attracted hundreds of flying ants, many of which became stuck on the oily parts of the plane 'like a gigantic fly-paper', Hinkler said.[4] Pet monkeys chattered around the plantation bungalows as the pilot's host showed him around the settlement, but all he really wanted was to sleep. Apart from his headache-enforced escape to bed in Cawnpore, this was his first early night, after twelve days in the air.

He lifted off early the next morning, bound for yet another British stronghold – Singapore, 850 miles distant. Not long into the journey, while passing over Georgetown, on the island of Penang, he saw four RAF seaplanes and myriads of small boats bobbing gently at their moorings in the sun. 'It was as peaceful a scene as could be wished for,' he wrote.[5] Thirteen years later, that serenity was to vanish as Japanese warplanes pounded Penang with daily bombings and the European population was evacuated, just before the whole of Malaya and Singapore was overwhelmed by a surge of Japanese forces against surprised British and Australian troops.

Hinkler had not flown far from the sunlit scene at Georgetown when he saw masses of black cloud ranged across the sky ahead. 'I could not help the fancy they were waiting for me,' he recalled.[6] Then the rain started. Heavy drops were soon pelting into the cockpit, stinging his face. Around him, thunder rumbled and roared, and brilliant lighting slashed through the clouds.

He ploughed on, wrestling the bucking plane, only to discover that what he'd so far endured was merely the outrider of the main storm. Closer to Singapore, he hit the real thing: a boiling mass of angry black cloud that seemed to fill the sky entirely.

Hinkler circled 50 miles north to try to skirt it, without success. At higher altitudes he was flying blind, and if he dropped below the storm clouds, the Avian was soon brushing the treetops. He looked around for a possible site for an emergency landing, but nothing was visible through the gloom. He was forced to go on through the storm itself.

Surely after all he'd been through and flown across, and having chafed at the bit for years to get this venture under way, he was not to be stymied now?

Finally he was able to manoeuvre to a relatively clear area behind the wall of black, and was cheered by the sight of trailing white cloud caught on the trees below 'like bits of cotton tangled on a hedge'.[7]

When he reached Singapore, he had to outfox another rainstorm, so it was with great relief and near exhaustion that he finally put G-EBOV down on the official landing ground. But only for a moment. Officials rushed over to tell him that the *operational* landing field for Singapore was the racecourse, over at Farrer Park, just as it had been in 1919–20 for competitors in the £10,000 race to Australia. When Hinkler headed over there, another challenge awaited him – the local turf-club track was set around a golf course, and the holes were protected by hurdles. He was forced to weave the biplane around the greens as he came in. 'I jolly near holed out in one,' the Queenslander reported, 'but missed by inches, just rimming the tin.'[8]

There to greet him were Bill Lancaster and Jessie 'Chubbie' Miller, still waiting for their Avian Mark III to be repaired after the crash in the Dutch East Indies five weeks earlier. Several local supporters of the *Red Rose* venture resented Hinkler's arrival, feeling that he was taking advantage of the couple's misfortune to steal the England–Australia light plane record. Lancaster himself would have none of it. Clustered under umbrellas against the constant rain, he and Jessie helped Hinkler check his first generation Avro Avian by torchlight, and the three then went out to dinner. 'They were generously glad I had fared so well,' Hinkler said later.[9] That night Lancaster slept in the plane to safeguard it from any of his supporters who might have felt inclined to sabotage it. In the morning, he passed on to his fellow aviator several strip maps of Australia he'd been carrying for his own flight in *Red Rose*.

In Australia, newspapers were capitalising on the increasing public interest in Hinkler's progress. After all, there'd been only three successful flights from England to Australia, all of them in bigger aircraft with a crew of at least two. The previous May, Colonel Charles Lindbergh had captured the world's attention and been dubbed the 'Lone Eagle' for his solo flight across the Atlantic in a purpose-built monoplane. Australians saw in Hinkler their own 'lone eagle', scudding across the skies in a fragile, open-cockpit biplane, and destined, it seemed, to break the record time set by Ross and Keith Smith back in 1919. 'Hinkler coming fast,' announced the Melbourne *Sun-Herald*.[10] Meanwhile, in England the *Daily Mail* reckoned it had worked out what made Hinkler an ideal long-distance pilot: that he was utterly fearless, small, active and had a schoolboy grin.

* * *

If races had been planned at Singapore's Farrer Park racecourse for Monday, 20 February, they would've been abandoned on account of the heavy track. Continuous rain had made the ground soggy, so much so that when Hinkler refuelled the Avro in preparation for day fourteen, the additional weight pushed its wheels 3 inches into the mud.

The track was so sticky and the weather outlook so unpromising, he even considered postponing his departure.

He was no stranger to dirty flying weather, of course. During World War I, he'd been involved in fighting a determined enemy from icy cockpits at high altitudes over France and Belgium, and in the relatively benign post-war atmosphere of air races in England, he'd had to contend with fogs that obscured landmarks and competitors' planes alike, often turning flying into guesswork. As a member of the British Schneider Cup team in 1925, he'd seen the competition disrupted by violent weather on the American east coast and his own participation brought undone by the lingering after-effects. Before his current flight his most recent experience of foul weather had been in the *Princess Xenia*, when his planned trip to India with Captain McIntosh was brought to a shuddering halt in Poland.

With those sorts of experiences behind him, Hinkler considered his options in Singapore. Not only might the take-off be less chancy if he deferred, but the weather might improve for the upcoming flights, much of which was over extended stretches of ocean. On the other hand, the field was only going to become soggier, surely, which could mean a delay of several days. Although he was now five days ahead of the Smiths' record time, there was no guarantee that the remainder of the journey would pass without mishap. He decided to risk a take-off. A crowd gathered behind the running rail to watch.

Hinkler gave a final wave to Lancaster and Miller, and opened the throttle. The aircraft didn't move, its wheels held firmly by the clinging mud.

Hinkler eased off the throttle and sat there for a moment, pondering his next move. Then he turned to the watching crowd, beckoning them to come over and give the plane a shove. Next moment, a mass of willing bodies was pushing on the Avro's silver-coloured wings and tail, grunting with the strain, their feet skidding and sloshing on the slippery ground. Finally the turbo-boost of people power had an affect, and the plane began to move slowly forward.

As the aircraft gathered speed, Hinkler waited as long as he dared, and when the Avian was close to the end of the makeshift runway, he pulled back on the joystick. The plane shook itself free of the mud, as if glad to be away, clearing first the fence and then the surrounding trees, like a steeplechaser over the jumps. As the Avro rose into the steel-grey sky, Hinkler swung it around over the racecourse to give the crowd a thank-you wave, then headed south for the Dutch East Indies port city of Batavia (now the Indonesian capital, Jakarta).

The assurances in Singapore were that he'd be leaving the rain behind, but weather forecasting was not an exact science in the '20s, so he wasn't surprised to run into more storms. As he climbed high to avoid trouble ahead, Hinkler saw a hole in the clouds below and immediately swooped through it. Miraculously, he found a clearway that led him into blue skies.

A little further on, he flew over the Thousand Islands, a spectacular mass of emerald atolls fringed with white sand, sitting in the deep blue of the Java Sea. Hopeful that the worst of the weather was behind him, Hinkler started to count the islands below, but gave up when he reached 100. He was willing to accept that the person who'd first counted them hadn't made a mistake.

Just when it seemed that he'd avoided the storms, banks of cloud appeared ahead – sitting over Batavia, and lined up like an army battalion. They were too wide to fly around, so he darted through the thinnest patch, only to be met by pelting rain that felt to him as if he was being whipped by twigs. With the military aerodrome of Bandeong near Batavia seemingly unreachable in the conditions, he detoured to the airstrip at Kalidjati, 50 miles east of the capital, and the site of a flying school for the Royal Dutch East Indies Army. Even then, low-lying storms interfered, and it took him an hour and a half of dodging bad weather before he could land. The Dutch commandant and his wife spoke a little English and made him welcome.

Prior to this stop, Hinkler had apparently managed to circumvent the British Air Ministry requirements and keep local authorities aware of his movements on a day-to-day basis, by telegraphing ahead from one overnight stop to the next. When he made the diversion from Batavia, however, the strategy broke down. The first the British Consul-General there heard about Hinkler's intention to land in the Dutch East Indies was via a press-agency bulletin after the pilot had left Singapore, already on his way. The Consul-General was concerned, because all the Dutch East Indies airstrips were controlled by the military.

After a flurry of diplomatic consultations, he and several Dutch officials hurried to the Bandeong Aerodrome at Batavia to await Hinkler's arrival. To no avail, of course. 'It appears that Captain Hinkler had passed over [Batavia],' the British diplomat complained to the Foreign Office in London, 'either because he could not identify the landing ground or because he wished to proceed further before dark. He was unable to get as far as the military aerodrome at Bandoeng, and had therefore alighted at Kalidjati, where he was altogether unexpected, and had literally descended from the clouds.'[11]

The Air Ministry then had to explain to the Foreign Office why the requisite telegram had not been sent, and asked for an apology to be conveyed to the Dutch administration.

* * *

Apparently unconcerned by his lack of advance notice and unaware of the ripple of annoyance among the diplomats, Hinkler left Kalidjati at 6 am the next day, heading for Bima, on the eastern tip of the Dutch East Indies. It was day fifteen, and the plane purred along, as it had throughout the flight, nurtured by Hinkler's careful maintenance.

The weather was mostly fine, but cloudy, and at one stage he plunged into cloud so thick he felt like 'a fly crawling into icing sugar'.[12] He tried dropping below the cloud, and discovered that the air underneath was quite cold, but if he dropped further, towards sea level, it became quite warm. The result was a strange phenomenon where the Avro was continually sucked up into the clouds, and even when Hinkler turned off the engine, the plane didn't immediately lose height, but continued forwards.

After 900 miles, he landed at Bima, where a myriad of brown-skinned 'coolies', colourful in red and yellow, immediately surrounded the aircraft. Some time later, a car appeared, and with one mighty roar the locals told him that the Dutch Commissioner had arrived. The commissioner had a Roman bath at his home, 15 miles from the airfield, and Hinkler enjoyed soaking in the concrete tub so much, he found it difficult to go back to service the Avian. When he did, the plane was merely an angular shape in the encroaching darkness, and he finished up working by lamplight.

This time it was not flying ants but mosquitoes that were attracted to the site, and their size impressed the visitor. 'Several times I thought the engine had started,' Hinkler wrote in his newspaper account of that day's flying. 'Four hefty ones could have swung the propeller. Some, I'll swear, could have bitten through the tank and started the petrol leaking.' When he went to bed, the insects followed him, despite there being a net. 'I didn't sleep a wink all night,' he joked, 'but neither did the mosquitoes, so that was fair enough.'[13]

By now he was well ahead of the Smith brothers' time. At Singapore he had been five days in front; by the time he reached Bima, the difference was eleven days, the Vickers Vimy in 1919 having made more overnight stops and been delayed by a boggy airfield.

In Australia – just 900 miles away now – interest in the flight had reached a new intensity. The story that had begun as a series of minor items on inside pages was now high-profile news. 'All Australia on tiptoes for Hinkler,' trumpeted one newspaper headline.[14] Maps of his route were splashed across front pages, and predictions made about how many days he would lop off the earlier time. The federal government was also following his progress with interest, even though official policy discouraged such ventures. Newspapers reported that the Controller of Civil Aviation,

Colonel Horace Brinsmead, would greet the Queenslander on his arrival at Bundaberg. It seemed that everyone in the nation knew Bert Hinkler was on his way to a new England–Australia record.

* * *

After a breakfast of two bananas (the only food available), Hinkler headed off next morning on what he hoped would be the final leg of the flight – to Darwin. In the half-light before daybreak, the fully fuelled Avian struggled to clear the mountains bordering Bima, and by the time it levelled off and turned south-east, the exhaust pipe was red hot with the effort. Early in the afternoon, Hinkler passed over Kupang (in today's West Timor) and set course for Australia, across the emptiest sea he'd ever seen.

Just after he'd left Croydon two weeks before, an aunt in Melbourne, Beatrice Bonney, who had previously added her weight to the push for Hinkler to receive his war gratuity, had written to the Australian Minister for Defence, Major General William Glasgow:

> Now that Bert Hinkler (my nephew) has started his flight to Australia, can you arrange for a war boat to watch for him on the last long sea flight of his trip. We are all naturally anxious and would feel more secure if we knew there was a likelihood of him being picked up if he is forced down. Trusting you will be able to arrange it: I have the idea if you issue an order, it is obeyed.[15]

The minister had replied that it was not possible to agree to her request. There were a number of reasons, he explained: sending a ship to the north of Australia would seriously interfere with the RAN's training program; it would take time for a ship to proceed there; Mr Hinkler might be delayed; deploying a vessel could involve considerable expense; and there was a great difference in speed between a ship and an aeroplane. Three days later, however, the Navy sent a message to its Darwin base advising that Hinkler was expected there on 22 February, noting that he didn't carry a wireless transmitter, and asking that they use their discretion to assist him as they could. HMAS *Melbourne* was sent out to watch for him. Officially, it was on a training cruise.

No such veil of secrecy was required in the nation's newspapers. The press had picked up on the fact that Hinkler sometimes sang to break the monotony of flying, so C.J. Dennis, best known for his 1915 verse novel *The Songs of a Sentimental Bloke*, wrote a poem about the incoming 'Singing Ace':

There's an Aussie in the zenith where the Timor spills its flood.
Alone with sea and sky he rides the air.
He is homing to his own land with her spirit in his blood,
And only sea-birds mark his passing there.
But he's singing, gaily singing, with a heart aflame with hope,
And his eyes fixed on the far horizon's rim
Where tropic skies to tropic seas in azure glory slope
And the nearing shores of Homeland beckon him.[16]

After the long flight across the Timor Sea, if Bert Hinkler sang at all that day, it was probably when he spotted Bathurst Island in the late afternoon light. The pilot was elated. 'There was joy in the cockpit of the good ship Avro Avian, 16 days out from London,' he later wrote.[17]

In Darwin earlier that afternoon, hundreds of residents had gathered at the local airstrip (recently groomed by inmates of the nearby jail), their eyes straining out to sea for a glimpse of Hinkler's plane. No one was sure exactly when he would arrive, and after a couple of hours, their enthusiasm began to wane. Then came a message from HMAS *Melbourne*: G-EBOV had not been sighted. Most of the crowd went home, some no doubt concerned that something might've happened to the pilot. Back in England, a newspaper had arranged to have a car standing by, allegedly with the engine running and a reporter and photographer sitting inside; as soon as confirmation of Hinkler's arrival came through from Australia, the two pressmen would then speed off to obtain Nance's first reaction to the news.

Just before 6 pm in Darwin, there was the buzz of a small aircraft overhead in the sky. Hundreds rushed back to the landing strip at Fannie Bay, to the north of town, in time to see Hinkler's Avian circling above. Photographers had already set themselves up on perches to ensure they had the best view of the Queenslander's arrival.

Looking down from his open cockpit, the pilot himself was astounded by the number of people there to welcome him. 'I thought I'd arrived on a bad day, when it'd been booked for a picnic,' he joked afterwards.[18] As Hinkler came in to land, the photographers were knocked to the ground by the surging crowd, and even the town band had to scramble for cover to avoid the crush.

It was Wednesday, 22 February – fifteen-and-a-half days since he'd left foggy London town. Hinkler had broken the England–Australia record by an astounding twelve days. Powered by its Cirrus II four-cylinder engine, the Roy Chadwick-designed Avro 581E had covered around 10,500 miles at an average speed of 89 miles an hour, in a total flying time of 134 hours, or five days and fourteen hours. A cartoon in *Punch* magazine at the time showed a kangaroo jumping up and down on the shore, waving an Australian flag and calling to the incoming plane: 'Hinkle, Hinkle, little star, 16 days and here you are.'[19]

On the way, Hinkler had landed in darkness in Rome, had twice been forced to overnight in the desert, had fought daily against loneliness and boredom, and had nursed the little silver and green Avian across thousands of miles of ever-changing countryside and trackless ocean, while at the same time contending with storms that threatened to beat him and the plane into submission. All without a radio and detailed maps. And he'd done it by himself, with hardly a whisper of financial support, and against the doom-laden predictions of what he termed 'the croakers'.[20]

One newspaper summarised Hinkler's achievement and the esteem that was now due to him:

> Some quietly pronounced the feat that Hinkler set himself as unattainable, and expected the adventure to end on some rock-bound coast, or amid treacherous tribesmen of the desert. Day by day, he has steadily confounded all such doubters. Having casually left the English aerodrome without flourish of trumpets or the aid of the publicity man, and reached Australia well within the time he allowed himself, Hinkler has astonished a world whose capacity for astonishment was getting dulled.[21]

Hinkler would later talk about coming in to land at Darwin 'out of the heated sky', his heart 'as light as a feather'.[22] He reportedly said that his most important accessory had been his alarm clock.

The previous July, Bert Hinkler had told his mother and father that when all was quiet, he'd 'just come toddling along', but the nation wasn't about to let him sneak quietly into Australia. When he pulled to a stop on the runway at Fannie Bay, he triggered a national celebration that would last several months.

CHAPTER 13

The conquering hero

After a cursory customs inspection and a brief welcome at the landing ground, Hinkler was whisked off to the Victoria Hotel in Darwin, where, in the middle of a beer strike, the mayor shouted him a cold glass of Melbourne Bitter. While he was enjoying his drink, almost 500 telegrams arrived for him, an indication of the enormous interest that had been developing across the country and the world.

'Thank you very much,' he was quoted as saying, 'but I don't have time to read them at the moment.'[1]

This was an understatement from a man who'd hardly slept a wink the night before, had just flown 900 miles nonstop, and had been in the air solo every day for the previous two weeks. Not to mention the fact that, in Hinkler's mind, he still had to fulfil the promise he'd made to his parents, to land in Bundaberg. As the C.J. Dennis line went: 'Till he ends his long adventuring beside his mother's gate', although this time Hinkler hadn't promised he'd roll the Avian along Gavan Street as he'd done with the Avro Baby seven years earlier.

None of these considerations affected the plans of the good citizens of Darwin, who, having been deprived of an afternoon reception at Fannie Bay by their hero's late arrival, turned on an early-evening one at the Town Hall, on Smith Street. It's an indication of Hinkler's temperament that he went along with the arrangements (after first having a bath).

The 500 telegrams turned out to be the vanguard for hundreds more over the next few days. One of them was from Nance in England. 'Bravo beloved,' she wrote. 'Please do rest awhile. How proud I am wonderful reception. My love mater. All longing know when you are returning. I need you so much. Lovingly yours, Nance.'[2] She told reporters that she'd slept for the first time in a fortnight after hearing the news of his safe arrival. Hinkler's 'wifie' might've been disconcerted, though, to read a certain telegram he received from Port Augusta, in South Australia. 'You ball of muscle, are you any good', the senders asked before signing off with: 'Batchelor [sic] admirers'. There was also a cable from his old workplace: 'The Hamble Avro workmen rejoice in your success.'[3]

King George V and the Australian Governor-General also sent messages of congratulation, as did the Australian Prime Minister, Stanley Bruce, who complimented Hinkler, on behalf of the Government of the Commonwealth and the people of Australia, on completing 'the hazardous undertaking with skill and intrepidity'.[4] As the newspapers had already reported, the Controller of Civil Aviation, Colonel Horace Brinsmead, was instructed to go to Hinkler's next stop, Bundaberg, to greet the flyer on behalf of the federal government.

The Queensland Premier, William McCormack, was not to be denied either, announcing just the previous day that there'd be a state reception in Bundaberg to celebrate Hinkler's successful flight. In London, Secretary of State for Air Sir Samuel Hoare rhapsodised about the feat in the House of Commons, and the flags at Australia House flew on every available mast.

Even the British Deputy Director of Civil Aviation, whose officers had jousted with Hinkler for the previous twelve months over his non-payment of telegram fees, acknowledged that 'the earlier difficulties . . . should not be allowed to stand in the way of a telegram of congratulation.'[5] (Shortly afterwards, the Air Ministry went back to enforcing the Treasury regulation, sending Hinkler a bill for the telegrams he'd cabled from Tehran and Malta on his way over. John Lord, at A.V. Roe and Company, who had settled Hinkler's earlier bill, agreed to step in once more.)

The London *Daily Mirror* of 23 February crammed its front page with photographs of Hinkler and his plane, and there was a shot of Nance reading congratulatory telegrams, all under the banner of 'Captain Hinkler wins more laurels for Britain'. The *Evening Standard* speculated that Hinkler might team up again with Robert McIntosh for an east–west crossing of the Atlantic in an all-metal, British-built seaplane. 'He is very keen to do this,' they insisted, 'because all the rest of the contemplated attempts are to be with foreign machines . . .'[6]

* * *

Hinkler stayed in Darwin for two days, catching up on sleep and otherwise recovering his equilibrium. Newspapers throughout the world waited breathlessly to report his every move, and sub-editors scrambled to outdo each other with epithets about him.

'Hero of the hour', 'Monarch of the air', the headlines shouted. As a result, most of the world knew that Hinkler left Darwin on Friday, 24 February, on his way to Bundaberg. But only a few knew he was wearing Stella Nelson's shorts.

As he headed into the humid tropics, Hinkler had gradually discarded his English winter wardrobe, yet he still arrived quite unprepared for the heat of Darwin in February. At that time of year, daily temperatures in the northern city range from a minimum of 25 Celsius up to a maximum in the early 30s, which must have been a shock to the system of a man who'd spent the past 15 years of his life in the cooler climes of the northern hemisphere. When he'd lifted off from London 16 days earlier, the mercury had struggled to reach four degrees Celsius in the middle of the day.

A local federal MP in Darwin, Ern Nelson, lent the diminutive pilot a pair of shorts that his daughter, Stella, had left behind when she moved to Melbourne. Ms Nelson was subsequently obliged to explain to the press that women wore shorts in the Northern Territory for motoring and for picnics.

The record-breaker planned to reach coastal Bundaberg in two hops through Queensland: via Camooweal, a dot on the Barkly Highway in the north-west of the state near the Northern Territory border, and then Longreach in the central west, the town where the first Qantas flights originated.

Hinkler didn't arrive at Camooweal as planned, however. By late afternoon that day, the last sighting of his silver Avian had been over Katherine Waters at around 9 am, two hours after take-off, and now the level of anxiety was rising. Widespread joy was replaced by public concern: Hinkler was missing. The local Shell representative had planned a celebratory dinner in

Camooweal for that evening and chartered a plane to look for him, but without success. Motorists gathered to light Camooweal's airstrip in case Hinkler turned up in the dark.

Colonel Brinsmead, who was on his way to Bundaberg to welcome the record-breaker, assured the public that Hinkler had probably repeated what Cobham had done in 1926 – followed the north–south telegraph line and missed the turn to the east because of the lack of navigational features on the ground. Their hero had most likely landed at a remote location that had no communication, Brinsmead suggested, and would turn up safely the next day.

In Bundaberg, the rain spattering on the roofs seemed to increase the gloom of the local residents as they gathered outside the post office and the mayor's chambers for the latest news. It was arranged that the fire bell, which was to have been rung to alert citizens as Hinkler approached his hometown, would now be rung to let them know that he was safe.

Next day came good news. Brinsmead had been right: after coping with the volatile conditions he'd encountered between London and Darwin, Hinkler had been confounded by the extremes of his own native land. Soon after passing over Katherine, he'd been enveloped in a huge dust cloud, a strong headwind had slowed the plane, and the sun had scorched his face and arms. Hinkler would later describe the fierceness of the heat and the continual haze as being beyond belief: 'It was difficult to distinguish between a house and a waterhole.'[7]

After five hours of making little headway, and without an adequate map, he became concerned about the engine and decided to land. He set the plane down beside a windmill, and drank more water than he knew was good for him, but found no one around. Later, an Aboriginal stockman who chanced along was able to give him a rough idea of where he was, and Hinkler opted to stay there the night and take off in the cool of the morning. Once again, he dragged out his rubber dinghy to use as a mattress.

In the morning, he flew 40 miles to Alexandria Station homestead, where he had breakfast. He then reached a relieved Camooweal community just after midday, and stayed overnight. A photo taken at the time shows him standing beside G-EBOV, dressed in a shirt and tie, a jacket, a pair of shorts (presumably Stella Nelson's), short black socks and sandshoes. On his head he has a pith helmet – perhaps the one that caused him problems on his way from Karachi to Cawnpore. A reporter from the *Sydney Morning Herald,* who'd been waiting with increasing concern at Camooweal, suggested, 'It requires a finer nerve sometimes to "play safe" than to rush recklessly into danger; and in deciding to alight at Alexandra [sic] rather than risk disaster for the sake of a few hours, Hinkler simply proved himself the master of his fate.'[8]

'Master of his fate' is the perception that the public had of Bert Hinkler: the cautious, unflappable, competent pilot and mechanic who wouldn't take chances, and scrupulously looked after his machine, carefully calculated the odds in any situation and made considered decisions. And Hinkler had already shown that while he could work in teams, such as in the 1925 Schneider Cup and with McIntosh, he would much rather be master of his own fate.

As he hopped across rural Queensland, he was as modest and affable as he'd been in his circuit of towns around Bundaberg seven years earlier. When he landed at Longreach, accompanied by the Qantas mail plane from Cloncurry, the town band played

'See, the Conquering Hero Comes', a tune that Hinkler was to hear often over the next few weeks.

In the rush to welcome the conquering hero, a woman was almost trampled in the crowd, another went close to a whizzing propeller, and mothers wanted to sit their babies on the Avro's wings. An enthusiastic fan snatched his goggles, which were recovered when Hinkler appealed for their return. He may've been concerned by the 'coolies' swarming around his plane as he came across the world, but the locals in Australia made him anxious too. Post-flight, he was always keen to house the machine as quickly as he could.

From Longreach, Hinkler called his mother by telephone, the first time he'd spoken to her in person for seven years. With son Jack and daughter Queenie by her side, along with several other Bundaberg citizens, Frances Hinkler begged Bert to hurry home. At the start of the conversation she was serene and contained, but towards the end her voice broke with the emotion of the occasion, bringing tears to the eyes of those clustered around. Next day, the fire bell sounded in Bundaberg to let the excited residents and the huge number of visitors know that Bert had left Longreach and was heading for his hometown. There he would not only receive an affectionate welcome from his overjoyed mother, but discover that Frances Hinkler had struck up correspondence once more with her local state MP regarding the thorny issue of her son's unpaid war gratuity.

For his arrival in Bundaberg that Monday afternoon, Hinkler discarded Stella Nelson's shorts in favour of a suit. And what an arrival it was. A crowd variously estimated at between ten and twenty thousand welcomed back their favourite son with bunting in the streets, fire bells, whistles, tooting car horns, several bands, and extended cheering that rolled out across the town and down the Burnett River. A special train brought people up from Maryborough, 60 miles south, and a citizens' guard was drafted to help the police control the excited masses. Radio station 4QG broadcast proceedings from the back of a truck. Frances Hinkler, persuaded to say a few words before her son arrived, told listeners that she and Bert's wife were the happiest women in the world. She broke off when she saw the speck of the Avro Avian in the sky. A few minutes later, Hinkler circled over the town under a blanket of low cloud, before spiraling down and rolling the plane to a halt on the recreation reserve at North Bundaberg.

There were too many people for him to be able to taxi over to Woodbine Villa, as he'd done in the Avro Baby in 1921, but Frances Hinkler, Jack, Queenie and other relatives were there to greet Bert as he climbed out.

Enthusiastic onlookers carried him, shoulder high, over to a specially constructed platform, hung with a huge Australian flag. There, he was officially welcomed by Colonel Brinsmead, the Governor of Queensland, and the mayor. Brinsmead passed on Prime Minister Bruce's offer of Australian Government support, the governor gave him a cheque for £500, and the band played 'See, the Conquering Hero Comes'.

Next, Hinkler was bundled on top of a decorated truck for the short trip through the surging crowds to his mother's house in Gavan Street, its front almost hidden by an oversize British flag. This time the band played 'Home Sweet Home'. One reporter wrote that the people of Bundaberg still saw Hinkler as 'the same enthusiastic but unassuming boy who used to make gliders in his mother's back yard, grown a little older'.[9] Hinkler had not long turned thirty-five.

At the civic reception that evening, selected citizens were introduced to the record-breaking pilot, having been issued in advance with gold-printed souvenir cards to capture his signature. Hinkler was suitably moved by the occasion, and the press reported his words to the assembled throng:

> It is the proudest moment of my life to have successfully reached Bundaberg and home. As an Australian, I am proud that my flight has brought England nearer to Australia than ever before, and as a Britisher, I am particularly proud that only British workmanship and British enterprise have been utilised the whole way. Though almost every night I came down in a different country, I was astonished to find the British flag so strongly represented at every stop.[10]

Not all that many years later, he might've been surprised to see how quickly it had disappeared.

In proposing the toast to Hinkler's health, Brinsmead declared the 'dark days of depression'[11] were passing and that in aviation they were now approaching a time when they would 'experience complete success'. Brinsmead was no doubt referring to the recession that was affecting Australia at that time. Despite post-war stability and prosperity, repaying a high federal government debt and a decline in primary produce prices had led to stagnation of the economy. In addition, there was bad blood between employers and workers over wage levels, and a series of disputes in different parts of the country in the early 1920s had intensified into significant strikes by the middle of the decade. Unemployment rose, and in 1927 the Australian Council of Trade Unions had been formed to try to better protect workers' rights.

Brinsmead's optimistic prediction turned out to be premature. He was not to know that the following year would bring the great stock-market crash and that the consequences for the world, and for the dreams of pioneers such as Bert Hinkler, would be significant.

In February 1928, however, local entrepreneurs were soon producing postcards of Hinkler's arrival in Bundaberg – the forerunner across the nation of a string of souvenirs more often associated with royal visits. Among the letters he received were a variety of business offers, including £1000 a year (about £30,000 today) to become a travelling salesman for a business company, and £100 a week for twelve weeks to appear in a movie. One promoter claimed that Hinkler could make £10,000 on a lecture tour and still give the promoter a profit; if he went to the United States, it was suggested, he could make £20,000. An aviation company offered him £5000 per annum for five years to act as its field manager and technical adviser.

Frances was reported as saying that when Hinkler was there seven years before, he'd had to go back to England to compete in the Aerial Derby, but this time, he would stay longer because he was tired out and needed a rest. Returning to her role as his de facto publicity agent, she also supplied the press with some insight into her eldest son's upbringing:

> Bert and I were more like pals than mother and son. When he went down the street he would buy little things for me, and I would do the same for him. When he broke the wheels of his glider after trying it out on Sandhills Beach, I scraped together two guineas to buy him a new pair from Melbourne. I never repressed or deceived my children, and they have always been

> happy and dutiful. Bert never had a penny of assistance from anybody all his life. He won through with his own hard work and determination.[12]

Over in England, Nance had been inundated with requests for interviews, and allegedly had to flee from Mon Repos. When finally cornered, she told a reporter that she was expecting her husband to fly back to England, but without trying for any records.

Following his late afternoon arrival in Bundaberg, at 1 am the following morning, Hinkler and his mother made a radio broadcast to Britain, through the BBC. His message included thanks to all those who had helped him along the way, and acknowledgment of the reliability of the Avro aeroplane and its motor. Near the end of the broadcast, he asked everyone to 'put your receivers down as I am going to speak to my dear wife, who I am sure is listening'. It was reported that he then spoke to Nance 'affectionately and encouragingly' over the air.[13]

Frances told listeners that having her son home was the greatest joy she had ever known. 'I counted the days when he would return, and now he is with me,' she said.[14] The manager of radio station 3LO in Melbourne, which organised the event, claimed that 2 million people listened to the broadcast.

The Anglican Archbishop of Brisbane made a special journey to Bundaberg to 'convey to the intrepid aviator the congratulations and blessings of the Church'.[15]

* * *

While Hinkler was in Bundaberg considering business proposals, the Australian Government invited him to come to Canberra at a later date for an official welcome in the national capital, and announced that it would present him with a cheque for £2000 and a memento of his visit. Prime Minister Bruce's carefully worded statement to the House of Representatives, recorded in Hansard, tried to justify a decision that went against government policy.

After noting Hinkler's 'very wonderful accomplishment', Bruce declared: 'By that accomplishment he has established the fact that the small aeroplane, which, possibly, up to the moment has been regarded as a toy, is really very valuable, and a great aid to the whole science of flying. Unquestionably his accomplishment is not merely a stunt or freak performance, but one which has contributed materially to the whole science.'[16] And so on, to cheers from the members.

The Leader of the Opposition, Matthew Charlton, agreed fully with the PM's remarks, and said his side of the House was especially proud that Hinkler was Australian. The Cessnock (NSW) branch of the Australian Labor Party subsequently censured Charlton for supporting the £2000 payment, contending that the money should've been spent on unemployment relief.

To add to the government's cheque, newspapers and other organisations set up funds to collect donations for Hinkler, and the Royal Geographical Society announced that it would award him the Thomson Foundation Gold Medal for his flight. Another gift to mark the occasion, this time to the nation, came from Sir Charles Wakefield: an Avro Avian aeroplane. The Australian Government gratefully accepted the offer, putting the New South Wales Aero Club in charge of the new machine. The Australian parliament also paid Hinkler the rare honour of extending an invitation for him to be seated on the floor of the House of Representatives, in order to acknowledge his achievement; Hinkler accepted, and a date was scheduled for the middle of March.

By the start of March, an east coast itinerary was emerging for the record-breaking pilot: Brisbane, Sydney, Canberra, Melbourne. The other states were soon scrambling to make sure they were included. Nance was on her way by ship, courtesy of the Orient Line, with plans to meet up with Bert in Perth. Eventually it became a frenetic national tour lasting through to June, and Brisbane set the pace. All the while, Hinkler hoped that the financial return would be sufficient to make his future clearer.

* * *

Although grey skies greeted the people of Brisbane on Tuesday, 6 March, thousands of them streamed into the city to secure the best vantage points for the procession that afternoon. Adelaide Street was closed to traffic, but trams clanged their way down Queen Street as the crowds built up, and lorry drivers negotiated busy laneways to complete their deliveries in time. Flags fluttered from almost every building as white-helmeted policeman began lining the route. Despite an occasional rain shower, the crowd waited with patience and good humour.

At around two o'clock there was a volley of excited shouts: 'He's coming!' Fingers pointed and thousands of eyes turned skywards.

And there he was, a black speck against the grey cloud, with another speck alongside – his Qantas escort – heading for Ascot Racecourse. On his way south from Bundaberg, Hinkler had circled over major towns en route, where the residents had gathered for the occasion, alerted to his imminent arrival overhead by the whistles of local mills.

At the racecourse, Hinkler brought the plane to a stop directly over the white cross painted on the ground for that purpose. An hour or so earlier, traffic was four abreast on the main thoroughfare to this temporary landing ground, early-model cars competing with buses, vans, small runabouts, limousines and trucks to disgorge their passengers in time, while little motorbikes snaked their way through. It was a holiday for schoolchildren, but besides them, a huge excited crowd packed the grandstand and its surrounds. One reporter suggested, tongue-in-cheek, that a lot of grandmothers must've died that day, given the number of young men at the course.

The cheering that had started as Hinkler landed doubled in decibels when he jumped down from the cockpit, 'sunburnt and smiling',[17] to be met by the mayor. His mother was also there to welcome him, throwing her arms around his neck and hugging him as if this was the first time she'd seen him since he arrived from England. Hinkler was subjected to 12,000 voices singing 'For He's a Jolly Good Fellow', instigated by the mayor, followed by a brief welcome from the Governor of Queensland. After a quick response from Hinkler, in which he called himself a 'disciple of flying',[18] the crowd insisted on singing 'For He's a Jolly Good Fellow' again, and Frances gently waved the bouquet she'd been given.

The now-famous pilot took all of this in his stride as he climbed into a car with Australian and British flags draped across the bonnet. G-EBOV sat on a truck behind with its wings neatly folded. Preceded by a troop of mounted police, the little procession set off for the city, the dignitaries' cars bringing up the rear.

By this time, the crowd was twelve-deep in Queen Street, there were faces at every window, and people perched themselves on lampposts and scaffolding.

The crush was so great that a string of trams was trapped down one side of Queen Street – to the annoyance of those who'd been waiting there for hours. Several men risked their lives by clambering onto the roofs of the stranded tram cars, dodging the lethal wires close to their heads.

When the procession arrived, the crowds surged forward, and Hinkler, standing in the lead car, waved and smiled, occasionally chatting to his mother beside him. A number of spectators commented on his dusky skin – Hinkler's complexion was nearly always listed as 'dark' on ships' passenger lists, but on this occasion he was also tanned by the sun after sixteen days in an open cockpit.

On occasions, the horde broke through the police line, causing Hinkler to glance apprehensively at his precious plane.

The noise and tumult continued unabated along the streets as he passed, and after ceremonies at the Town Hall (where he was described as 'the idol of the whole empire'[19]), the police had trouble controlling the thousands of spectators, and several people fainted in the crush. In one instance, mounted police rode their horses into the crowd, bringing screams but no injuries. The occasion was likened to a visit the previous year by the Duke and Duchess of York, where the crowds were so overwhelming that the royal guests were forced to enter a function through a rear door. There was none of that with Hinkler, though, and as his car drove off, the crowd closed in behind it.

On a visit to the *Courier* two days later, to receive a cheque for £1000 from the newspaper's Hinkler fund for citizen donations, the pilot told the small distinguished group assembled for the occasion that aircraft travel was the ideal way to cover the sorts of vast distances Australia had, and that a network of airports would 'fill the back-blocks'[20] and help keep the nation safe.

Before he left Brisbane, Hinkler, his mother and Queenie were guests at an afternoon tea hosted by Maude 'Lores' Bonney at her home, 'Montana', in the then prestigious inner-city suburb of Bowen Hills. Lores was married to Bert's second cousin, Harry Bonney, a well-off leather goods manufacturer. In keeping with the fashions of the day, the hostess wore a hand-made French frock of ivory net and lace, with pastel flowers embroidered at the waistline, set off with ribbon streamers at the shoulder. A large black hat completed her outfit. Frances Hinkler was in cyclamen and wore a felt hat, while Queenie chose a frock of green crepe de chine, and a small hat.

Lores Bonney was five years younger than Bert, and had a keen interest in aviation. They hatched a plan for him to take her up in the Avro so she could drop flowers to a friend in another Brisbane suburb. Next day, they took off from Eagle Farm Aerodrome, Lores clutching a bunch of roses. With his cousin shouting and pointing the way, Hinkler soon located the house, where the friend was standing in the front yard, waving her arms about like a windmill. Hinkler circled, made a slow swooping descent, and his passenger launched the bouquet over the side and into the woman's arms. Inspired by Hinkler, Lores Bonney went on to become a famous pilot in her own right, but she never saw cousin Bert again.

* * *

Hinkler's England–Australia record-breaking flight brought not only national adulation, but a spate of souvenirs, along with a rush of (mostly forgettable) poems that were published in newspapers across the country. In Victoria alone, fifty budding poets responded to Hinkler's inspiring feat with odes sent to radio station 3LO, which then forwarded them to local newspapers. In 'Hinkler: He'll Do Me' by 'Whisker', the poet was keen to claim him as a country boy:

Now 'e's the sort ter imitate,
The sort 'oo'll get ter grips with fate,
'E does a thing right on 'is own,
'E's not afraid ter go alone,
'E's got the strength an' got the push,
The sort they breed out in the bush.[21]

The Numismatic Society of Victoria commemorated the event with a medal, showing Hinkler's head on one side and a map of his journey on the other, encircled by a Latin phrase that translated as 'Borne on swift wings to Australian shores'.

One of the more intriguing spin-offs was the 'Hinkler hat', designed for women, and allegedly based on the shape of Hinkler's flying helmet. It was in two-tone felt (including black and oyster, rose beige and crushed rose, and putty and dark brown) and retailed for 27 shillings and 11 pence at Grace Brothers in Sydney. Another unusual item was a pair of salt and pepper shakers moulded in the shape of Hinkler's face.

Babies were named in the pilot's honour – Ronald Hinkler King was born in Horsham, Victoria, and Bert Hinkler Pearton in Nabowla, Tasmania – while plant breeders named a variety of gladiolus after him. Out on the town, trendsetters were keen to dance the Hinkler Quickstep, and diners could allegedly order a 'Consommé à l'Hinkler'.

There were also numerous musical tributes, and the best-known song of the time was 'Hustling Hinkler', a foxtrot by two well-known American songwriters, L. Wolfe Gilbert and Abel Baer.

The media seemed to have no issue with mentioning the products that Hinkler used on his trip, and advertisements using his name popped up in newspaper classifieds, including the regal-themed 'Bert Hinkler: King of Aviators; Granny Smith: Queen of Baking Powders'.

In an era before licensing agreements, the man who inspired such creativity doesn't appear to have made any money out of this sort of commercial exploitation of his England–Australia flight. Apart from the direct gifts, and payment for his syndicated account of the journey, there was only the Orient Line's provision of sea travel.

CHAPTER 14

Modesty is seldom rewarded

As he arrived in the skies over Sydney on Saturday, 10 March, several planes joined the Avro to escort Hinkler across the harbour and south to Mascot Aerodrome. A huge crowd, estimated at 100,000 people, was there to welcome him. Asked by reporters about his future plans, Hinkler said they were 'indefinite', apart from arrangements already made to visit Canberra, Melbourne and Adelaide. He was hoping to make return visits to Brisbane and Sydney, he said, but when these might take place it was difficult to say, because he wasn't sure how long he would remain in Australia. 'It seems to me there is a possibility of my being required for aeronautical developments in other directions,' he added enigmatically. 'However my future plans are quite unsettled. That is all I can say.'[1]

At the time, there were at least two 'aeronautical developments' in the wind. One was the skywriting business he'd discussed with Major John Savage in England, back in 1923–24. After Hinkler's arrival in Bundaberg, Savage sent him a telegram, saying that George 'Dopey' Lingham had recently arrived in Sydney with full skywriting equipment, and suggesting that Bert 'communicate with object [of] joining us if your plans permit'. In the proposal he'd originally discussed with the former RFC major, Hinkler saw himself as the director of operations, with a business manager to look after the financial side. Working with another pilot sent by Savage was an entirely different scenario, and as Hinkler had long ago made clear, in the context of serving with the RNAS during the war, he didn't want to be just 'one horse in a team'. Perhaps for that reason, he rejected the Englishman's offer.

Another possible venture was a trans-Atlantic flight. Hinkler had received a telegram from London that read: 'Practically certain can arrange Short boat Atlantic. Are you in?' The sender was 'Macinherski', who assured Hinkler that he was getting drunk while toasting his health. The telegram probably came from Robert McIntosh, with the signature an in-joke regarding their Polish escapade during the aborted trip to India. 'Short boat' was a reference to the revolutionary triple-engined, metal-hulled seaplane designed in Britain by Short Brothers Ltd – the S.8 Calcutta – which had literally just come off the production line.

Hinkler telegraphed back: 'Most sincerely appreciate congratulations from worthy partner; will inform you when definite about return.'[2] However, piloting a Short S.8 across the Atlantic was another prospect that came to nothing.

For Hinkler, these hectic months following his triumphant arrival in Darwin were a topsy-turvy period. His need for a more concrete future had to be balanced against the expectations of an adoring public and the demands of politicians eager for the conquering hero's presence at official dinners and ceremonies.

'My future plans are quite unsettled' might well have been his catch-cry.

In Bundaberg, Horace Brinsmead had advised Hinkler not to make any business decisions for two weeks, leading to speculation that the Australian Government was going to offer him a job. The Melbourne *Herald* claimed that federal politicians from all parties supported the idea of Hinkler being appointed to a government position. When asked by reporters, the Prime Minister said he knew nothing about it, and the Minister for Defence said there was no need to engage Hinkler to arouse interest in aviation.

There was a groundswell of public support in Australia for Hinkler to be knighted, however, and politicians on both sides voiced their approval. There were precedents – Ross and Keith Smith had each received the honour for making the first-ever England–Australia flight, and Cobham had been knighted for his services to aviation on his return to England after flying from London to Darwin and Melbourne and back.

Despite the widespread support, the federal government made no immediate response. The Prime Minister later replied to a letter from a proponent for a knighthood for Hinkler that the government had carefully considered the circumstances surrounding his flight, and 'with a keen appreciation of his services to aviation, and Australia in particular', had decided the awarding of £2000 was appropriate.[3] There was some feeling among the populace that the lack of government interest in recommending a knighthood had something to do with the Queenslander's working class background, as in this letter to the *Brisbane Courier*: 'The Smith brothers and Cobham were knighted upon arriving in Australia, both having the advantage of huge planes, skilled mechanics and laid-out routes. Yet Hinkler flies out in a "flivver" [i.e. cheap or second rate] plane in record time. Is it because he is a son of the people, or have they run out of knighthoods?'[4] The editor of Sydney's left-wing *Daily Guardian* was even more direct in a telegram to the Prime Minister: 'Understand government have refused recommend knighthood Hinkler on account his humble birth. Is this true? Would appreciate denial.'[5]

In the same wartime letter home from the Western Front in which he'd lamented his status as 'one horse in a team', Hinkler had suggested that his path in the military might've been smoother had he 'started life on a different plane' and how instead, he found himself on the 'lower deck', where his opinions were not held in high regard. It's difficult to know whether any perception of social class was a factor in the decision about a knighthood eleven years later, although one newspaper columnist amiably suggested that Hinkler was better off without the honour because the aviator didn't have the wherewithal required to maintain such a status.

The more likely explanation is that the nature of his relationship with Nance Jarvis was the main stumbling block. When Kingsford Smith was knighted in 1932, he was divorced and had remarried, and his knighthood was opposed by those who believed a divorced person should never be honoured in that way, whatever the circumstances. In Hinkler's case, Nance was divorced, had a child, and he lived with her in a de facto relationship – a double 'whammy' in the eyes of such conservatives.

In any event, intervention from the mother country saw recognition for Bert Hinkler take a different path. King George V, who'd taken a close interest in the flight, indicated he'd like to award the airman the Air Force Cross. Instituted in 1918, the Air Force Cross was awarded for acts of courage or devotion to duty carried out in non-combat situations. The king had made the same award to another pilot, Richard Bentley, for flying solo from London to Cape Town the previous year. When Stanley Bruce was asked by the Secretary of State for Dominion Affairs, Leo Amery, whether he supported the King's proposal, Bruce quickly cabled back, 'Answer is in the affirmative.'[6]

There was no immediate response from England, and the Prime Minister was becoming nervous about the growing intensity of public calls for a knighthood. Three days later, he cabled Amery again. He suggested that the king's announcement of the conferring of the Air Force Cross be made as soon as possible to mitigate 'certain agitation arising in Press' that a knighthood should be conferred. Bruce told the Secretary he personally considered the Air Force Cross a much more suitable award and believed the public would support that view. 'Agitation for knighthood might however gain strength if announcement delayed,' he added.[7]

After more hasty correspondence between the Australian and British governments, the Governor-General announced on 10 March that it was His Majesty's pleasure to award the Air Force Cross to 'Captain Hinkler', in recognition of the 'distinguished service rendered to aviation' by his record-breaking flight from England to Australia.[8] The erroneous rank afforded Hinkler in the citation was a minor detail in the politicians' rush to ensure that the announcement was made, and on the very day that he was being lauded for his achievement by tens of thousands of Sydneysiders. As for the investiture, when asked, Hinkler said he'd like the presentation to take place in England.

The Australian Government also gave Hinkler an honorary title: squadron leader in the Royal Australian Air Force. In the hastily drafted RAAF memorandum of recommendation, the recipient's first name is shown as 'Bertram' instead of Herbert, and a handwritten note amends the recommended rank from flight lieutenant (which he had been in the RAF) to squadron leader. He was asked to make a written application to join the Royal Australian Air Force, presumably to formalise the honorary title. Next to 'married or single', he very firmly wrote *Married*, and for his next of kin, *Nance Hinkler, wife*.

As things transpired, due to King George being too ill to attend, the AFC investiture in London was postponed from its scheduled date in late November, and eventually the Prince of Wales presented the award, on 21 December. By then the British authorities had discovered that Hinkler was an honorary squadron leader in the RAAF, not a captain. Coincidentally, on the same day that Hinkler received his award, US President Calvin Coolidge signed an approval for the award of the Distinguished Flying Cross to Orville Wright and the late Wilbur Wright.

* * *

On the afternoon of 17 March, 1928, just over three weeks since he'd arrived in Darwin, Hinkler landed in drizzling rain on the Review Ground – later renamed York Park – in Canberra to receive official acknowledgement of his solo feat. When he alighted from the plane 100 yards from the rotunda where the welcome would take place, he was greeted by a roar from the throats of some two-thirds of the population of the capital (then around just 8000), and mounted police had to clear a path for him. In addition to the Prime Minister and other dignitaries and their wives, also there to welcome him were members of his own family – his mother Frances, brother Jack, and sister Queenie, along with Frances's sister, Beatrice Bonney. The government footed the bill for the family's stay in Canberra. Hinkler skipped up the rotunda steps and gave his mother a hug and a kiss before being introduced to the official guests.

The focus then moved to the steps of Parliament House, where the Prime Minister presented the record-breaking pilot with the promised cheque for £2000 – the equivalent in today's currency of over $80,000. At the point of handover, the drizzle turned into a downpour that might've reminded Hinkler of the drenchings he'd endured on his way through the tropics.

In return for the cheque, Hinkler handed the Prime Minister a letter that he'd carried from the Australian High Commissioner in London, which began, 'I am handing this letter to Mr Hinkler, the airman, in the confident hope that he will be able to carry it by aeroplane. . .'.[9] It was the first international air letter ever delivered in Australia, Hinkler said, but the forerunner of many.

Bruce then escorted Hinkler inside the building where the President of the Senate, Sir John Newlands, invited him to take a seat on the floor of the house – an honour accorded to only one other person, Nobel prize-winning author, Patrick White, in 1973, who refused the invitation. Frances Hinkler and the other members of the aviator's family observed this unique recognition from the public gallery. Thirty minutes later, the Speaker of the House of Representatives welcomed Hinkler to that chamber in a similar manner. At an official reception that evening, Stanley Bruce presented the record-breaking pilot with a gold cigarette case bearing the Australian coat of arms, as a memento of his visit to Canberra (cost to taxpayer: £35).

While its generosity didn't extended to recommending him for a knighthood, the government soon added a bonus to the figure of £2000: the Imperial Service Grant, or war gratuity, that he'd pursued unsuccessfully for five years up to 1926. Frances Hinkler's recent efforts had led to another letter reaching Frank Forde at Parliament House, who dutifully passed it on to the Prime Minister, for his 'personal consideration'.[10]

At Bruce's instigation, a schedule of earlier actions and responses was again compiled, ending with the advice that 'no further extension' had been granted. An officer subsequently reviewing the case concluded that Hinkler's claim should've been disallowed definitely back in 1921, since he hadn't complied with the conditions, and that the then Minister for Defence had no authority to grant any of the extensions that had been given.

The PM agreed – but he went ahead anyway. At a Returned Soldiers' League luncheon in Canberra for Hinkler, Bruce said that although the time had long passed since applications for war gratuities could be admitted, the federal government had decided to make a special decision in Mr Hinkler's favour. He then handed over a cheque for £153, 5s and 9d to the cheers of the assembled diggers.

Inevitably, this decision raised the question of whether the twenty or thirty others who'd had their claims refused after failing to return to Australia by the required date were also entitled to a payment. In reply to one such query, William Glasgow, the Minister for Defence, said the Prime Minister had made it clear that Hinkler had not met the conditions, but the government had waived them because of the 'very unusual circumstances under which he eventually returned'.[11] Bruce added that since those special circumstances didn't apply to anyone else, the conditions would not be waived for anyone else.

* * *

Having delighted the good citizens of Bundaberg, Brisbane, and Newcastle, spent a week being feted in Sydney, and been suitably honoured in Canberra, Hinkler continued on what had become a tour of the continent. When contacted by a church leader in Melbourne objecting to his intention to arrive in that city on a Sunday, the Sabbath, he tactfully replied that he was content to leave arrangements in the hands of the local organising committee. In the state capitals, that committee usually included a member of the Imperial Oil Company, still only too happy to provide him with Shell aviation spirit.

Hinkler obligingly touched the Avian down in the rural towns of Cootamundra and Wagga Wagga on his way to Melbourne, where another huge crowd assembled at Flemington Racecourse to greet him, on Sunday, 18 March. In the southern capital he again met up with his mother and other family members, who continued to share in the celebrations, and Jack apparently had a hand in making advance arrangements for his brother.

The day after his arrival in Melbourne, Bill Lancaster and Jeannie 'Chubbie' Miller landed in Darwin in their repaired Avro Avian Mark III, and Hinkler sent them a congratulatory telegram. It had taken them five months since leaving England. Although they were well outside Hinkler's time, and *Red Rose* had missed out on being the first light aircraft over the route, the press were excited by the fact that Miller was the first woman to fly across the equator and the first to travel from England to Australia by air.

Among his many engagements during the 12 days he spent in Melbourne, Hinkler joined an air pageant at Essendon Aerodrome, where 5000 coloured balloons were released in welcome. He also made radio telephone contact with Nance, who was en route by ship from England, and arranged to meet her when the *Orama*

Above: Pupils at North Bundaberg Primary School, c. 1900. Bert is the small boy in the middle of the second row, eighth from left in the sailor jacket. *John Oxley Library, State Library of Queensland*

Right: Bert, the young man about town, aged about 18, with his sister Mayme. *John Oxley Library, State Library of Queensland*

Hinkler, strapped to one of the two full-size gliders he built and flew as a teenager on Mon Repos Beach, Bundaberg. *John Oxley Library, State Library of Queensland*

Above: Hinkler trundles the Avro Baby up Gavan Street, Bundaberg, to his parents' home after his flight from Sydney, 1921. *John Oxley Library, State Library of Queensland*

Above: Hinkler in 1918 as a pilot in the RAF; on his chest is the DSM (Distinguished Service Medal) he won as an air gunner in the RNAS. *Courtesy Hinkler House Memorial Museum & Research Association and Hall of Aviation*

Mon Repos, the house where Bert and Nance lived in Southampton from 1925; it was later dismantled and brought back to Bundaberg and reassembled. *Courtesy Hinkler House Memorial Museum & Research Association and Hall of Aviation*

Above: The inset photo shows Hinkler in an Avro 504N for the 1925 King's Cup race. On the right is Alan Cobham, whose mechanic was shot en route to Australia in 1926. *Courtesy Flightglobal Archive*

British Schneider Cup team members at Chesapeake Bay, Maryland, USA, October 1925, in front of the Supermarine-Napier S4. Hinkler is second from left. *Courtesy Flightglobal Archive*

Above: Hinkler in an Avro Gosport with John Leeming, of Lancashire Aero Club, with whom he landed in another Gosport on Helvellyn peak in the Lake District in December 1926. *Courtesy Flightglobal Archive*

Hinkler in Riga, Latvia, in August 1927, having flown a record 1200 miles non-stop from London in G-EBOV. He was awarded the badge of the Latvian Air Service. *Courtesy Flightglobal Archive*

Above: Hinkler at Camooweal, Queensland on his way to Bundaberg in 1928. The pith helmet may be the one that almost caused him to conk out over India. *John Oxley Library, State Library of Queensland*

Above: The Hinkler family home, Gavan Street, Bundaberg, awaiting Bert's arrival after his 1928 England–Australia flight. *National Library of Australia*

Right: Hinkler in 1928 with his mother; behind are his sisters Queenie (left) and Mayme (Mrs Eadie), and brother Jack. Missing is his other brother, George. *John Oxley Library, State Library of Queensland*

Above: G-EBOV with its wings folded in the enthusiastic welcome to Hinkler in Queen Street, Brisbane, March 1928. *John Oxley Library, State Library of Queensland*

Below: For his 1928 flight to Australia, the Federal Government presented Hinkler with a cheque for £2000, signed by the Treasurer and the Prime Minister. *National Library of Australia*

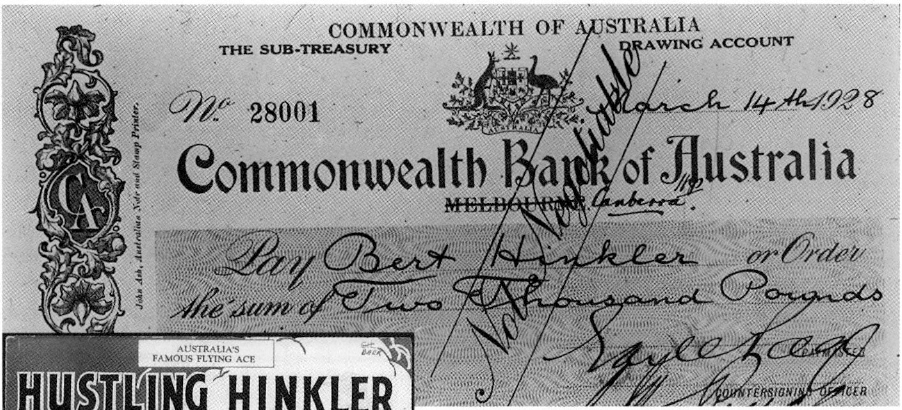
COMMONWEALTH OF AUSTRALIA
THE SUB-TREASURY DRAWING ACCOUNT
No. 28001 March 14th 1928
Commonwealth Bank of Australia
~~MELBOURNE~~ Canberra
Pay Bert Hinkler or Order
the sum of Two Thousand Pounds
Not Negotiable
John Ash, Australian Note and Stamp Printer.
COUNTERSIGNING OFFICER

Left: The most popular of the songs written to celebrate Hinkler's record 1928 flight was 'Hustling Hinkler', by L. Wolfe Gilbert and Abel Baer. *National Library of Australia*

Right: Among the numerous mementos and products that took advantage of Hinkler's popularity as an aviator was the Hinkler hat, shaped after the pilot's flying helmet. *National Library of Australia*

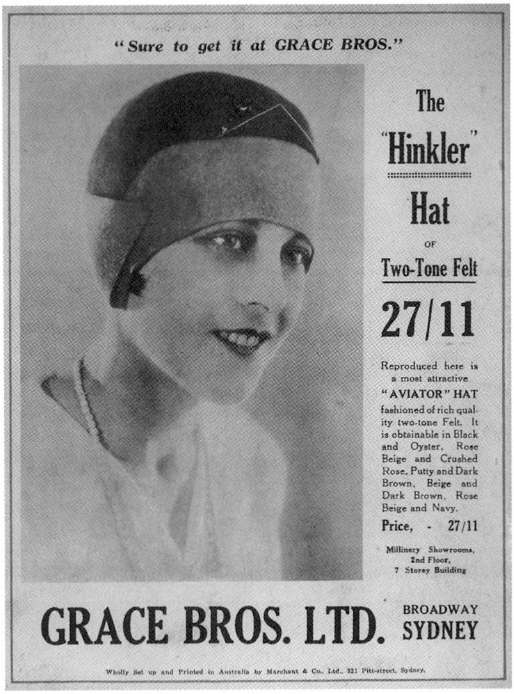

Above: Katherine Hinkler (whom Hinkler secretly married under an assumed name in May 1932) with her nephew, Bill Ross Jr, in 1943, ten years after Bert's death. *Courtesy Jean Costa.*

Above: Hinkler with Nance (otherwise known as Hannah Jarvis), the woman the world knew as Mrs Hinkler, at one of the many functions they attended in Perth in April 1928. *State Library of Western Australia*

Above: The wreckage of Hinkler's Puss Moth, found in April 1933 amidst melting snows on the slopes of the Pratomagno mountains, Italy, three months after he disappeared. *National Library of Australia*

Above: Mussolini's government gave Hinkler a full military funeral. The ornate hearse made its way through silent, respectful crowds in Florence, Italy in May 1933. *National Library of Australia*

docked at Fremantle, and to fly back to Melbourne with her in the Avro.

He took three days to fly to Perth, overnighting in the tiny Nullabor Plain railway town of Cook in South Australia, and Merredin, in Western Australia's wheat belt, and waving to the passengers as he passed the transcontinental express on its long rail journey through the desert. Long hops in the Avian were still possible because of the supplementary fuel tank that had helped him fly halfway across the world. With Nance soon to be a passenger again, however, in Perth he arranged for the front cockpit to be restored, and fitted a 12-gallon booster tank, a quarter of the size of the previous one.

Before he reached Perth, the managers of both racecourses had declined to make them available as a landing ground for his arrival, and one of them, A.E. Cockram, from Belmont Park Racing Club, publicly stated that the charity to which the gate takings would go would be Hinkler himself. The pilot refuted the claim, and the organisers announced that the proceeds would be divided equally between charities and the Hinkler fund. When he landed at Perth Oval on April Fools' Day, 1928, 20,000 people turned out to welcome the record-breaking pilot. Sitting in the radio cabin on the SS *Orama*, making its way steadily across the Indian Ocean towards Australia, Nance listened with interest to a broadcast of his arrival at the ground.

As the ship docked at Fremantle two days later, Hinkler leapt across before the gangplank was lowered, to the delight of the waiting crowd. Passengers, too, cheered when they saw him, and there was no possibility of greeting Nance in private, but they were both clearly pleased to see each other again. A newspaper described the newly arrived Englishwoman as 'a shy retiring woman of slender build, with dark eyes and black hair, and taller than her husband'.[12]

Although Nance had seen Hinkler feted in Britain, she was unprepared for the size and enthusiasm of the crowd that gathered noisily on the wharf for the official welcome, and froze after just a few words of thanks to them. 'Of course, I am tremendously proud of him,' she later told reporters, away from the hubbub, 'but my chief feeling during his flight to Australia was one of anxiety. He told me not to worry; but it was hard sometimes not to do so.'[13]

From that time, Nance accompanied her famous partner to many of the numerous functions organised for them in Perth. At each event there were the usual speeches and a toast, followed by a response from Hinkler, and the presentation of a cheque. Their half-share of the proceeds from Bert's arrival at Perth Oval was £350.

After nine days in Perth, Hinkler spent the morning of Tuesday, 10 April trying to pack the belongings his partner had brought with her by ship into the nooks and crannies of the Avian, in preparation for their flight to Adelaide. Although Nance had often flown with him in England, this would be the first time she had accompanied him on long flights, and across landscapes with little habitation or vegetation.

Their track took them to Northam, nowadays a town on the outskirts of the Western Australian capital, and to the gold mining town of Kalgoorlie, its declining fortunes shortly to receive a boost when the Great Depression saw gold prices soar. From there they headed steadily east, touching down overnight at the railway siding of Hughes and the next night at Ceduna. Nance was amazed by the aridness of the country, and passed the time counting telegraph poles – '25 to the mile,'[14] she smilingly told reporters in Adelaide – and looking out for kangaroos, but the only wildlife she saw were rabbits.

With the smaller supplementary tank, at one point Hinkler was concerned whether they had enough petrol to reach their next destination, and landed at a railway fettlers' settlement seeking more fuel, but without success. He eventually decided that they would make it anyway, with what was in the tanks, but it must have been an especially anxious time for Nance, unused to the vagaries of long-distance flying.

Also approaching Adelaide, but from the east, and by train, were Frances Hinkler and her son Jack. Although Jack had met Nance in England when he was in the AIF, this would be the first time Hinkler's mother would meet her 'daughter-in-law'. The Bundaberg matron told reporters she was excited about the prospect. No doubt there was anxiety on both sides, however. And the first occasion was not ideal – in front of thousands of cheering spectators when the Avian spiralled out of a clear blue sky to land at Adelaide's Morphettville Racecourse, a short tram ride from the city centre. There had been a ripple of applause when Frances had arrived earlier, 'in her demure black frock, with worn face and tired eyes smiling behind glasses', as one reporter described the recently widowed 61-year-old.[15] Later the two women would meet in private, and Frances would approve of her son's partner.

From the time of their arrival in Adelaide on Wednesday, 4 April until their departure for Melbourne four days later, Bert and Nance fulfilled another whirlwind of engagements. At the Lord Mayor's reception, hundreds of unemployed locals took the opportunity to stage a demonstration against the government, resulting in intervention by mounted police. It was a sign of the economic times.

Hinkler was also considering his economic future. Although he was content enough for the moment to accept the accolades and gifts, and maintained the outward affability with the Australian people he'd displayed from the time he arrived in Darwin, he was hoping that more rewarding, longer-term opportunities would present themselves. Heeding Colonel Brinsmead's advice, he'd been cautious about the burst of proposals he'd received when he first arrived in Australia, and eventually nothing had come of any of them. Even when he did corner a contract, his business naivety scuppered it. A Melbourne publisher signed him up for exclusive newspaper serialisation of the account of his flight for £300, with a further £200 plus royalties for a book, and the promise of more for international rights. However, Hinkler ingenuously gave an interview about his flight to a rival newspaper chain, putting the original deal in jeopardy. Eventually he settled for £150 for the serialisation rights, and the book never eventuated.

Across the Pacific, Hinkler's fellow solo distance-flyer, Charles Lindbergh, had become almost instantly wealthy through the generosity of his fellow citizens, following his New York-to-Paris flight, and had also been given a well-paid government civil aviation position. He reportedly asked the US Congress not to use public moneys for projects such as the purchase of his family home for conversion into a museum, nor to grant him $500,000 to undertake development of aviation.

In Adelaide, Frances told the press that her son had not received any firm government or business offers, but she was confident that if a satisfactory proposal came forward, he would stay in Australia. His brother Jack was more forthright: 'If the

Australian Government has anything to offer him, it should speak out – make it plain.'[16] Jack made it clear that otherwise Bert was just wasting his time and might as well return to England.

For the moment, Bert had accepted an invitation for him and Nance to visit Tasmania, and he housed the Avro at a private aerodrome at Coode Island, in Melbourne's west, to prepare it for the flight. His brother Jack helped him fit a new oil tank to the plane. When the tank was connected, however, the oil didn't flow through to the engine. They discovered that the problem was a blockage in the line: a ball of cotton waste stuck partway along the connecting tubing. Jack cleared the blockage and Bert, seemingly unconcerned, let the manufacturer know what they had found.

Apparently Jack was suspicious about the incident, though, and believed it was a case of sabotage: an intentional effort to block the oil and cause the aircraft to crash as it crossed Bass Strait. Aviation author Ted Wixted identified the alleged perpetrator as Dopey Lingham, John Savage's skywriter friend, who was in town for a dinner where Hinkler was guest of honour. Wixted claimed that Lingham's involvement was part of a wider conspiracy, related to Hinkler's final flight in January 1933. However, Lex Rowland, a Bundaberg engineer and Hinkler historian, has a more straightforward and plausible explanation for the oil tank incident. In those days, cotton wadding was used to clean out oil pipes for engines (like a pull-through on a rifle), and this was most likely a case of sloppy work – the wadding hadn't been pushed all the way through in the final cleanout at the manufacturer's.

After negotiating rain squalls across Bass Strait, Bert and Nance spent eight cool autumn days in Tasmania, where Frances

Hinkler's parents had once lived. Schoolchildren across the state were delighted by an unexpected half-holiday when the couple arrived in their town. In Devonport, on the island's north-west coast, 6000 paying spectators excitedly leapt from their seats when the plane landed and followed it up the showground – obviously unaware of what was either acceptable or advisable behaviour on such occasions. When Hinkler swung the Avian around and headed towards them, they turned as one and hot-footed it in the opposite direction.

Hinkler continually propounded the role of aviation in linking the continent, a message that was well received in moated Tasmania. Although their accommodation in Australia was mostly provided gratis, and Shell was supplying fuel and oil for the Avro, by now Hinkler was becoming more hard-nosed about the financial return from his national tour. Perhaps seeing his hopes of a government position or business deal in Australia fading, he began to insist on a minimum payment before he agreed to touch down in smaller towns. On the Apple Isle, he negotiated a payment of £30 to land at Wynyard, on the north-west coast, before heading back to Melbourne on Monday 14 May.

Once back on the mainland, Hinkler and Nance began to wend their way north to Bundaberg.

When the couple landed once again on the Review Ground at Canberra on 20 May, there was no one there to greet them, even though their arrival was expected. It was a big difference from just two months earlier. That evening Bert and Nance were guests at a dinner hosted by the Secretary of the Prime Minister's Department, Percy Deane, at which one of the other guests was the former Prime Minister, Billy Hughes. So Hinkler would've heard up close the 'big, noisy Welsh mouth' he'd been so critical of back in 1919, while waiting impatiently for the go-ahead for the £10,000 air race.

* * *

By the time he and Nance returned to Bundaberg, Hinkler was beginning to tire of the travelling life. His trusted Avro 581E had covered some 30,000 miles since he'd acquired it from the company in late 1926; around 5000 miles of that was in Australia alone. He wasn't keen on continuing to tour, owing to what he called 'the unsatisfactory nature of the results'.[17] What Hinkler meant was that the financial return was diminishing. As time went on, people were less prepared to pay to see him, and not all organisers were prepared to pay the 'appearance fee' he had begun to expect.

There was also competition from other aviators. When *Red Rose* arrived in March, Lancaster and Miller attracted national attention, and the federal government invited them to an informal reception at Parliament House in Canberra. Like Hinkler, the two flyers were keen to exploit their story commercially, and soon Jeannie negotiated a contract for a two-month lecture tour of Australia's capital cities and main towns, at £150 a week. Newspapers reported the pair's subsequent progress, although not as extensively as they did Hinkler's. However, in June 1928, public interest in the feats of all three flyers was overtaken by another record flight.

On Wednesday 9 June, two Australians already known for their aviation exploits in Australia, Charles Kingsford Smith and Charles Ulm, along with two Americans, Harry Lyon and James Warner, flew into Brisbane after flying 7500 miles from Oakland, California in the *Southern Cross* to complete the first air crossing of the Pacific Ocean. Among the crowd of 15,000 there to greet them at Eagle farm Aerodrome was the redoubtable Mrs Frances Hinkler. Unlike her son, Smithy was not one to hide his light under a bushel, and the flight received tremendous publicity every day they were in the air. When the intrepid four arrived in Sydney the next day, an estimated 300,000 turned out. Smithy and Ulm received over £20,000 in cash from various sources, as well as aviation awards.

As the hullabaloo over Lindbergh's flight the year before had shown, this was a time when the public were hungry for heroes. When Hinkler flew into Darwin, one writer said: 'At a time when wonderful flights succeed each other with bewildering rapidity, Hinkler has leapt to a coveted fame which is harder and harder to capture . . .'.[18] But the fame was also fleeting. He was the hero of the day – but the next day might bring a new one.

Advances in the design and technology of planes after World War I were exploited by newspapers that offered prizes for risk-takers, and encouraged by governments for both nationalistic and military purposes, particularly over long distances. Concern for the welfare of pilots who failed was offset by the excitement generated in the press for those who succeeded. And each new record seemingly demanded another; one that would push man and machine even further, and excite new superlatives.

In the face of the declining interest in his flights and the emergence of new heroes, Bert Hinkler considered his options. Despite all the touring and back-slapping, no one in Australia had come forward to offer him a job, the burst of business proposals had come to nothing, and he hadn't taken up Savage's invitation to join the skywriting team. There was money in his bank account from the gifts and donations, but that wasn't a livelihood.

Hinkler considered shipping the plane to San Francisco and doing a series of hops through towns across the States, collecting donations on the way as he had in Australia, and then heading back to England from the US East Coast. He approached the Australian Government about sponsoring the trip, but they baulked at the freight cost, and asked shipping companies if they might be prepared to transport the Avro without charge. The Union Steamship Company was willing, but due to a mix-up with mail at Woodbine Villa, the confirmatory letter from the Prime Minister's Department didn't reach Hinkler before he left Australia.

On 20 September the record-breaking pilot had slipped out of the country almost unnoticed – 'without a cork popping', as one newspaper put it, in contrast to the fanfare receptions he'd received in Darwin, Canberra and the state capitals earlier in the year.[19] He left the Avro behind, electing instead to accept the free passage to England the Orient Line had offered him and Nance on the SS *Orama*. As they boarded the ship in Adelaide, he emphatically refuted a charge that he'd personally benefited from payments for his autograph, insisting that organisations he had visited in Australia had conceived of the idea to benefit charities. He told a reporter that he deplored the fact that Australians were not interested in aviation, when it had so much to offer them, and that he had nothing to say about his future plans.

On 20 October, a month after the couple's departure, Frances Hinkler wrote to Percy Deane, Secretary of the Prime Minister's Department, to express her disappointment that her son hadn't been offered a job to keep him in Australia. 'There was nothing doing here, and the money he got he needed for inventions to make aviation safer for the next generation,' she lamented.[20] 'Bert never thinks of self – to prove it see how he came alone all those

12,000 miles to prove what can be done by man. As you know, he was never rewarded enough for what he'd done; no one opened their hearts to give him £5000. Modesty is very seldom rewarded.'

No doubt conscious of how Lindbergh's achievement had been recognised, she said Bert would've received better treatment in America.

CHAPTER 15

Flight of the Ibis

Having taken fewer than 16 days to fly from England to Australia, Hinkler had mixed feelings about the four weeks he and Nance spent on the SS *Orama* on the return journey. 'Pleasant, restful and monotonous'[1] was his description of the voyage via Colombo, in a letter to his mother from Mon Repos. The testiness he'd displayed in response to reporters' questions before embarkation in Adelaide emerged again when the ship arrived in London on 25 October. Her Majesty's Customs demanded he pay duty of a penny per foot for 2000 feet of film depicting his landings in Australia, even though he insisted it was for private use. His response was that he would rather leave it in the shed on the wharf than pay the tax.

Interviewed shortly afterwards by the Australian Press Association, following a long discussion he'd had with Thomas Trumble, secretary to the Australian High Commission in London, Hinkler maintained that his future was undecided, and he ridiculed a suggestion he'd been engaged by an Australian company flying

German aircraft. 'I am a freelance,' he protested. 'Numerous propositions have been submitted, but I won't tackle anything unless I can be absolute director, running things in my own way.'[2] He assured the interviewer he had no interest in flying the Atlantic or making another flight to Australia.

The London correspondent of the *Sydney Morning Herald* was bemused:

> While Sir Alan Cobham is the busiest airman in London, another famous comrade of the air who has accomplished the flight from England to Australia is one of the least occupied. This is Mr. Bert Hinkler. Unheralded and unsung, he arrived in London last week on his return from Australia . . . Mr. Hinkler evidently lacks a publicity agent. He does not know yet what he is going to do, and if nothing else turns up he might take another lone flight. In the meantime he has nothing to do.[3]

That wasn't the picture Hinkler wanted to give his mother. 'Since our return we have been running round quite a lot,' he wrote in the same December letter. 'Down here at Mon Repos we manage to hang out over the week-end, but during the rest of the week we are caught up in the rush of dodging into various places in London.' Both the Royal Aero Club and the Royal Aeronautical Society held dinners in his honour, as did Sir Charles Wakefield. But none of these events were advancing Hinkler's financial situation, as he told Frances: 'I must hasten to add that in the midst of all this running about, I am not collecting fees right and left.'[4]

Hinkler claimed to have turned down business proposals in England because he was 'making some headway with one of the best firms to build the machine of my dreams'. Although he had told the APA reporter in October that he had no intention of making another flight to Australia, six weeks later he was so confident his new creation would be capable of soon making such a journey, that he told his mother there was no point in her coming over for a visit in the northern summer, beginning six months hence.

The reality, however, was that Bert Hinkler was thirty-six years old and unemployed, with no apparent prospects except an idea in his head for a new aircraft, which he was still discussing with potential manufacturers.

A few months after his return to Mon Repos, he offered his record-breaking Avro Avian to the Queensland Government as a donation, which it gratefully accepted for display at the Queensland Museum. His mother chastised him for giving the plane away. 'I had no further use for it,' Hinkler countered, 'and owing to the sentimental interest of a generous public, I couldn't very well have sold it to anyone.'[5] However, he retained the precious blue log book in which he'd charted every mile of his journey across the globe.

That flight had shown him the limitations of the Avian for long-distance flying, even with the numerous modifications he and Chadwick had carried out beforehand. Hinkler had begun to conceive of a small aircraft for private use that was sturdy, reliable and economical across the sort of distances he'd flown in Australia, and adaptable to different environments, including being able to land on water. He believed that such a plane would appeal to the increasing number of private pilots as well as to small commercial operators.

With the Avian still fresh in his mind, he sat down and began to draw. He had help from his friend Roland Bound, an aeronautical engineer, but Hinkler apparently carried out most of the design for the new plane. The wings, however, were the work of Basil Henderson, a respected aircraft designer and engineer who had been employed by A.V. Roe and Company for four years prior to the Hamble plant's closure in 1928. The resulting configuration was a cantilever monoplane with a boat-like fuselage. Most radically, there were two opposed engines – that is, the motors were set back-to-back, the forward one driving a tractor propeller, the other a pusher propeller, in a concept known as push–pull – and these were mounted on struts above the cockpit, with the aim of minimising engine noise in the crew area. The plane had an enclosed cabin with two seats side-by-side, for the pilot and one passenger. Eventually two floats would be added to make the craft amphibious.

Hinkler gave his new design a name, just like the big manufacturers. 'I call my machine an Ibis,' he told Frances. 'An Ibis aircraft is a type of small aeroplane which is at home in all three elements, whether flying in the air, landing on the ground or else on the water.' He confided that the 'many difficulties' put up with in the Avian had helped him design 'the first really useful small aeroplane.'[6] The aircraft's name was a recognition of the (sometimes fatal) role played by the local birds in Bundaberg in his glider designs many years before.

Unfortunately, British aircraft manufacturers didn't share Hinkler's enthusiasm for the Ibis. Whatever negotiations he had with them came to nothing. For them, the push–pull engines and unusually shaped fuselage made the plane an unorthodox light aircraft and not one that they were prepared to take risks with, whatever the reputation of Hinkler as a pilot. Early European experiments with push–pull motors had encountered an ongoing problem with overheating in the rear engine, which had not yet been overcome.

What's more, the economic climate was turning ugly. Britain was already struggling after years of recession, and the United States went into economic depression early in 1929, a decline that was to culminate in the infamous Wall Street Crash six months later. It was not the time to be investing in risky ventures.

As the early months of 1929 drifted by, and his approaches to manufacturers floundered, Hinkler reluctantly decided he'd have to build a prototype of the Ibis himself. Perhaps once the aviation companies saw the new machine, they'd be convinced of its potential, he reasoned. With the help of Roland Bound, he started to construct the Ibis in a shed on the property at Mon Repos. He estimated that the prototype would take 50,000 man-hours, partly because he had to rely on access to other facilities for such tasks as machining parts – jobs that would've been routine and quick at an aircraft works. While he was working on the plane as summer approached, Nance occupied much of her time in the garden at the Thornhill house.

In June, Hinkler took time out from the project to attend a ceremony in Copenhagen. There, in further recognition of his landmark England–Australia flight, the Fédération Aéronautique Internationale presented him with its Gold Medal for the finest air exploit of 1928. In his acceptance speech, Hinkler was reported as saying that he was busy planning new adventures in which he would embody the 'priceless lessons learned in his flight to the Antipodes'[7].

He was excited when the two 40-horsepower Salmson engines arrived from Paris in October 1929. 'They are two really dinky little spinning tops,' he enthused to Frances in a letter that month, 'with nine tiddley cylinders round the crankcase . . . like so many tea cups with gills on.'[8]

It was reported that, when Hinkler installed the opposed engines, the propellers should've been of different pitch for maximum performance, but that he couldn't afford the cost of the experiments needed to determine the best combination of pitch and diameter for each blade. Another limitation of Hinkler's do-it-yourself approach was that the plane's fuselage had to be made of waterproofed timber because he didn't have the equipment to shape metal.

Flight magazine commented cheekily that there was no evidence to support the rumour that some of the smaller items for the Ibis were moulded using Nance's clothes wringer.

An article in *Flight* in December 1929 predicted that planes with enclosed cabins would eventually have an amphibious undercarriage as standard, thus opening up a market for private owners. It was forecasts like these that kept Hinkler's hopes alive.

* * *

By this time, there had been another significant development in the small-plane market: the DH.60 Moth, designed and built by Hertfordshire-based de Havilland Aircraft. Launched in 1925, this two-seater biplane with folding wings, and initially powered by a Cirrus engine, quickly became popular with UK aero clubs, and some aviation historians later described 1927 as 'the year the Moth took over'[9]. Its popularity was enhanced with the introduction of the Gipsy engine from 1928, and the aircraft's basic design would shortly lead to the famous DH.82 Tiger Moth.

By now Hinkler's 1928 record had been broken. Charles Kingsford Smith and Charles Ulm, with Harold Litchfield and Thomas Williams, touched down at Croydon Aerodrome in the *Southern Cross*, on 10 July 1929, after leaving Australia 12 days and 18 hours before. The same team the previous September had made the first flight from Australia to New Zealand, the route that Hinkler in the early 1920s had considered pioneering as a commercial proposition. Nevertheless, *Flight*'s editor pointed out, the *Southern Cross* flight to London had the advantages of three engines, four crew-members, and wireless communication; Hinkler's flight stood 'as an unbeaten individual achievement, and in this respect it will possibly never be beaten'. On arrival in England, Smithy paid a 'warm tribute' to his fellow Queenslander.[10]

Although Hinkler's record for a solo effort was still intact, the number of assaults was increasing as small planes became more sophisticated and reliable. Early in 1930, Francis Chichester flew solo from England to Australia in a de Havilland DH.60 Moth, although he failed to get close to Hinkler's fifteen-and-a-half days. In May the same year, Amy Johnson became the first woman pilot to make the same trip solo, also in a DH.60. Although she beat Hinkler's London-to-Karachi record by two days, Johnson took four days longer than he had to reach Australia. Still, the 26-year-old Yorkshire woman was feted wherever she went, with *Flight* describing her as 'the centre of a whirlpool of enthusiasm and admiration, which the aviation world has not experienced since Bert Hinkler's similar exploit, or Charles Lindbergh's lone flight across the Atlantic'.[11]

Johnson was better at exploiting her flights than Hinkler was. En route to Australia, she lost her way and made a clumsy landing on a playing field just north of Rangoon: the de Havilland ended up in a ditch, and the propeller, wing and undercarriage were severely damaged. Amy was unhurt, and although some observers regarded the incident as an example of pilot error and a serious mishap, she sold the story to Britain's high-circulation *Daily Mail* for a reported £2000.

* * *

Hinkler continued to spend most of his time on the Ibis. In May 1930, eighteen months after he'd returned from Australia, the plane was ready for its first, unofficial, air trial. Hinkler loaded the aircraft, now bearing its G-AAIS British registration, onto a trailer behind his Riley, and towed it along to a local field. He'd fitted a conventional undercarriage for the occasion; the floats would be added when the time came for the airworthiness checks.

Once he'd climbed into the cockpit and strapped himself in, he must have sat there for a moment, savouring the feeling. The Australian had tested numerous aircraft in his years with Avro, from the tiny autogiro to massive bombers, but this was the first time he would fly a plane that he'd had a major part in designing and building. This was *his* plane, the fulfilment of the dream he'd had since his teens.

After take-off, it was straight into professional mode: Hinkler checked the sightlines, tested the responsiveness of the controls, and watched for signs of overheating in the rear engine. He decided that a brief circuit over the Hampshire countryside was sufficient for the inaugural flight, and soon brought the aircraft back down. The Ibis rapidly became a common sight around Southampton, however, trundling behind the Riley on its trailer, just as he'd once trundled his homemade glider to Bundaberg's Mon Repos Beach behind a horse and buggy.

Some of the press became prematurely excited. Shortly after the trial, the *Northern Territory Times* proclaimed, 'Squadron Leader Bert Hinkler will begin a flight to Australia this week in a monoplane amphibian of his own design.'[12] As encouraging as the air trial had been, the reality was that the Ibis had yet to qualify for an official airworthiness certificate, and Hinkler didn't have enough funds to pursue its further development.

The editor of *Flight* had optimistically suggested in December 1929 that the Ibis 'may very well be the means of starting a movement which will be as far reaching as that which was virtually brought about by the introduction of the original Cirrus-Moth'.[13] Six months later, the signs were not promising. Despite the continuing recession, competition was increasing as the number of small plane owners grew. In mid 1930, a list of almost 300 private owners of planes in Britain showed the majority of the aircraft were various species of de Havilland Moth, and there was a plethora of other commercial brands, including Avians, Bluebirds and Woodpigeons. The single Ibis looked very lonely among them.

Hinkler became increasingly pessimistic about his chances of developing and marketing the plane in Britain. As the effects of the October 1929 stock-market crash reverberated around the world, investment declined, production slumped, and workers were laid off. The coal, steel and manufacturing industries in northern England were particularly hard hit, and by the beginning of 1930, around 1.5 million British workers were unemployed. Hinkler knew that even though he'd demonstrated the initial flight capabilities of the Ibis, there was no likelihood that British manufacturers would change their minds in the deteriorating economic climate.

If he couldn't develop the Ibis for the moment, Hinkler reasoned, perhaps he could persuade a manufacturer to let him use one of its existing aircraft: the company would benefit from the Australian's international reputation, and the arrangement would help keep his name in the public eye. By now A.V. Roe was under new ownership, with its operation concentrated in the north of England, so Hinkler approached a smaller company, Westland Aviation, based at Yeovil, in the West Country.

He had his sights set on a Widgeon, a high-winged monoplane of which only a small number were built. Negotiations broke down, however, because, in the words of Harald Penrose, Westland's manager of civil aviation, the company was 'not very co-operative'.[14] The reasons for this aren't clear, but two issues are hinted at: Penrose thought Hinkler was difficult to work with, and Westland refused to agree to his insistence on using Castrol oil, made by the company headed by his occasional benefactor, Sir Charles Wakefield. Whatever the reason, Hinkler once again found himself up the proverbial creek.

Since he had no regular means of support, the nest egg from his Australian trip was now dwindling. His situation was becoming desperate, and Hinkler decided to look beyond Britain, the country where he'd lived most of his adult life. Despite the bleak economic outlook across the world, Hinkler thought North America might be a more receptive market for the Ibis.

He'd designed the plane with Australian conditions in mind, but knew that there were similar environments in Canada and the United States. He'd also been to America five years before with the Schneider Cup team, and he had aviation contacts there from his wartime days. He was hardly unknown to the general public in that part of the world, either, since his record flights had been reported in American newspapers.

Frances Hinkler had said when he left Australia that Bert would do better in America. He was about to put her belief to the test.

* * *

At the end of August 1930 Hinkler boarded the TSS *Tuscania* at Southampton, bound for New York. Nance stayed at Mon Repos. Her de facto husband initially gave his intended address as care of the Cunard Steamship Company, Broadway, New York, but during the voyage he changed it to a hotel in the city. Although Hinkler indicated that he intended to stay in the United States for the usual sixty days allowed under the conditions of a visitor's visa, he would remain in North America for over a year.

He visited potential backers for his Ibis venture in the United States and Canada, but the manufacturers shook their heads even more emphatically than their counterparts in Britain. The US share market had been highly inflated when it crashed twelve months earlier, and hundreds of banks had begun closing their doors as borrowers reneged on their loans and customers demanded their savings. Unemployment was on the rise, and a general pessimism about the ability of the country to overcome its woes led to a spiral of economic decline that would only be arrested by the impact of World War II. It seemed that, at least for the time being, the Ibis would have to remain in its shed at Mon Repos.

This realisation must've been a big blow to Hinkler. The dream that had spawned the Ibis had begun on a beach in Bundaberg 18 years earlier, been confirmed during the time he spent with Wizard Stone, and then sustained throughout his service in World War I and in the post-war years as an Avro test-pilot and air-racer. The record flight to Australia had helped him fine-tune the design he held in his head. Subsequently, when British aircraft-makers had baulked at supporting the venture, Hinkler had shown enough belief in the project to take it on himself. When the prototype took to the air, Hinkler's hopes rose with it, only to be dashed on the twin rocks of manufacturer apathy and worldwide economic depression.

As if to rub salt into his wounds, in October 1930 Charles Kingsford Smith smashed the solo England–Australia record. Flying a heavily modified, Gipsy-engined Avian Mark IVA, christened *Southern Cross Junior*, the much-travelled pilot arrived in Darwin after just nine days and twenty-one hours aloft. Hinkler was among the first to send his congratulations, but for the hero of the 1928 flight, it might've stung all the more to read an assessment in *Flight* magazine declaring Kingsford Smith's achievement as 'perhaps the most noteworthy light 'plane flight that has yet been made'.[15] The editor added that so many pilots were heading to Australia from England, or vice versa, that year, it was a sickness that deserved a name: 'Antipodes Aeronitis'.

Flight's editor was full of praise for Smithy:

> We prefer to regard those two great Australians, Hinkler and Kingsford Smith, apart. Comparison would be as futile as it would be odious. Hinkler's laurels, won as test pilot, racing pilot, and pioneer of great solo flights, will never wither. Kingsford Smith stands out as the greatest modern touring pilot of the world . . . Outside the Polar regions, he has made almost every great flight which could be made.[16]

Unlucky in business and seemingly eclipsed in the air, Bert Hinkler once again considered his future.

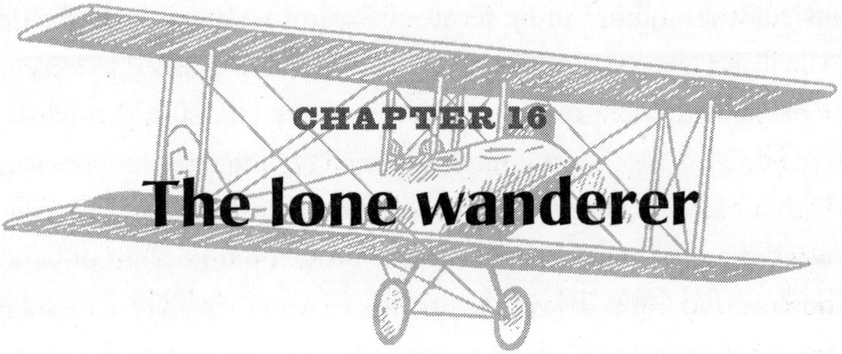

CHAPTER 16

The lone wanderer

When Hinkler turned thirty-eight on 8 December 1930, his outlook might've seemed as bleak as the weather in New York, where temperatures that month plunged below zero for days on end. In the past, he'd usually been ready to tell reporters (and his mother) that he was considering several aviation developments. Now there was nothing on the horizon.

He had friends on New York's Long Island, just east of Manhattan, and at one stage considered setting up an air charter service there. Ultimately he decided that it wasn't a commercial proposition, however. On 29 December, Nance arrived from England on the Cunard liner *Ausonia* to join him.

In January, almost 2 feet of snow fell in New York, and Hinkler may have felt as weighed down as the trees in Central Park as he tried to decide his next move. A month later, he'd made up his mind. Apparently without Nance, he headed north across the border, to de Havilland's Canadian operation in Toronto, Ontario. Although the company's sales had suffered across the world in the early years of the Depression, they had held up in Canada, thanks largely to orders from the Royal Canadian Air Force. Hinkler would've felt the bite of the Canadian winter in its coldest month, but he received a warm welcome from the de Havilland general manager, Bob Loader, when he asked to look at a plane he thought might suit his needs: the DH.80A Puss Moth.

The Puss Moth was a single-engined high-winged monoplane, with a metal fuselage and an enclosed cabin that could be configured to seat two or three people. From a pilot's point of view, the inverted Gipsy III engine provided greater visibility across the nose, the wings folded for storage, and the undercarriage struts could be rotated 90 degrees, allowing more control for landing in confined spaces. With good fuel economy, the DH.80A was a popular choice for both private and commercial operators.

Of the nine Puss Moths that had been shipped to Canada the previous summer, seven had already been sold and one was the company's demonstrator. Hinkler snapped up the last one: number 2049, for $6800 Canadian – around $100,000 Canadian in today's currency. It came with the engine, instruments, upholstery and controls in place, and a wooden propeller to bolt onto its ready-for-use Gipsy Mk III motor. Sir Charles Wakefield reportedly helped with the purchase.

Hinkler wrote to his old friend Edward Hart in Australia. 'I was hoping to resurrect the Ibis under the Stars and Stripes,' he told the journalist. 'Well, the ideal touring ship is still a long way off completion and altho I have great hopes of acquitting myself by its aid, at the moment I fear I may not be able to hold out long enough. Therefore the Moth seems to provide a fitting fillup.'[1]

Hinkler didn't say what he intended to use the new plane for, but hinted that it would be a commercial venture: 'My finances being what they are, I am prevented from the great joy of flying just for pleasure.' He knew he'd have to return to England, the 'land of smoke and fog', sometime, he added, but since travelling by ship was never his preferred option, he would probably use the Moth for the purpose.[2] What Hinkler didn't say was which way he'd be travelling to reach his adopted home, or whether Nance would go with him.

At its Downsview Park base, in the north of Toronto, de Havilland prepared Puss Moth number 2049 for handover to the new owner, and applied for airworthiness and registration papers. On delivery, the plane was painted with a basic coat of red-brown dope, ready for the owner to apply his preferred colours. Hinkler chose silver, with dark red struts, using the minimum of coats in order to keep the weight down. The new plane's Canadian registration, CF-APK, was emblazoned in red across the underside of the wings, and repeated in smaller letters on both sides, towards the rear of the fuselage. A company test pilot flew it on 28 April 1931, and declared it airworthy. Hinkler immediately wanted to give it his own test, and Bob Loader arranged for a temporary flight permit to allow him to fly the new plane to the US the very next day. This was the first of a number of flights that Hinkler made to North Beach, Long Island and Providence, Rhode Island, and he often brought back a supply of a particular brand of ginger beer he liked.

After formally taking delivery of his Puss Moth, Hinkler began to customise it with his own modifications, as was his wont. The de Havilland general manager allocated him a wooden storage hangar at Downsview, and placed the company's facilities at his disposal, including the machine shop, the fabric shop, and woodwork specialists. How Hinkler would've liked to have had access to those sorts of amenities when building the Ibis. Soon the 'dark haired little guy in the white overalls',[3] as one staff member described him, looked like one of de Havilland's own technical staff, chewing gum as he worked away. The harder Hinkler worked, another worker said, the harder he chewed.

There was speculation that the Australian was preparing for another record flight attempt, but he wasn't giving anything away. When he landed in Buffalo in upstate New York, a week after his first flight in the DH.80A, reporters asked him if what they'd heard from airport workers was true – that he was planning to fly to Africa via Buenos Aires. Hinkler replied that he wasn't in a position to make any statements about his plans, and that any reports were unauthorised. 'Whenever I use my plane,' he said brusquely, 'people immediately rush to the conclusion that I must be going on an important flight, and if I have not decided where I am going, they decide for me.'[4] Next day, *Burnie's Advocate* proclaimed: 'Hinkler plans flight across Atlantic? Won't talk.'[5] Some newspapers reportedly dubbed him 'No-news Hinkler'.

If he did discuss his plans, it might've been with his good friend Charles Browne, manager of the Canadian operation of Wakefield's Castrol Oil Company. Hinkler also kept in touch with Charles Sproatt, the former RNAS officer who had selected him as a gunner and recommended him for pilot training back in 1917.

Wherever Hinkler was going, he was in no hurry. Over the next few months from May 1931, workshop employees at Downsview Park became used to seeing him around – borrowing tools and arranging for little welding jobs. Twenty years after his experiments in the backyard shed at Gavan Street, he'd not lost his love of tinkering.

He applied a coat of wax to the new aircraft, which gave it a distinctive appearance. One day a visitor walking past remarked to a colleague, 'What an awful looking aeroplane.'[6] Hinkler emerged from behind the Puss Moth and told them firmly that it was his plane and that was exactly the way he liked it.

* * *

At the end of May, Nance returned to England by ship. Mystery surrounds her relationship with Hinkler during the five months she spent in North America, since there is no mention of her in accounts of the period when he resided in Toronto.

Just as he had once in London, Hinkler travelled around the Canadian city on a motorbike, until someone who had a contact at General Motors arranged for the company to lend him a car. The Toronto Flying Club made him an honorary member, but he was no social animal, keeping mostly to himself and spending a lot of time in the hangar and workshops. By comparison, when the celebrated British pilots Amy Johnson and Jim Mollison later came to Toronto, they enjoyed the hospitality of de Havilland Canada and the local flying fraternity, and hardly stepped inside the workshops.

The only signs that pointed towards what Hinkler had in mind were the modifications themselves, where his technical and inventive skills came to the fore. He removed two of the Puss Moth's three seats, the windows at the rear of the cabin, and also the navigation lights, the last of which suggested that he might be planning only daytime hops, as he'd done on his England–Australia flight. Long-range fuel tanks on the wings and a specially built tank wedged in the rear of the fuselage gave him almost six times the standard fuel capacity of the Moth. He mounted a second compass on the cabin roof, behind the pilot's seat, which he viewed though a mirror. De Havilland's John Slaughter helped him replace the original tail skid with a wheel. The skid was intended to help slow the Moth on landing – as it had with his Avro Avian – but it also impeded the take-off, and Hinkler wanted more acceleration for the aircraft when it was heavy with a full load of fuel.

He also initially replaced the compression struts of the undercarriage with wire bracing, relying on the resilience of the tyres to cushion the landing. On the first try-out with a full load, however, both tyres blew as he touched down, and he abandoned the idea.

One disadvantage of the inverted design of the Gipsy III engine in the Puss Moth was high oil consumption, requiring regular refills of the external tank. In order to keep the oil topped up and fresh, Hinkler wanted to be able to replenish the supply and regulate the flow from inside the cabin. To maximise the use of fresh oil, one of the de Havilland workmen, Harry Proctor, came up with the idea of setting the system up like an office water bubbler. All Hinkler had to do was keep a can of fresh oil within reach, and as one emptied, feed the next one in. The empty cans were disposed of by chopping them up with a pair of tin snips kept nearby, and throwing the pieces out the window.

During these months of modifications, Hinkler developed a reputation as a craftsman and a thorough and cautious pilot, constantly checking and re-checking the installations and their effect on the DH.80A in the air. The only time he sought help was when he needed another pair of hands. 'When you worked for Bert,' John Slaughter said, 'you were the helper – he was the boss.'[7]

The first official inkling of Hinkler's intentions came when he listed the plane's modifications in a letter to the Controller of

Civil Aviation in Canada on 4 July: 'Until the aircraft is returned to normal structural condition, it will be used solely for solo long-distance flights. My plans are at the present time in a somewhat nebulous stage and I am particularly anxious to avoid any premature publicity in any form and I therefore ask you to regard the contents of this as being entirely confidential.'[8]

Despite Hinkler's claim that his plans were still evolving, the media consensus was that his next long flight would be to Africa. Hinkler said nothing. As usual. Over the next few months, he continued to fly regularly to Long Island, and he continued to prepare the de Havilland for a long-distance flight.

* * *

Almost six months after he'd taken delivery of the Puss Moth, and more than twelve since he'd arrived in North America, Hinkler slipped out of Toronto on 20 October in what another aviator called a 'semi-furtive'[9] departure, and landed shortly afterwards at the airstrip on Long Island. That afternoon he called in at the Office of the Commissioner-General for Australia, and told the secretary, D.M. Dow, that he proposed to fly to Jamaica, Venezuela, Trinidad, British Guiana, French Guiana and south along the Brazilian coast. Dow was bemused by the visit. 'Mr Hinkler did not advise me fully relative to his objective in the flight to the British West Indies and ports in South America,' he reported. 'The flight appeared to me to be meaningless, unless he hoped to make business connections at various centres in the West Indies and South America.'[10]

No one else seemed any the wiser about Hinkler's plans when he lifted the silver Puss Moth off the runway at North Beach Aerodrome on 26 October, without a word to the press. Below, the maples, oaks and elms were glowing red and yellow in the afternoon sun, parading their autumn colours.

Despite the paring down he'd done in Toronto, with a full load of fuel the little plane was 500 pounds overweight, and struggled for height in the erratic winds over New York. Finally the bumps and the city were left behind, and Hinkler crossed the coast and headed south-east across the pulsing waves of the immense Atlantic Ocean. It was the first time he'd flown across a significant tract of water since his record-breaking flight to Australia, and this was a new aircraft that he hadn't yet had a chance to try out over a distance. With the additional tanks, he had enough fuel for twenty-five hours at 100 miles an hour.

Just after six o'clock, the sun slipped behind the horizon, and he found himself flying in darkness, the ocean somewhere below. Because he'd stripped off the navigation lights, which were mandatory for flying over the US mainland, Hinkler was forced to keep out to sea, and about 150 miles off the coast he ran into heavy cloud and unstable air. Twice the plane dropped towards the ocean before he was able to level out.

He decided to try climbing above the clouds, and after some anxious moments, the DH.80A emerged at 10,000 feet into bright moonlight that bathed the plane in a soft white glow. For the first time that night, Hinkler could see the instrument panel clearly. He soon ran into more cloud and the moon disappeared again, and for an hour he flew blind, guided only by his luminous compass. The plane droned on, over the area that would later become notorious as the Bermuda Triangle, and then across the island of Cuba – at that time, a country in political turmoil, but not yet under Communist rule.

As morning approached and the sky lightened, Hinkler sighted the shadowy shapes of sharks in the turquoise water below, and was thankful for the steady beat of the Gipsy engine. Soon he could see a mountain ahead, its apex wreathed in cloud. It was Blue Mountain Peak in Kingston, on the Caribbean island of Jamaica, then a British crown colony. When he touched down on the town's polo ground a few minutes later, he was just in time for breakfast.

Hinkler's skill as a navigator had once again paid off. He'd flown over 1800 miles in eighteen hours, most of it in the dark. And it was another record: the first nonstop flight from New York to Jamaica.

In a cable to the Australian Press Association, Hinkler claimed his destination was South Africa and revealed that he'd given the de Havilland a name. 'My airship, *Karohi*, is excellently suited for the task,' he wrote, 'so whether I make the trip is entirely dependent on being able to meet the expenses.'[11] *Karohi* was painted on the left-hand side of the plane, on the nose cowling, with an arrow slicing through the text. Photos show it wasn't there when the Puss Moth left Tornoto, however, so the name must've been added during his six-day stopover in New York. Hinkler claimed it was Aboriginal for 'Lone wanderer'.

The long-distance flyer spent almost a fortnight in Jamaica, delayed in the second week by unfavourable flying weather on his forward route. Newspapers quoted New York sources who claimed he would probably continue through to the city of Natal, Brazil, and decide there whether he would fly across the Atlantic to Africa. His only public obligation in Kingston was a dinner organised in his honour by the Mayor. At the end of his stay, he again avoided the press, taking off late on Monday 9 November into the night sky.

For a while Hinkler flew in moonlight, on a south-eastern course across the Caribbean Sea, but then dark clouds moved in. Inside the black clouds, the plane ran headlong into a serious of rain squalls, which seemed to have been waiting for him. They played with *Karohi* like a cat with a mouse, pelting the cockpit with rain and sending out claws of fierce wind that pushed and pulled at the tiny craft. Hinkler struggled to keep the Puss Moth on course, and resorted to heading for a certain time in one direction, then for the same amount of time in the opposite direction, guided by a compass and the clock on the control panel. Sometimes in the darkness he glimpsed clouds for long enough to calculate his rate of drift and then take more precise corrective action.

At daybreak the plane emerged from yet another squall, and there below was a large city. After flying blind for 600 miles, Hinkler had come out exactly where he'd intended: Maracaibo, on the edge of its eponymous giant lake, in the north-west of Venezuela.

After a brief touchdown in the South American city, he flew east and made an overnight stop on the island of Trinidad, where another Moth owner unexpectedly flew out to greet him.

For the moment, Hinkler was content to fly in easy stages around the north-east coast of South America, first to Paramaribo in Surinam, and then on Saturday, 14 November to Belém do Pará, the so-called 'city of mango trees', in northern Brazil. It took Hinkler an hour to fly over the delta of the Amazon River, and from Belém he cut across the jungles of northern Brazil, his path punctuated by bright flashes of colour as birds darted across the sky or sought refuge in the greenery below from the noisy intruder in their skies. Enormous flocks of scarlet ibis wheeled below the Puss Moth, perhaps reminding him of the 'dream machine' he'd left behind in England.

A little further east along the Brazilian coast, on Wednesday, 18 November, he landed at Fortaleza. It was mid afternoon; the officials welcomed the Australian and asked to see his visa and authority to fly over Brazilian territory. Hinkler had neither. He was taken into custody and the aircraft was impounded. Newspapers quickly picked up the story.

When the British Chargé d'Affaires at Rio de Janeiro was advised, he alerted the Australian authorities in New York. From there, an irritated Secretary Dow wrote a missive to the Prime Minister's Department in Canberra: '[Hinkler's] detention by the Brazilian authorities in Sao Paulo [sic] has provoked a situation which could have been avoided. The free and easy methods characteristic of the Australian aviator have led him into an embarrassing but, I trust, not serious situation.'[12] The official's tone was reminiscent of that of the British Consul-General in Batavia, when Hinkler arrived there unannounced in February 1928.

Newspapers reported that the pilot was languishing in jail. Hinkler's reputation as an international aviator proved to be an asset, however, and the British Chargé d'Affaires soon arranged the necessary paperwork. After two days' detention, the pilot was free. Asked later about his confinement, Hinkler reportedly downplayed the incident, claiming that his two-day 'arrest' amounted to going for walks and drinking beer with the governor.

Despite the attention afforded his Brazilian interlude, he continued to maintain his silence with the press. Asked, as always, for an indication of his intentions, Hinkler said his future arrangements were very indefinite. It was fast becoming a stock response – almost the same as the one he'd given journalists in Australia three years before, and in Buffalo the previous May.

Hinkler's final stopover in Brazil was Natal, a city on the far eastern tip of the country, before the South American coastline curves west again, to wind down past Rio de Janeiro to Uruguay and Argentina. Natal is renowned for its towering white dunes and spectacular beaches, but Hinkler wasn't there for the scenery. He'd finally decided that this would be his departure point for the flight the media had long suspected he was planning: to the west coast of Africa, almost 2000 miles away across the South Atlantic Ocean. Once more he'd be flying without lights and, more significantly, without a radio. He sent a telegram to Nance: 'Here's hoping.'[13]

CHAPTER 17

A bold, bad little pilot

As Bert Hinkler prepared for a mid-morning take-off from Natal on Wednesday, 25 November 1931, the temperature in the Brazilian city was heading as usual towards a steamy 30 degrees Celsius. The conditions might have reminded him of his few days in Darwin almost four years before, when he'd been forced to borrow a woman's shorts to stay cool.

The fuel tanks on the Puss Moth were filled to the brim, and he was anxious to get away. Crouched in the back of the plane, among the pilot's belongings, was a marmoset monkey that Brazilian admirers had given him for company on the flight across the Atlantic. Once again the Australian had been uncommunicative about his exact destination, but airport workers and journalists alike believed it was Dakar, on the western-most tip of the then French territory of Senegal.

As the Puss Moth gathered speed along the unsealed runway, Hinkler felt the tail-trim lever slip, on account of the heavy load and the rough terrain. Unbalanced, the monoplane threatened to nosedive into the ground even before he'd taken off.

He gave the control stick a hefty pull, and managed to lift *Karohi* into the air, but thought the undercarriage had given way. Once aloft, his fears proved to be unfounded – the combination of the tail-trim fault and the uneven field had merely given the impression that something vital had collapsed. From the way it was flying, he was confident the plane had emerged unscathed. Hinkler breathed a sigh of relief, but he was still worried that there might be a structural problem somewhere.

The white beaches below glistened in the mid-morning sunshine as he crossed the coast and headed north-east over the green swells of the Atlantic Ocean, bound for West Africa. As precedents went, beginning with Portuguese military flyers Sacadura Cabral and Gago Coutinho in 1922, all successful flights across the South Atlantic had been made in the opposite direction, east to west, and in airships or seaplanes that had touched down on the way – in Sacadura and Coutinho's case, even involving a change of planes. In addition, all of these flights carried at least two crew members, often with external support groups to monitor progress and assist if something went wrong. True to form, Hinkler was alone in his heavily loaded single-engined de Havilland, without a radio or back-up of any kind.

Several hours after leaving the Brazilian coast, he saw a mass of clouds ahead, stretched across the horizon like a football team defending its line. Within minutes he met the full force of a South Atlantic storm. Gale-force winds whipped at the plane and rain lashed the windscreen.

With the little craft unable to climb easily due to the heavy fuel load, Hinkler's only option was to burrow under the cloud front. Down he went – only to discover that the cloud mass extended to within 100 feet of the ocean. Not daring to go back into the seething mass above, he levelled the plane out above the foam caps, and concentrated on maintaining height and staying on course.

The storm raged on. As darkness fell, Hinkler could no longer see the churning ocean, so he had to go up or risk smashing into the waves. His first thought was to try to get above the storm, but as he angled up, and up, and up, it became apparent that the cloud mass stretched high into the sky, perhaps to 20,000 or 30,000 feet, like huge blocks of concrete. There was no chance of the Puss Moth being able to reach that altitude, and he decided to level out at around 12,000 feet.

As he wrestled with the pitching aircraft, vivid yellow bolts of lightning hurled themselves across the sky like telegraph poles, and any moment he thought they'd slice *Karohi* in two. 'It was like being in a glass box plastered with paper, dimming the light, people throwing buckets of water, and a few elephants taking hefty kicks at you,' Hinkler said later.[1]

As if that wasn't enough, the windscreen started dripping water. With the plane lit up by intermittent flashes of lightning, he ploughed on, his hands fighting with the controls.

Suddenly Hinkler felt something grab him from behind. He looked round with a start, then let out a sigh of relief and turned quickly back to his task. It was the marmoset, which had abruptly leapt onto his shoulder, attracted by the water dripping from the windscreen.

The Puss Moth eventually emerged from the storm into welcome moonlight, which lit up the ocean below like silver foil. Soon afterwards, he identified a small outcrop as Saint Peter and

Saint Paul Rocks, and a small 'Yes!' might've escaped his lips as he realised how accurate his navigation had been. Hinkler was now some 60 miles north of the Equator and about a third of the way across the Atlantic.

He headed steadily north-east once more, hoping there'd be enough fuel left after his long battle with the storms. The previous year, a French pilot named Jean Mermoz and two companions had flown a commercial seaplane across the South Atlantic in the opposite direction, but in retracing their path were forced to ditch into the sea. Fortunately, they'd had radio communication, and were rescued.

Colonial authorities in West Africa were on the lookout for Hinkler, but when CF-APK didn't arrive in Dakar by early morning, expectation turned to concern, because the long-distance pilot had now been in the air some twenty hours. That is, if he was still in the air. A *Sydney Morning Herald* headline on 28 November alerted Australians: 'Mr Hinkler – Flight across South Atlantic – Fears for his safety.'[2]

Karohi was indeed still airborne. As the moon disappeared, the fingers of a new dawn reached across the horizon towards the plane. Hinkler sighted a cargo ship chugging a steady path through the deep green waters below, and knew he must be over the coastal trade routes of West Africa, and therefore not far from his goal. Elated, he swooped down alongside the ship, waving to the no-doubt startled sailors as he flew past. He read the name emblazoned on the ship's stern – *Nyassa* – before taking the Puss Moth back up and heading for the coast.

A few hours later, some 3500 miles to the north, in Thornhill, near Southampton, England, Nance received a brief telegram: 'Landed at Bathurst, Gambia. O. K. Bert.' Entirely surrounded by Senegal save for a 50-mile stretch of coastline, tiny Gambia was then a British Crown colony with Bathurst (now Banjul) its capital.

Hinkler had just flown close to 2000 miles in twenty-two hours, and in doing so had broken three records: first west–east crossing of the South Atlantic; first solo flight across the South Atlantic in either direction; and first trans-Atlantic crossing in a light aeroplane – Lindbergh's specially built Ryan monoplane of 1927 did not officially fall into the 'light' category. Nance was quoted as saying that the only advance information she'd had about the flight was Bert's telegram from Natal. 'For all I knew,' she said, 'he might have been heading to Patagonia.'

Some newspapers reported that Hinkler had been aiming for Dakar but ended up in Bathurst because he'd been blown off course. Nance would have none of it: 'It is not a question of bad navigation. He went to Bathurst because it is British.'[3] Perhaps feeling the need to fill the gap left by her partner's reluctance to talk to the press, Nance told reporters that Bert had gone to America to buy a plane and set up a business there, but that the financial downturn had put paid to that. Then when another project didn't work out, she said, he'd decided to make the flight across the Atlantic. She implied that Bert had invested the money he'd received from his Australian trip, and had used the proceeds to fund the purchase of the Puss Moth.

Word quickly spread that Hinkler had made the first solo flight across the South Atlantic, and from west to east. Cables to British newspapers from local reporters in Bathurst brought a new burst of media attention. But still the pilot avoided the press. He set off again, this time heading north-north-east for Casablanca in Morocco, with brief stops in between. On the last leg, he flew high to avoid Moroccan tribesmen, fearing they might take pot shots at his plane.

In 1931 Casablanca was a tawdry market town, far removed from the glamorous portrayal it would receive eleven years later in film-maker Michael Curtiz's hands. But it at least gave Hinkler an opportunity to overhaul the de Havilland, as well as play a round of golf. The ruling French received him warmly, and their Commissioner presented him with the Moroccan Cross for what a local newspaper called '*un exploit sensationnel*'. Casablanca's aero club hosted a reception for him.

Despite the public attention, Hinkler continued his stand-off with the press, leaving the French reporter to write that he was heading to 'a destination he wants to remain secret'.[4] As it turned out, there was no great mystery – he was going back to England. Plane, pilot and monkey duly arrived there a few days later, through a series of relatively straightforward hops via Spain and France, with just a short delay in Tours because of the weather.

* * *

Fifteen months had passed since Bert Hinkler was last in Britain, and he touched down at west London's Hanworth Air Park on 7 December 1931, one day before his thirty-ninth birthday. The weak winter sun glinted on the silver wings of the DH.80A Puss Moth as it rolled up to the roped-off enclosure. Among those there to greet the Australian were the Under-Secretary of State for Air, Sir Philip Sassoon, other senior government officials, several pilots who'd also conquered the Atlantic, and a large contingent of policemen to maintain crowd control. The king sent a message of congratulations, but Hinkler might have been just as pleased with the one from his mother in Bundaberg: 'Proud of your achievement. Wonderful.'[5]

Nance was also present, dressed 'most becomingly in black with a black hat, and a white fur around her neck', according to Frederic Robertson's feature in *Flight* magazine. Hinkler, on the other hand, was wearing a dark suit 'somewhat the worse for the attentions which he always pays to his engine when aground', and a woollen sweater under his coat. In his lapel gleamed the maroon button of the Moroccan Cross he'd been awarded in Casablanca. 'One cannot imagine,' Major Robertson continued, 'Bert Hinkler buying new clothes in the course of a flight in order to make a well-groomed appearance on arrival.'[6] It was an image that dogged Hinkler, but it didn't seem to bother him.

As it turned out, the police presence wasn't required – because there was no crowd. While Hinkler had been in Toronto, the public's attention had been diverted by other significant aviation achievements. The England–Australia record had been broken several times: in April that year, C.W.A. Scott piloted a DH.60 Gipsy Moth to break Smithy's 1930 record of ten-and-a-half days by seventeen hours, Arthur Butler later bettered that by two hours, and in August, Jim Mollison (soon to become Amy Johnson's husband), flying in the opposite direction, touched down in England in under nine days. The editor of *Flight* drily suggested that the England–Australia record should now be measured by stopwatch rather than tear-off calendar.

Despite the small numbers at the official welcome, there was no shortage of support for Hinkler in Southampton, where the mayor and a large crowd gave him an enthusiastic welcome five days later. Nor did they think any less of him at Croydon: 'This latest flight undoubtedly ranks with some of the greatest flights undertaken, and it was all-British,'[7] their newsletter enthused. The Croydon Aerodrome representative added that although they hadn't seen him for a while, he was 'as popular as if he were one of our happy family'.

In *Flight* magazine, Robertson mentioned Hinkler's subsequent purchase of clothes from Burberrys, a well-known London store, and joked about his penchant for modifications: 'We do not know if he induced Burberrys to introduce a few "Hinklerisations" into his greatcoat, but possibly we shall soon see a new model, known as the "Bert Burberry", and possessing several novel improvements.'[8]

Later, the British Aeronautical Society presented Hinkler with the Segrave Trophy for the most daring flying feat of 1931, and other aviation organisations, including the Royal Federation of Aero Clubs of Australia, and the Guild of Air Pilots and Air Navigators, also made presentations to him in recognition of the record-making flight. The Royal Aero Club not only awarded him the 1931 Britannia Trophy for the most meritorious performance by a British aviator – which he'd also received in 1920 and 1928 – but its Gold Medal for outstanding achievement. The recipients of the Aero Club's first gold medal, 23 years earlier, were Wilbur and Orville Wright.

A Brisbane woman, Winifred Stephenson, believed that Hinkler's latest feat was worth more than medals and trophies, however. She took the matter up directly with King George V: 'May it please your Majesty to make Bert Hinkler a knight? Could it be possible to have an Order of Flying Knights?' she wrote. 'We get so sick of these political knights and feel we would like some men to be knighted for bravery and wonderful deeds.' She assured the king she didn't know anything about Hinkler personally, but still felt that it would be 'nice to have the little man as one of an Order of Flying Knights if it would please your majesty at all'.[9]

The King didn't respond to Winifred's plea, but his son Edward, the Prince of Wales, invited Hinkler to dine with him at York House in London, along with two Arctic explorers, Gino Watkins and Augustine Courtauld. The two explorers produced maps and charts of their expedition, which the prince showed great interest in. When Edward asked Hinkler about the maps he'd used on his Atlantic flight, however, the pilot embarrassedly explained he didn't carry any charts at all – although it seems likely he would've at least have had his *Times* atlas with him.

While it had travelled all the way from South America with him, and had gone through the same storms, thunder and lightning, the marmoset received no telegrams and no awards. It reportedly struck up a friendship with the Hinklers' three-legged cat (rescued from a rabbit trap), but died in February, unaccustomed to an English winter.

* * *

In a speech at the Royal Aero Club dinner in his honour, a few days before Christmas 1931, Hinkler said that many people had told him he was lacking in a sense of publicity, so he had compiled his own list of achievements from his recent flights. The list went as follows: the first British aircraft to arrive in Jamaica; the first nonstop flight of any nationality to Jamaica from New York; the first land [non-airship or -seaplane] machine to touch down in Jamaica; the first British aircraft to fly over the Caribbean Sea; the first nonstop flight between Venezuela and Trinidad; the first British aircraft to fly to the coast of South America; the first land aircraft to fly eastwards along that coast; the first aircraft to land at Pera on the Amazon; the first British aircraft to land at Ceará, in Brazil; the first solo flight across the South Atlantic; the first British machine to fly over the South Atlantic; the first west–east successful flight over the South Atlantic; and the first Canadian-registered aircraft to arrive in England under its own power.

It was and is an impressive catalogue, and serves to highlight Hinkler's unhappy lot. Namely that his outstanding aviation achievements didn't lead to improved career prospects or, in the long term, a better bank balance. Nor did they assist in the development of the Ibis. Other British pilots who were sympathetic to his situation pointed out that less-difficult flights had received more attention than Hinkler's, because their publicity had been better organised. On the other hand, a petulant Hinkler response such as 'any reports are unauthorised' and his continuing avoidance of the press indicate an increasing irritation with the journalistic profession.

In an interview with reporters in London not long after his return from West Africa, Hinkler was at pains to stress that he had carefully planned the South Atlantic flight, that it was not a 'harebrained stunt', but an opportunity to demonstrate the workmanship of a British aircraft. One young journalist then asked him if he expected to crash at any minute as he flew above the waves. Hinkler turned fiercely to him. 'Haven't I been saying that I took every precaution possible, tested the ship in every way, calculated what she could do and what she could carry?' he snapped. 'Why should I be expecting to crash, except [if] something I couldn't control intervened?'[10]

At the RAeC dinner, Hinkler played down his South Atlantic flight as largely a 'joy ride', since other pilots were slogging away daily with commercial airlines, doing much more than he'd done. Asked why he'd made the flight, the record-breaker reportedly grinned and replied, 'I don't know.' Perhaps it was because of this apparent flippancy, and because they knew personally the risks involved in long-distance flying, that some aviators were critical of his actions. At the tribute dinner, Charles Kingsford Smith said he was proud to claim Hinkler as 'a brother Aussie', but at the same time he rebuked his fellow Queenslander for the chances he'd taken in flying across the South Atlantic in a Puss Moth.[11] In Canada, Hinkler's wartime friend Charles Sproatt also congratulated Bert on his latest achievement when he met him later in Toronto, but urged him not to undertake such dangerous flights.

However, it was the editor of *Flight*, a long-time Hinkler supporter, who took him to task most severely.

> He has been almost our *beau ideal* of what a pioneer long-distance pilot ought to be. Consequently we are shocked and pained to learn that he has sunk to the level of a trans-Atlantic flier. We must now write him down as a bold, bad little pilot, who has risked, not merely his life, but also the fair reputation of the aeroplane, by taking a chance which staked more in the event of failure than it stood to gain in the event of success.[12]

Disregarding the accolades and brickbats Hinkler received over his South Atlantic flight, the outcome was that, after the initial flurry of publicity, after all the dinners and speeches and presentation of medals, his future in England was no more settled than it had been when he'd left in September 1930.

When asked at the Hanworth welcome whether he intended to continue with development of the Ibis, Hinkler had said he would if he could raise the money. In January 1932, *Flight*'s editor put his finger on the problem that Bert now faced: although the back-to-back engine arrangement had been relatively novel when he'd first designed the plane, three years had elapsed, and 'nowadays the arrangement is apt to pass unnoticed'.[13] Also, although one advantage of pusher-type engines was that they were behind the cockpit and thus made for a quieter flight for its occupants, the propeller of the front (tractor) engine was ahead of the cockpit in the twin-engined Ibis, an arrangement that the same editor thought resulted in the blades being too close to the windscreen. Nevertheless, he hoped that Hinkler would be able to develop the Ibis for commercial production.

Aviation design was moving on, however, and by now Hinkler could see that there was no immediate prospect of a market for the Ibis, and therefore still no likelihood of financial backing. Having earlier declared that he would consider only projects where he was in charge, he was also increasingly pessimistic about his chances of employment in England. On 24 December 1931, the *Sydney Morning Herald* reported that the famous pilot had given Britain a month to make up its mind whether it would employ him. If nothing eventuated, he would go to the United States. 'I hate the idea of "boosting" foreign aeroplanes, but flying is my bread and butter, and I must live,' Hinkler had said.[14]

CHAPTER 18

Fallen onto hard facts

By January 1932, Hinkler's challenge to the British to find him suitable employment had not been answered, so the 39-year-old declared he was going to America. Contrary to press speculation, he had not made any advance arrangement for aviation work in the U.S. or an attempt on a distance record, but he had high hopes something would eventuate. The conqueror of the South Atlantic decided to leave the Puss Moth in England for the time being, and bought a ticket for himself to New York for a February departure of the RMS *Mauretania*. He booked his Riley below decks as cargo. Nancy would remain at Mon Repos.

When the liner docked in New York on 16 February, a reporter asked Hinkler what he intended to do in North America, but the Australian would give only his oft-repeated response that his plans were unclear. Braving the cold weather, he headed north in the Riley, and shortly afterwards, turned up at de Havilland's works in north Toronto. The staff at Downsview Park were understandably chuffed about the South Atlantic record he'd created in one of their aircraft, and Hinkler gave an impromptu lunchtime question-and-answer session about the flight. But this was no social visit. He had structural concerns regarding the DH.80A, and talked to one of the company's test pilots about the problem experienced during take-off at Natal, with *Karohi*'s tail-trim lever.

In March, Hinkler visited the Royal Canadian Air Force headquarters, probably to discuss a serious incident that one of their pilots had been involved in, at the controls of a Puss Moth. During a manoeuvre, the left wing had separated from the fuselage. This was the fourth such accident with a DH.80A, and the only one in which the pilot had survived. De Havilland subsequently decided that the problem was serious enough to warrant a correction, and in April they sent a letter to all Puss Moth owners, including Hinkler, requiring them to modify the lift struts on the wings.

A month after he'd arrived in America, Nance followed him across. They returned to England on the *Baltic* at the end of May, although Nance boarded in New York and Bert came aboard in Boston. It would seem that Hinkler had achieved little during his trip to North America. If he still had hopes of resurrecting the Ibis in that market, the response must've been the same as on his previous visit; and no one apparently offered him the chance of 'boosting foreign aeroplanes'. Apart from the information he'd gleaned about the Puss Moth in Toronto, and renewing friendships, he appears to have come away empty-handed.

While Hinkler tried to sort out his aviation future, the industry itself continued to move ahead. In 1931, the year he flew the South Atlantic, there were fifteen attempts at long-distance records in or out of Britain, the country had almost sixty officially recognised landing grounds, and there was a significant jump in the number of private pilots, even with the downturn in the economy.

Aircraft were becoming more powerful, too. British RAF pilot, George Stainforth, having helped the British team win the Schneider Cup in 1931 – the last year the competition would be held – set out on 29 September that same year to create a new air speed record in a Supermarine S.6B. Powered by a 2600 brake horsepower Rolls Royce engine fed with a mixture of petrol, methanol and ethyl, the super-sleek plane rocketed over four timed miles in opposing directions to achieve an average speed of 407.5 miles an hour, making Stainforth the first man in the world to fly faster than 400 miles an hour.

By 1932 there were regular air services across Europe, mail was being delivered by air from London to India and to South Africa, and the Russian civil fleet, renamed Aeroflot, already had numerous aircraft. Britain's Imperial Airways and the Dutch carrier, KLM, were both exploring routes to Australia. In the United States, several airlines had set up passenger services during the 1920s, and the US Post Office, which introduced regular cross-country flights after World War I, was delivering millions of articles annually across the nation from midway through that decade.

In the private aviation field, small planes continued to break records, the England-to-Cape Town route seemingly as popular a challenge as the track to Australia. American flyer Amelia Earhart wrote herself into the record books on 21 May 1932 when she flew nonstop in a Lockheed Vega from Newfoundland in Canada to land fifteen hours later in a farmer's field in Ireland, thus becoming only the second person to do the crossing solo (after Lindbergh) and the first woman. In August that year, Jim

Mollison completed the first solo crossing of the North Atlantic in the opposite direction, flying a Puss Moth.

Nevertheless, the older generation of pilots struggled to find work for themselves as commercial aviation developed in an economic environment where business acumen was more important than barnstorming skills and seat-of-the-pants flying. Hinkler's friend and Schneider Cup team-mate Henri Biard, who was about the same age, lamented the lack of opportunity for experienced British pilots. 'One Schneider winner is now living on the dole,' Biard would soon write in his memoir, *Wings*. 'A Schneider pilot who was in one of the Trophy races with me is scraping a living in a Midland city as best he can, unable to find a flying job, though he is a magnificent pilot; another once world-famous flyer is a baker's roundsman; another is driving a bus.' Biard added that none of these pilots had lost the flying skills that had once been regarded as 'almost magical': 'It is just that they have fallen out of the limelight on to hard facts. Flying is a young man's game now!'[1]

Hinkler was in exactly that situation. There'd been suggestions in Australia that he and Kingsford Smith should be given commissions in the RAAF, but the idea didn't wash with Sir George Pearce, the Minister for Defence. Hinkler had recently turned thirty-nine, and Smithy was almost forty-five; they were too old, said Pearce. His response resulted in a public outcry, and ridicule in the press – but no commissions. 'If I am too old,' Hinkler countered, 'Sir George ought to alter the Australian old age pension regulations enabling me to qualify now instead of at 65.'[2]

Then there was speculation that Hinkler might join his old friend Captain McIntosh in an attempt to fly from London to Cape Town in three days, via the west coast of Africa. Nothing came of that, and over the northern summer of 1932, no new opportunities arose.

By September, Hinkler's career had once again reached a critical point. The Ibis was still in its shed at Mon Repos, untouched and without an airworthiness certificate, let alone any funding support. In addition, the pilot had spent most of his savings on the Puss Moth, had no regular income or offer of employment, and was considered too old for a government position in his homeland. It was a dispiriting time for him.

'He was as keen on success as ever, but he did not care what happened to himself,' his friend Charles Grey would say following Hinkler's death. 'He was thoroughly fed up with everything, and everybody. He realised that nobody wanted to employ him, and he could see no way of making a good living on his own account.' Grey lamented the waste of Hinkler's talent, suggesting that he had a genius for invention. To Grey, the editor of *The Aeroplane*, the best use of this talent would've been if some big firm had taken the Queenslander on as 'a kind of experimenter' and allowed him a free hand.[3]

On arrival at Karachi during his 1928 flight to Australia, Hinkler had already broken three records, and he later wrote of what that success had meant: 'What I expected had come to pass – thenceforward I was to be a sort of hero, proving to the world the excellence of English machines and engines. I was no more a hero than when I started . . . but once you begin to excite the public by doing the unexpected, they turn you into a hero.'[4]

Since then, his record on the England-to-Australia route had tumbled, but now he had a better aircraft, with an enclosed cockpit and custom modifications, the plane that had helped him set a new record across the South Atlantic. So, with no other prospects in sight, the man who had once been seen as master of his fate, decided to create his own opportunities. The press were always chasing after him, wanting to know where he was going next, making things up – well, he'd give them a story, a real story, but only after he'd done it. Just like before, he wouldn't give them a sniff in advance. A second record-breaking flight to Australia would grab the headlines, and might even make him some money. Perhaps even enough to reinvigorate the Ibis project. Wait till they found out that Hustling Hinkler was on his way again . . .

* * *

In late September 1932, Hinkler advised the British Air Ministry that he would be making another flight to Australia, beginning on 14 October. It would initially be from London to Vienna, he said, then to Sofia in Bulgaria, and on to Constantinople, and it would take about the same amount of time as his earlier flight. The thought of again taking on the England–Australia challenge excited him. 'I've got a chance of doing one more long-distance stunt before I die,' he told Henri Biard. 'It'll get me a few meals anyway. I thought I was going to starve till this came along.'[5]

The October date turned out to be optimistic. *Karohi* needed re-certification, and in November he booked it in for a full service at the Hendon-based aviation company owned by John Savage, the skywriter. Hinkler took the opportunity to upgrade to the more powerful Gipsy III engine and longer-range fuel tanks, along with making further modifications. One of these was a 'flowmeter' – a glass tube connected to the petrol system, to help him calculate fuel consumption – and another a plywood frame to secure the oil cans for the 'bubbler' oil-circulation system he'd used over the South Atlantic. During that flight to West Africa, the worrying tapping of two cans continually touching on the floor had sounded like engine knock, which was hardly something a pilot wanted to hear above the ocean in the dark. He also installed a small blue light in the cockpit to illuminate his instruments, with a shield over the bulb to avoid glare on the windscreen.

Because the Puss Moth was Canadian-registered, the paperwork was forwarded to Canada, where a senior official suggested that since Hinkler was resident in England, he should instead apply for British registration. A brief exchange of bureaucratic ping-pong ensued, during which the London office supporting the application emphasised that 'Squadron Ldr. Hinkler's plans are to return to Canada via Australia' and that he 'does not wish his projected flight to receive any publicity. It is requested please, that it be treated as confidential.'[6] The Canadian re-registration was approved; CF-APK could take to the air once more.

By mid November, he was still not ready to leave – to the annoyance of the civil servants who had to arrange the telegrams to foreign governments. As in 1928, Hinkler was supposed to bear the cost of these cables, and once again he was reluctant to pay the deposit. He said he'd discuss the matter with his solicitors. Nance sailed for New Zealand on 18 November, apparently in order to be able to meet him when he reached Australia.

In early December, the press tried to pin him down about his plans. 'There is no telling where we might go,' Hinkler replied, using the royal 'we' to refer to himself and his plane, as he often did. However, he did say, enigmatically, that there were warmer places to be than England at that time of year and 'altogether, there were plenty of reasons for going, and not very many for staying'.[7] He also divulged that he was contemplating some long flights between touchdowns, and that this might mean some night flying.

On 8 December 1932, his fortieth birthday, Hinkler informed an Air Ministry official that he planned to take off six days later, and would now make Athens his first stop, flying over Paris and Marseilles. He requested dispensation to use navigation lights over England, asking if they could seek a similar waiver for France. The official told Hinkler that he'd left it until the last moment, as usual, but he'd see what he could do. Publicly, Hinkler continued to deny that he had any immediate plans to fly to Australia. Such reports were premature, he said, claiming he was busy organising a program of aviation displays throughout England for the following year.

Again he delayed his take-off, and set a new date: 7 January 1933. And again he changed his mind about the route. He still planned to fly from London to Athens, but then to Istanbul, and on to Konia, Cyprus; thence to Aleppo in northern Syria, to finally arrive in Darwin on 17 January. On the face of it, this wouldn't beat Mollison's record of eight days and nineteen hours, but Hinkler had already indicated his intention to take the longest possible hops. He told government officials that he might bypass two stops and fly direct from Athens to Aleppo via the Mediterranean coast of Turkey.

With yet another change of plan, the Foreign Office in Whitehall had to send more telegrams to their international counterparts, just a week before the revised departure date. Whether they managed to extract any payment from the Australian is not clear. Whatever the case, once again the officials weren't pleased, and told Hinkler that since it was the Christmas–New Year period, it was unlikely that all the approvals would be received in time.

He said he'd take his chances.

* * *

It was late afternoon on Friday, 6 January when Hinkler arrived at Great West Aerodrome, Heathrow. There was scattered cloud overhead but the rain from the day before had disappeared, and a pale moon occasionally broke through. After supervising the refuelling of his Puss Moth, Hinkler rolled it into a hangar and thoroughly checked the engine.

At dinner that evening, Mrs Harris, the aerodrome caretaker's wife, asked him if he needed anything to take with him the next day, and he requested three pints of strong coffee, without sugar or milk, which she put in separate vacuum flasks. She also provided him with a flask of drinking water, two cheese and three tongue sandwiches, and four half-pint bottles of Guinness Stout. He gave one bottle of stout back to Mrs Harris, put two in the plane, and set the other aside for himself. During dinner, Hinkler told the Harrises that he was heading for Brindisi in Italy, and said he hoped not to reach the Alps too early, while it was still dark. He didn't mention his final destination, but said the trip might take him six days.

After dinner, Hinkler rang Major Savage and a telephone number in Glasgow. He reportedly sent a telegram to Nance in Auckland, telling her that he wouldn't fly unless the weather report was good, and that it was a 'business' flight to Australia – he wasn't trying to break any records. He also cabled his mother.

Mr Harris arranged a bed for him in the sick bay at Great West, and he retired at about 9 pm, asking to be roused at 1.15 am. It would not be a great amount of sleep before a 10,000-mile flight, with a proposed first hop of around 1000 miles. Just after midnight, two airport staff arrived, followed shortly afterwards by

John Savage and Dopey Lingham, responding to Hinkler's earlier phone call. This was the first the two had known that he'd be going that day, they said later.

Hinkler was awakened as requested, and after two cups of tea, he stowed the coffee, water and food in the cockpit of the plane, and dressed for the flight. The temperature in London the previous day had struggled to reach double figures, and he knew it was going to be even colder over the continent, especially when he reached the Alps. He decided to leave his fleecy pyjama shirt on over his singlet, and put a jumper over that. Then he donned the suit he liked to wear when he was flying, and zipped his flying jacket snugly over the top. A fur-lined flying helmet and gloves would complete the ensemble.

The silver and red DH.80A, but with *Karohi* no longer splashed across the port-side nose cowling, was wheeled out of the hangar. Hinkler climbed into the cockpit, went through the starting sequence, and the Gipsy motor roared into life, the noise rippling across the almost deserted airstrip. Lingham said later, 'As Hinkler prepared to depart and the Customs were absent, we learned that in conformity with his usual taciturnity he had passed the Customs at Croydon on Friday.'[8]

It was almost 2.30 am, and the airstrip wasn't equipped for night flying, so Savage and Lingham went off to do what Hinkler had asked of them: position their car headlights to illuminate the runway. As they headed off, Hinkler stepped down from the cockpit, shook hands with Harris, thanked him for his hospitality and asked him to also thank his wife.

He hadn't directly alerted the press, but the Australian Government, at least, were aware of his intentions. The day before, in Melbourne, the Secretary of the Department of Defence had received a message from London advising that Hinkler was probably leaving Croydon on 7 January for Australia and expected to arrive in Darwin on 17 January. The message included the Puss Moth's registration number, and indicated Hinkler was understood not to be carrying a wireless or firearms.

Climbing back into the cockpit, Hinkler taxied the plane towards the south-east corner of the runway, the throb of the engine still loud in the frosty air. About the same time, a mist drifted across, partly obscuring this path, and he was forced to wait until he could see the strip clearly enough for a take-off. The airport ambulance was on standby, just in case.

For forty minutes he waited. Suddenly the mist disappeared as quickly as it had come, and Hinkler immediately opened the throttle. In the muted yellow light from the cars' headlights, CF-APK roared down the strip and into the air. It was 3.10 am on Saturday, 7 January 1933.

The observers on the ground saw the aircraft caught momentarily in a shimmer of moonlight, like the flash of a silvery fish in a stream. Then it was gone.

Hinkler was on his way to Australia. Again.

CHAPTER 19

Wrapped in a shroud of snow

Twenty-four hours later, there'd been no word of Hinkler. Not from Italy or Greece, not even from nearby France. Silence.

No one was quite sure where to look for CF-APK. Or even whether they should. Which way had he gone? Did he make it across the Channel? Was he *really* flying to Australia? Perhaps he'd force-landed at a remote airstrip without communication facilities? Or had he gone down in the sea and been picked up by a passing ship?

Days passed with no contact.

On 10 January, three days after take-off, there was no longer a chance that he'd landed at an isolated airstrip and continued on. Although the Australian Air Liaison Officer in London discussed Hinkler's disappearance with the British Air Ministry on 11 January, no official request for a search was made because, the ministry claimed, they didn't know if he'd come down on French, Greek, Italian or Swiss territory or crashed into the sea.

An English solicitor, Leslie Pearkes, said to be representing Hinkler, released an itinerary to the press, which indicated a first stopover of either Brindisi or Athens, depending on the weather, the state of the engine, and how the pilot was feeling. Although British Civil Aviation officials had received a similar schedule, for some reason they speculated that Hinkler may have tried for the London–Cape Town record that McIntosh had proposed a few months earlier.

The press also began to speculate. One newspaper declared that Hinkler was prone to making statements that cloaked his real intentions, that his plan had been to fly to Australia in five days, and that he'd said the result of the first day's flying would decide his subsequent plans. The paper claimed that the Australian had once indicated a more leisurely trip 'including acceptance of a long-standing invitation to spend three days shooting in India'.[1]

On the other hand, the editor of Broken Hill's *Barrier Miner* suggested that, despite the Queenslander being one of the world's premier airmen, '[he] took a tremendous risk in surrounding his flight with a cloak of secrecy, which as yet has not been lifted, and it is to be feared may not be raised in time to rescue him alive.'[2]

The mayor of Bundaberg said he deplored the delay in mounting a search when the oil companies who laid down supplies in advance must've known about Hinkler's route and that he'd therefore not arrived. Shell-Mex, which was providing his fuel supplies, initially said it was bound to secrecy, but on 11 January, the company released an itinerary identical to the one announced by Pearkes. The *Daily Mail* lamented the 'amazing position when no one in England is prepared to take the responsibility of inaugurating a search, as Mr Hinkler has no financial backers and is using his own machine'.[3] In Italy, the Aviation Ministry issued an alert to all airfields, asking pilots to keep a lookout, but pointed out that if Hinkler had crashed in the Alps, he might not be discovered for a long time, citing a recent example where an Italian pilot wasn't found for two months.

In Auckland, Nance said she believed that winds might've carried him past his destination, but she had great faith that his skill would keep him safe. She was said to be upset by a report emanating from England that Hinkler had told a friend before the flight, 'I am going to break the record or break my neck.'[4] To her mind, Bert would never have said such a thing. A few days later, Nance left New Zealand for Bundaberg. 'My husband's mother has sent for me, and I must go,' she said.[5]

During the first week of the pilot's disappearance, a postman discovered that Hinkler's home at Thornhill, Hampshire, had been broken into. The press reported that the house was trashed, and a photo of Frances Hinkler was found on the floor 'with the face trodden in'. There were concerns that the plans for the Ibis might be missing, which 'would be of greatest value to thieves able to place them in the right quarters'.[6] Considering how little commercial interest the plane had attracted over the previous three years, Hinkler might've found that suggestion laughable. The shed housing the Ibis had also been broken into, but the aircraft itself appeared undamaged. All that was definitely missing were 8 gallons of petrol, and possibly a boomerang bearing the inscription: I HOPE YOU WILL RETURN SOON, BERT.

Inevitably, there were reports of sightings and suspected sightings on the day he disappeared: over Kent, over France, over Switzerland. A particularly promising report came from Monsieur M. Saby, Inspector of Waterways and Forests at Sens, about

60 miles south-east of Paris. Saby had heard an aircraft overhead on the morning of Hinkler's departure, and on learning of the airman's disappearance then tracked a plane via informants across his district. He was convinced that Hinkler had come down in the rugged Monts du Morvan area. 'The obvious conclusion,' he told the British Air Ministry, 'is that the aeroplane was stopped by fog and the dark, because a pilot like Bert Hinkler could easily have landed by day.'[7]

* * *

The only organised search attempted from England was through a private consortium, and it turned out bizarrely. A week or so after Hinkler's disappearance, a group of supporters in England, desperate to do something that might shed light on the mystery, responded to a report of a plane being sighted over Switzerland at about the time that CF-APK could've been in the area. The 'Hinkler Search Committee' began to plan a search by a respected British flyer, Captain Wally Hope, three-time winner of the King's Cup and director of an aerial taxi service, with experience of flying in southern Europe.

Flying his own Puss Moth, Hope arrived in Switzerland on 17 January, ten days after Hinkler had taken off from London, and set himself up at Lausanne as a base for his operation. The Swiss Aviation Office in Berne advised the British authorities that Hope and a newspaper photographer named Heanly would be conducting ground searches for Hinkler in the Diablerets region, in the west of the country.

Within twenty-four hours, Hope and his companion were also missing. A plane from the Swiss Aero Club searched for them all morning, and military aircraft were also alerted.

They were located the next day, the two men and the plane unharmed, but Hope and Heanly were not keen to answer questions about their disappearance. An account of their search for Bert Hinkler appeared in the following day's (London) *Daily Mirror*.

According to the story told by the photographer, Hope and Heanly set off to check out the Wetterhorn, a 3600-metre mountain in the Swiss Alps, because that's where Hope thought the Australian was most likely to be found.

But the two Englishmen quickly ran into trouble, Heanly wrote:

> Although the sun was shining brightly when we took off, we speedily flew into terrible weather. We encountered low black snow clouds which reduced visibility to a few yards. Every moment we were afraid that we might crash headlong into the mountainside. Great winds sprang up and shook the aeroplane like a leaf, and fierce gusts, which Captain Hope estimated had a velocity of 100 miles an hour, struck the aeroplane, carrying it out of its course. On two occasions, only by clever side-slipping did Captain Hope prevent us, by the smallest possible margin, from being smashed against the great black rocks on the mountainside as a fly is brushed against a window pane.[8]

'For six hours we continued our battle with the snow, clouds, and the gale,' the account went on, 'with death in a new form appearing every minute.'[9]

But they found no sign of Hinkler.

Arriving in Brisbane from New Zealand on her way to Bundaberg, Nance said that words could never express her gratitude to Captain Hope. She knew him well, she said, and what he'd done 'was done with a thoroughness that could not have been bettered'.[10] In England, the Hinkler Search Committee regarded Hope's actions as 'evidence of a British officer's loyalty to duty at the risk of sacrificing his own life'.

The reality was quite different, however, according to a subsequent complaint the Swiss Aero Club lodged with its counterpart in Britain. Hope and Heanly had shown very little interest in searching for Hinkler, they said, and the *Daily Mirror* story was pure fantasy. The real version of events was that after their initial arrival in Lausanne, following a thirty-minute flight from Basle, Hope declared that he would not be flying again that day, despite the clear skies and good weather. The next day, pilot and photographer rose just before midday, claiming later that the concierge had failed to wake them as requested. They then flew a short distance from Lausanne to the village at which they were eventually located, where they booked into a hotel and went sightseeing.

The following day, 20 January, they apparently spent an hour over the Rhone Valley searching for Hinkler, and that was the sum total of their efforts over four days of mostly clear skies.

A subsequent inquiry by the Royal Aero Club concluded that Captain Hope had not carried out a serious search for Hinkler in Switzerland, and was guilty of 'carelessness and lack of consideration thereby causing trouble and anxiety to the Swiss authorities'.[11] Hope was cautioned by the RAeC, but no severe measures were taken against him. The reasons for his behaviour in Switzerland weren't disclosed. Nor were the reactions of Nance and the Hinkler Search Committee.

* * *

In Australia, Nance was critical of Prime Minister Joseph Lyons' government for not pushing the British authorities to carry out an official formal search. She believed that Bert's achievements as a pilot and an Australian entitled him to some consideration. The government defended itself, saying that Stanley Bruce, now the Commonwealth Resident Minister in London, was the contact point and he had kept in touch with the relevant parties.

The British Government did offer some assistance – six days after Hinkler's disappearance, it asked the BBC to send a telegram to national broadcasters in Europe, asking them to broadcast an appeal to listeners for information of any aircraft accident or the passage of an unidentified airplane. This message went out to thirteen countries, including some away from the pilot's likely route, such as Holland, Russia, Germany and Rumania. Germany pledged to have its radio stations broadcast twice-daily SOS bulletins. All to no avail.

Several weeks went by without news, and the Hinkler Search Committee abandoned its plans for a ground search. Instead, it began planning a memorial service. The service was to be held in early February at the City Temple, a well-known nonconformist church in central London. Then a rumour sprang up that Hinkler had been found in an alpine hut in Switzerland. The consensus among the committee and aviators alike was that there was no truth to the story. Nevertheless, Arthur Bishop, chairman of the memorial service committee, said the service would be postponed, just in case. A short while later, however, solicitor Leslie Pearkes announced that, acting on instructions of a relative of Hinkler, the ceremony was not postponed, but cancelled. The relative's name was not revealed. In Bundaberg, Nance denied that she'd had anything to do with the decision.

On 3 February, almost a month after Hinkler took off, the Director of Civil Aviation sent a copy of Monsieur Saby's letter to Pearkes – his explanation for doing so being 'in case you have any means of following the matter up'.[12] In other words, the British Government would not be organising a search.

The *Sydney Morning Herald* reported that Hinkler's London friends weren't surprised by the indifference shown in England where, they said, his disappearance was given less space in the press than was the search for a murderer. This attitude was put down to Hinkler's increasing reticence about disclosing his plans. The aviation correspondent of London's *Morning Post* claimed to have spoken to the missing pilot shortly before he left, and said that Hinkler planned to break all records to Australia by a substantial margin, but had vowed he would keep the flight secret until he had achieved his goals.

France's Air Attaché in London later told the Air Ministry that Saby's investigations had been followed up in the Morvan area by land searches and aerial surveys, without success, 'in spite of the favourable atmospheric conditions, the lack of leaves in the forest areas, and the strong will of the crew to find their lost comrade'.[13]

At the end of March, Nance decided to return to England. On her way from Bundaberg to board the liner *Strathaird*, she told reporters: 'I cannot believe that my husband is lost until I have absolute proof. I still hope and believe that when the snows of the Alps melt after the winter, it will be found that he is safe in some snow-bound place in the mountains.'[14] However, when the ship stopped over in Melbourne on Anzac Day, she would lay a wreath for Hinkler at the Cenotaph.

On 21 April, Pearkes wrote to the Director of Civil Aviation, stating that he'd been in touch with Saby and the Swiss authorities, and had concluded that Hinkler had most likely crashed on the Italian side of the Alps, where Pearkes understood a snowstorm had been raging at the time the pilot was probably in the area. He also noted that the search by Swiss authorities had been hampered rather than helped by Hope's efforts. Pearkes asked if there were any official reports from the Swiss or Italian authorities (there weren't), and declared his intention to make an early application to the court to presume death.

* * *

Six days later, 25-year-old Gino Tocchioni was making his way down a spur of Tuscany's Pratomagno range in Arezzo province, which is in the middle of the mountainous spine known as the Apennines and which runs the length of the country. His eyes were peeled for timber he could burn and sell as charcoal, at that time used extensively in Europe for cooking and heating. Although the range was still white-capped, he was thankful for the warmth of the spring sun, because it meant the snows were melting on the lower slopes, revealing vegetation that had been hidden during the winter months. As water trickled past him, he noticed a flash of white on a ridge higher up. Intrigued, Tocchioni clambered up through the scrubby bushes and leafless trees of the rocky mountainside towards it. Shortly afterwards, among a scattering of beech trees, at a height of about 5000 feet, on the sloping side of the mountain, he found the wreckage of a small silver plane with red markings.

The machine was a crumpled mass, like a tin shed that had been flattened by a cyclone. Its frame was contorted, as if a giant had grown angry with his toy, and twisted it in his hands before dashing it to the ground. The engine was pushed back into the body of the aircraft, with only the tail and one black-tyred wheel poking up grimly through the buckled silver panels. Various personal items were strewn around the site, and higher up the slope a detached wing lay forlornly.

Some 80 yards from the wrecked plane, in a grassy area sheltered by a juniper bush, the Italian discovered the body of the pilot, lying on his back and clad in a torn suit and flying jacket.

As he scrambled down the slope to report his find, Tocchioni met another charcoal burner, 41-year-old Raffaello Cari, and the two men returned briefly to the wreck site. They then headed down the mountainside to alert the local Carabinieri. A small group from the police station at the nearby town of Strada di Casentino, some 30 miles due east of Florence, arrived at the site early on Friday 28 April. The police party, led by Carabinieri Marshal Romeo Aureli, took care not to disturb the body unduly, but, as recorded in the official report, they found a leather wallet containing a passport 'through which we identified him at once as the aviator Herbert John Louis Hinkler, born at Bundaberg, Australia, on the 8 December, 1892'.[15] The missing pilot had been found.

Tasmanian writer Bertha Southey later penned a poem for the *Bulletin*:

High on the shoulders of the Apennines,
Where only grey wolves roam,
They found our Hinkler 'mid the twisted pines,
Ten thousand miles from home.

Only the pale stars, and the wailing winds,
That lay the pine trees low,
Knew where he slept through the long winter nights,
Wrapped in his shroud of snow.[16]

CHAPTER 20

Vale, Hinkler!

The day the news of the discovery of Hinkler's body came through, the RMS *Strathaird* was standing off Fremantle, prior to picking up the final passengers for England. On board, Nance was having a cup of tea with friends when she was handed a telegram from a Perth newspaper, offering condolences and asking if she could give them a comment. She dropped her cup and dashed from the room. 'I never gave up hope that Bert would turn up,' Nance said tearfully the next day, 'until I got that wire. Oh, why did he go in such weather?'[1]

Frances Hinkler was travelling by train across the Nullabor, to stay with a niece in Western Australia and farewell Nance. She was alerted to the news en route via a telegram sent by the fourth of her five children, George. The following day, the discovery of the body was front-page news across the world. Jockeys in the Hinkler Handicap at Brisbane's Ascot Racecourse donned black armbands.

When Bert Hinkler's body was found a little way from the plane, his gold watch was lying nearby, stopped at ten minutes past five, its glass face shattered. One official at the scene said the site was subject to terrible wind buffeting and another suggested that Hinkler's body had been propelled to the place where it was found by 'the fury of the wind dragging on the snow'.[2]

By Friday, 28 April, when the first Carabinieri officers arrived, the body was badly decomposed, although this had been slowed by the cold conditions in the earlier months, and there was some mummification. Extremely severe head injuries suggested that he'd been thrown from the aircraft and died instantly, the consensus of all the officials at the scene. There was no hat or helmet. Part of one arm was missing, possibly due to a wild animal chancing upon the body, and some bones were found nearby; there were noticeable injuries and probable fractures to his lower back. The front of his jacket was torn and there was a gash in the back of his suit. When, at her request, the wireless operators on the *Strathaird* gave Nance more information about the discovery of the body, they considerately suppressed some of these details.

In the style required of official reports, the police listed individually the personal items of the late Bert Hinkler that they found at the scene, providing an insight into the trappings the pilot considered important to him on what became his final long-distance flight. On, or near, the body, the police found:

> i) A wallet of black leather, with several compartments; ii) A leather belt which appears broken; iii) A collapsible Bayer flask, without label which gives particulars; iv) A red coloured leather cover, containing a document of identity, carrying the date 2 November, 1932, from Shell Corner London, in the name of H. J. L. Hinkler, and printed instructions; v) 10 photographs, the subject of which were pictures of women;

> vi) 7 films of 4/1/2/6 [possibly negatives], corresponding to several of the above photographs; vii) A certified permit for carrying firearms dated 2 November 1928, issued in the name of Bert Hinkler for carrying a pistol No. 56480 and ammunition; viii) Collection of small coloured geographic cards of Europe and the world; ix) Small map containing typewritten course instructions and routes; x) Another small map with pencil writing with the address; xi) A note paper from Hendon aerodrome London, with numerical calculations; xii) Another note paper containing pencil annotations apparently pertaining to the route; xiii) A private letter written in English dated 12 December beginning with the words 'My Dearly Beloved'; xiv) An English newspaper clipping, size 10cmx10cm; xv) 13 Bank of England notes issued London 25 August 1931 for 5 pounds from Serial no. 20469 to no. 20481 inclusive; xvi) A lottery ticket No. 83407 Dublin; xvii) 2 stirling (sic) banknotes No. R37046464 and 046453; xviii) Two typewriter sheets in English containing telegraphic addresses, telephone numbers in various localities throughout the world for Shell agents; xix) Another small English newspaper cutting, size 10x8cm containing atmospheric conditions in various world localities; xx) A half page of letter paper containing on its lower edge addresses of various localities and various dates from 6 January 1933 to 26 January 1933; xxi) A small carte de visite, size 6x9 with a mounted photograph of a woman, lifting from the humidity.[3]

One can only speculate on the significance of some of the items, including the ten photographs of women, and the letter that began, 'My Dearly Beloved'.

Newspapers at the time claimed that Canadian bonds were also found in the plane, but the Carabinieri's inventory makes no mention of those. In addition, although he had a permit to carry a pistol (apparently obtained after his return from the Australia flight), and one of the police reports states that an empty holster was found, no gun was retrieved with the body.

* * *

After the Carabinieri's examinations were completed and photographs had been taken that first day, Hinkler's body was wrapped and placed in a locally made zinc coffin. Because of the rough terrain, the coffin was carried down the mountain by donkey before being transferred to a car for transport to a nearby hamlet. The zinc casket was then placed inside a walnut coffin, and a crowd of Young Fascists, local dignitaries and numerous others accompanied the body to the town of Strada, where the police party had come from.

There it lay in state overnight, watched over by a guard of honour. During the following day – Saturday, 29 April – villagers and townsfolk filed past, placing flowers beside the coffin, next to the wreaths left by the dignitaries. Flags were at half-mast, and the local women had joined together to sew a British flag from scraps of material. That evening, pilots from the Regia Aeronautica (Italian Air Force) carried the coffin, now draped in the British and Italian flags, in a procession led by the town band and including local leaders, community groups and other citizens brought in by air force bus from elsewhere in the Tuscan province of Arezzo.

On the outskirts of Strada, the procession stopped, and the band played hastily learnt versions of the British national anthem and 'Rule Britannia'. Hinkler's name was called, to which all those present gave the Fascist salute and answered '*Presente!*' ('Here!'). The coffin was then handed over to a staff officer sent from Rome by Italy's Minister for Air, and right-hand man to Mussolini, General Italo Balbo, for transport by truck to Florence. (Benito Mussolini and his National Fascists Party had been in power since 1922 – 1933 was officially year 11 in Italy.)

It was 10.30 pm and raining heavily when the coffin and its minders reached Florence that Saturday night. There waiting for them was a senior figure from the Florence Aero Club and other club members in uniform, along with a detachment of the dreaded paramilitary Blackshirts holding their banner aloft. These groups then formed up and escorted the coffin to the aero club, where a *camera ardente* (chapel of rest) had been set up. Blackshirts, militia and club members mounted a triple guard of honour.

From early the next morning, an almost constant stream of men and women went past the coffin, including the usual civil and military dignitaries, as well as the British Consul and local British residents. There were numerous wreaths, including one from General Balbo, who'd established an international reputation in aviation and had been a strong supporter of Italy's participation in the Schneider Cup competition.

The chief representative from the aero club arranged for a poster to be displayed across Florence: THE RESERVE PERSONNEL OF THE REGIA AERONAUTICA AND ALL THE MEMBERS OF THE AERO CLUB SALUTE THE BODY OF THE GLORIOUS BRITISH AVIATOR, HERBERT JOHN HINKLER, FLYER OF THE ATLANTIC, WHO FELL WHILE ATTEMPTING TO CARRY OUT A SUBLIME TASK IN THE SERVICE OF CIVILISATION AND PROGRESS.[4]

* * *

Following the discovery of the body, Italy's Ministero dell'Aeronautica (Air Ministry) announced that it was prepared to give Hinkler a funeral with full military honours. Since the British Embassy in Rome was handling the arrangements, the Australian Resident Minister in London, Stanley Bruce, cabled Canberra, asking whether Hinkler's widow wanted him buried in Italy or taken to England. The Australian Government said it would abide by the widow's wishes.

When Nance Jarvis had received the tragic news on board the *Strathaird*, a gloom had fallen over the vessel, and social activities were cancelled. On the Monday morning, Frances Hinkler arrived in Perth at the end of her railway journey across the Nullarbor, and rushed to the ship at Fremantle, where the two women comforted each other. They had met at Port Adelaide when the liner docked there a few days earlier, and had continued to encourage themselves with the belief that their Bert might still be alive. Now they had to deal with the awful truth. During the day, a Commonwealth Government representative met with Nance on board at Fremantle to ascertain her wishes about the place of burial. That evening, 1 May, the *Strathaird* sailed for England.

After a quick Cabinet meeting, Prime Minister Lyons announced that Squadron Leader Bert Hinkler, AFC, DSM, would be buried in Brisbane, in accordance with his widow's request, and that it would be a State funeral with full honours. He said the government would bear the cost of bringing the body home from Italy, and immediately sent a telegram to the British government to that effect. The Prime Minister told the British authorities that Nance

Jarvis was due to arrive in England by ship in four weeks' time, and that the Australian government would be grateful if the Italian government would take charge of the body in the meantime.

Not all Queenslanders were happy with the government's announcement. The state member for Bundaberg, George Barber, questioned why it was that the funeral was being held in Brisbane rather than the pilot's hometown. The Brisbane *Telegraph* reported that there was great indignation in Bundaberg at the slight, with residents there suggesting that it was the family's wish that Bert be buried next to his father, John.

But it was not to be – for either Bundy or the state capital. Arrangements already in train in Italy for the funeral continued uninterrupted, and Leslie Pearkes arrived in Florence from England to represent 'Hinkler's relatives'. Less than an hour before the ceremony was due to begin, the British Ambassador in Italy received a telegram from the British Foreign Secretary, communicating both the Australian government's advice that Nance wanted her late husband buried in his home country, and its request that the Italian government take care of the body until arrangements were made. When apprised of the contents of the telegram by Major McLean, the British Military Attaché, Pearkes said that he thought the funeral should still take place at the day and hour set by the Italian authorities. Thirty minutes later, the ceremony began as planned.

* * *

The Italians had taken over the funeral arrangements in grand style, and the full support of the government was brought to bear for the fallen airman. Il Duce himself sent an expression of sympathy to the British Ambassador for the loss to British aviation.

The funeral cortege set off at 6 pm on Monday, 1 May, and the event was conducted with all the pomp of the Fascist state. Across the city, huge blue and black mourning notices ordered shops to close and requested that citizens pay homage to Hinkler. Underlying the significance of the occasion, the four pallbearers were the Prefect of Florence, a general representing the Air Minister, the general commanding the local military division, and the Military Attaché from the British Embassy.

The city came to a halt and trams piled up as the coffin, draped in the British, Italian and Australian flags, was transported through the streets in an ornate funeral carriage, drawn by two plumed horses adorned in black velvet. The hearse was preceded by sixteen men on foot, carrying wreaths of flowers so big, it took two men to handle each one. A military band accompanied two infantry companies, along with a detachment from the Regia Aeronautica, and another of Fascist militia. Behind the carriage came Pearkes, and the local English clergy, followed by the British Consul, other members of the British community in Florence, and Italian military and civilian representatives.

Thousands of people lined the streets, silently and respectfully, many of the men giving the Fascist salute as the cortege passed by on its southward journey. It was a spectacular occasion as the ancient city, birthplace of the Italian Renaissance, rich in history and medieval culture, said farewell to forty-year-old Herbert John Louis Hinkler, the former foundry worker and trail-blazing aviator from the little coastal town of Bundaberg, Australia.

The procession halted at the city gates, where the accompanying troops presented arms while the band played the British national anthem, also hastily learnt. In a repeat of the previous day's *rito fascisti*, there was another rousing shout of '*Presente!*' after

Hinkler's name was called, and the British Military Attaché then shouted: 'Vale, Hinkler!'

The military guard withdrew, and the smaller procession made its way to the Allori, the English cemetery on the southern outskirts of Florence. This was a mostly British affair, with the graveside service conducted by three clergymen from the British colony in Florence. An Australian woman present described the final scene: 'The service was simple and sincere; and after we all joined in the Lord's Prayer, Bert Hinkler was laid to rest in that peaceful and beautiful bit of Tuscany. With him was buried a small Australian flag with a sprig of wattle pinned on, which I gladly gave; so he has on his coffin symbols of the land he loved and served so well.'[5]

There were suggestions in Australian newspapers that this was not intended to be a permanent burial, but a temporary interment until arrangements could be made for the pilot's body to be conveyed to Australia. Writing to the Foreign Secretary, Sir John Simon, after the funeral, the British Ambassador said that under Italian law the burial could not have been postponed, whatever the circumstances. In any case, he said it had not been possible to follow the wishes of Mrs Hinkler as conveyed in the secretary's telegram 'for reasons which Mr Pearkes, the legal representative of Mr Hinkler's relatives . . . will be in the best position to explain to the Australian authorities.'[6]

The meaning of this enigmatic statement became clear when Pearkes subsequently met with Australian government officials in London and told them that the relatives of Bert Hinkler he was representing did not include Nance Jarvis or Frances Hinkler and her family. He said he was acting on behalf of Hinkler's widow, and that the funeral in Italy had proceeded on May 1 at her request.

It must have come as a great surprise to the Australian government to discover that the solicitor was not talking about Nance Jarvis, whom they and most of the world knew as Mrs Hinkler, but one Katherine Hinkler, the late pilot's legal wife.

CHAPTER 21

The secret of Karohi

If Hinkler became notorious for being secretive about his aviation plans, he was even more tight-lipped about his liaison with the woman who legally became Mrs Bert Hinkler. He married Katherine in the US state of Connecticut in May 1932, seven months before his final flight, and she moved to England to be with him. They did not publicise the marriage, however, and Hinkler apparently continued to be sometimes domiciled at Mon Repos with Nance.

His relationship with his partner of 15 years had been in decline, however, since at least 16 December 1930. On that date, newspapers around the world reported that when Bert Hinkler flew to Jacksonville, Florida, to see his friend, Jeannie 'Chubbie' Miller, take off on another of her celebrated US cross-country flights, his passengers were John Held Jr, and Bert's wife. This came as a surprise to Nance, the woman then known as Mrs Bert Hinkler, because she was still at Mon Repos, preparing for Christmas.

Nance immediately booked a passage on the Cunard liner, *Ausonia*, and arrived in New York on 29 December to confront

Bert. She found that, contrary to the newspaper report, he was not married to the woman who'd been a passenger in his plane that day, but he *was* entranced by her. Her name was Katherine Rose, she worked as a secretary, and she lived in New York.

Hinkler likely met Katherine at a function hosted by the British Consulate in New York – where she worked – during the visit to the US by the British Schneider Cup Team in October 1925. A more romantic scenario, handed down by family members, is that the two met on board ship, introduced by Katherine's older sister, Jean. Her sister had married William Rome, the captain of the *Tuscania*, one of the newest and largest ships of the Anchor Line, launched in 1921 and designed to carry 2500 passengers. According to family folklore, Katherine was travelling with Jean on the *Tuscania* on one of its regular voyages between England and the States, and sitting as usual at the captain's table, when the captain (Jean's husband) invited Hinkler to join them. In that account, the relationship developed from there.

What is known for certain is that Katherine Milligan Rose was born in Edinburgh, Scotland on 31 December, 1901. In 1907, she emigrated to the United States with her mother, Isabella, her sister, Jean (10) and her brother, Robert (3), to join their father, Robert, a printing compositor, who had gone across the year before. Another brother, James, was born later. Her given name was Catherine, but at some point she decided she preferred to spell it with a 'K'. The family settled in New York, and when she left school, Katherine found work as a secretary and stenographer. One of her early jobs was with the British consulate, and she later worked for the US government, but she never became a naturalised American citizen.

If Hinkler harboured thoughts about the Scottish secretary after his return to England following the Schneider Cup loss, he must have kept them to himself, although he and Katherine may have kept in touch by letter.

Five years after their apparently first and only meeting, Katherine arrived in London from New York on 18 August 1930 aboard the *Tuscania*. In the ship's register, she gave her intended address as the London Metropole hotel. Before the ship sailed again for New York five days later, however, she managed to fit in a late summer visit to her cousin Peggy at Deerpark Gardens, Glasgow. She re-boarded the *Tuscania* at Liverpool on 23 August. The ship then wended its way around the coast to the port of Southampton where next day it picked up the rest of its complement for the voyage across the Atlantic. Among the passengers who boarded on 24 August was one Herbert John Louis Hinkler, long-distance pilot and frustrated aeroplane designer.

On 1 September, 1930, Katherine Rose and Bert Hinkler sailed into New York on the *Tuscania*, after a week on board. She was returning to her home on 8th Avenue, Astoria, in the metropolitan west of Long Island; he was seeking a new future in North America. Regardless of whether their relationship was kindled or rekindled on that voyage, within three months it had developed enough for Katherine to be flying around the US with Hinkler, in a borrowed plane.

When Nance arrived in New York on the *Ausonia* on 29 December, less than a fortnight after the news story appeared, the fears she'd expressed almost ten years before, asking Bert if he intended to come back to her after his sea voyage to Australia, might well have re-emerged. She found that the woman who had now captured Hinkler's attention had blue eyes and brown hair with a hint of red, and was 28 years old, some 9 years younger than Bert, a difference that would not have been lost on Nance, aged 49. Like Nance, Katherine was a couple of inches taller than the man they had both become entwined with.

If Nance had hoped she could convince Bert to end his affair with Katherine, however, she was to be disappointed. Before Nance arrived, he had already considered setting up an aerial charter service based at the North Beach aerodrome, Long Island, not far from where Katherine lived. When he bought the Puss Moth the following February and moved to Toronto to prepare the aircraft for its South Atlantic crossing, his very first flight in the newly registered plane, on 29 April, was to Long Island. He made numerous flights to the same destination in the months that followed.

Despite succumbing to Katherine's charms, however, he continued to make a place in his life for Nance. A month after her arrival in New York, he motored with her to Detroit, Michigan, in the Great Lakes region. While the pair were dining at a restaurant in the city, a case containing valuables was stolen from their car, parked on a nearby street, but the items were later recovered. It was shortly after this incident that Hinkler moved to Toronto, but alone. There he lived a quiet, single existence for eight months, apart from the regular flights to New York, and he gave no indication of what was happening in his personal life, including what continuing contact he might have had with Nance. She did not return to England until the end of May.

In October 1931, just before he headed to New York to begin the first leg of what would become his cross-Atlantic flight, Hinkler visited a Toronto solicitor to arrange for preparation of a will that named Nance as executrix and beneficiary of his estate. He failed to tell the solicitor Nance was not his legal wife.

Later that month, during the six days Hinkler spent in New York, he invited Katherine for a spin in the Puss Moth, prior to his departure for the Caribbean and South America. When they arrived at Long Beach aerodrome, he proudly showed her the name he'd chosen for the plane – *Karohi*, which was newly painted on the port side of the engine cowling. Other long-distance pilots had given names to their aircraft – *Red Rose*, *Southern Cross* – but Hinkler had never bothered to christen his planes. Later he told the press that *Karohi* was Aboriginal for 'Lone wanderer', and one newspaper reported it had a meaning in the Maori language. In New York, he told Katherine what it really meant, however – the word was derived from the first two letters of Katherine and Rose, and the first two letters of Hinkler. A cupid's arrow pierced the name from back to front.

During this time, however, he was still working on his relationship with Nance, who'd been back at Mon Repos since June. From New York he wrote to tell her about the preparations he was making for his South American trip, and explained about the will that he'd finalised with the Toronto lawyer. As the flight progressed, he kept Nance in touch with his movements by occasional telegram. Although she later claimed she didn't know where he was heading once he left Natal, she did know when he'd departed, and he let her know very quickly of his safe arrival in Bathurst, Gambia on 26 November. Asked at that time by reporters for her opinion of the flight, Mrs Bert Hinkler replied, 'I think he has done wonderfully, but then he is a wonderful husband.'[1] When Hinkler returned to England eleven days later, Nance was at Hanwood aerodrome to give him an affectionate hug and a kiss when he stepped from the plane.

After two months of English life he headed back to the States, however, having decided that there was still no aviation future for him in Britain. He intimated that there were better business prospects for him in America, but he now had another reason to go back – Katherine. Once again, Nance stayed behind in England.

When Hinkler arrived in New York on 16 February 1932, he gave a Toronto residential address, and he spent March and April in Canada, renewing acquaintances and checking out issues about the Puss Moth.

It appears that Katherine Rose's family by this time were becoming concerned about her relationship with Bert Hinkler. She seemed enamoured of him, but at the time of his arrival in February, it had been four months since she'd seen him, when he'd flown off towards the Caribbean with vague intentions, and her 'boyfriend' had eventually ended up back in England after a perilous flight across the South Atlantic. Through the newspapers, if not through Katherine herself, they also probably knew something of Hinkler's relationship with Nance.

Perhaps alerted that something was afoot, or simply concerned about Bert's ongoing relationship with Katherine, Nance arrived in New York on the *Olympic* on 15 March, a month after his ship had docked. She gave her age on the passenger list as 49, the same as when she'd arrived fifteen months earlier.

Nance was too late, however. Whatever pressures were applied, on 16 May a marriage licence was taken out in Connecticut, and five days later, on 21 May 1932, Bert Hinkler married Katherine Rose in a civil ceremony in Stamford, Connecticut. In order not to draw public attention to the union, however, Hinkler used the name Herbert Bonney. His new wife reverted to her given name of Catherine for the occasion. Coincidentally, the American pilot Amelia Earhart landed in Ireland the same day, to become the first woman to make a solo air crossing of the Atlantic.

Nance was still in North America at the time of the wedding, although why she came, where she was on the day of the marriage or whether she was aware of it are a mystery. Just a few days later, she boarded the White Star liner, *Baltic,* in New York, bound for England. She was alone. But not for long. When the ship called at Boston, further north along the coast, she was joined on board by Bert Hinkler and Catherine Rose, who used the original spelling of her birth name on the passenger list, and her maiden name. All three travelled cabin class.

So, when the *Baltic* docked at Liverpool, England, on 31 May, down the gangplank walked Bert with two women: his new bride, who had travelled on the voyage as 'Catherine Rose', and his long-standing de facto wife, Nance, who gave her surname as Hinkler. Bert and Nance gave their address as Sholing, Southampton, which meant Mon Repos. 'Catherine' said she would be staying at the Hotel Metropole, London.

Over the next few months, Hinkler spent time with both women. Sometimes he lived with Katherine at a Cricklewood address in London, and at one point they went across to Paris; some of the time he may have lived on the Thornhill Estate with Nance, who for public purposes continued to be known as Mrs Hinkler. Whether or not Nance was aware of the marriage, she would have known of Bert's continuing liaison with Katherine, and surely would have been affected by being usurped by another, younger, woman. For her part, Katherine, who occasionally journeyed north to visit her sister and cousin in Scotland, was obliged to keep quiet about her marriage to the record-breaking pilot. It seems that the other woman in Bert Hinkler's life, his mother Frances, at this point knew nothing about her son's nuptials or about his subsequent domestic arrangements.

Whatever words of endearment Hinkler had for each one of them, however, all three would have been aware that the one true love of his life was aviation. Any other passions had to take second place. And so it happened that none of the women who had a place in his heart was there to bid him farewell when he left London in the Puss Moth on 7 January 1933, having removed the name *Karohi* from the cowling during the preparation of the plane for the flight to Australia. Nance had arrived in New Zealand by ship, waiting for Hinkler to take off so she could join him in Australia, which suggests he planned to continue the subterfuge there. The press reported that Hinkler cabled Nance in New Zealand and his mother in Bundaberg to let them know he was about to head off. What the press did not know, however, was that the second of the two phone calls he made from the caretaker's cottage at Great West Aerodrome the night before he disappeared, was a goodbye call to his wife, Katherine, who was staying with her sister in Glasgow.

* * *

The month after the funeral in May 1933, Leslie Pearkes applied on behalf of Katherine for administration of her late husband's estate. Because of his marriage, the will Bert had arranged through the Toronto solicitor, naming Nance his executrix and benefactor, was invalid, and since he had left no alternative instructions, his estate was dealt with according to English intestacy law. In June, administration of his affairs was granted to Katherine Hinkler, of 17 Falkland Mansions, Glasgow, Scotland, the 'lawful widow and relict' of Herbert John Louis Hinkler. Her inheritance in England amounted to £906 10 shillings and 10 pence.

Although the Australian government had learnt of Hinkler's marriage from Pearkes soon after the funeral ceremony, whether they communicated this revelation to Nance or to Frances Hinkler at that time is not known. Finalisation of the estate in the English courts in June that year, however, ensured that if the two women were not aware beforehand of the ceremony that had taken place in Connecticut on 21 May 1932, they came face to face with it at that point, just over twelve months later. Nevertheless, the public continued to believe that Nance was Bert's widow, even when the Brisbane *Courier Mail* published a notice on 26 August 1933 from the legal firm of McGregor, McGregor, Given and Capner, of the intention to confirm in Queensland the grant of administration from the English courts for the personal estate of Herbert John Louis Hinkler on behalf of his widow, named as Katherine Hinkler.

As a result of the lack of public knowledge of Katherine's place in Hinkler's life, when his mother returned to Bundaberg in early September from a four-month stay in Western Australia, Frances was able to inform the press disingenuously that after consulting with their lawyers and considering how long it had been since the funeral, she and Nance – now back in Southampton – had decided Bert Hinkler's body should remain in Italy. She said returning the body to Australia would only cause unnecessary worry and expense.

Just a few days later, on 12 September, Australian government representatives in London met with Katherine Hinkler, the woman they now knew was Bert's widow, to seek her views on a possible re-burial in Australia. There was still public support for returning the body to his homeland, and the government was committed to the possibility. Under Italian law, exhumations could not take place in summer, so the earliest the body could be moved would be October. Katherine said she would think about it, and give the Australian government a written response.

In the meantime she'd been invited to the unveiling on Sunday, 17 September of a memorial to her husband, which had been instigated by the Aero Club of Arezzo, the largest town close to the crash site in Tuscany. As with the funeral, Pearkes represented her at the ceremony, and he and the British Military Attaché, Colonel Stevens – representing the Australian Government – left their car at the foot of the Pratomagno range and travelled by mule through the rocky terrain leading to the site. The monument was located on the crest of a hill, a few hundred yards from where the wreck had been found.

The memorial comprised a solid rectangular marble column that featured a stylised eagle in flight, and the simple inscription (in Italian) indicated the estimated date of the crash in Italy: 'To the long-distance airman, Herbert Hinkler, who fell here 8 – 1 – X1'.

In addition to the military and police presence, about 200 villagers turned up, despite the two-hour climb. This gesture was 'a very clear testimony,' the Military Attaché later reported, 'to the admiration and sympathy which Hinkler's exploits and tragic end have evoked in the hearts of these simple, intelligent, hardy, straightforward mountain folk'.[2] On the card that accompanied the wreath she sent for the unveiling, Katherine had written: 'In memory of my beloved husband, resting in Italy, whose people have my eternal gratitude because of their unsurpassable kindness.'[3]

Pearkes later wrote a letter to the English press, praising the Italians' efforts and lamenting the lack of a memorial to Hinkler in England, and the fact that no English flying club had been represented at the funeral ceremony or sent a wreath.

On 2 October Katherine gave her written response to the Australian government to their inquiry about a possible re-burial. She said flatly that she would not permit the body to be moved.

> Some time before my husband's body was found, but when it was no longer possible to hope for other than a tragic finding, I decided that wherever he was eventually discovered was to be the scene of his burial. It seemed quite apparent to me, with the information then available that only the most perfunctory concern was felt as to his fate – or at least no concern sufficiently great to arouse any practical activity. And since then nothing has come to me which would lead me to conclude that that information was not entirely correct.[4]

Katherine acknowledged that there was no obligation for a government to search for a civilian airman, but while she didn't expect that anything more should've been done for Hinkler than for anyone else in similar trouble, 'it was my feeling that there could be no greater tribute, no finer gesture, than for some step to be taken which might or might not result in the finding of a man who, it was finally discovered, crashed directly on his route . . .'.[5] Nance had said something similar about the government in January, when Hinkler was still missing, but not as forthrightly.

Now, five months after her husband's body had been found, the 32-year-old widow didn't think 'any worthwhile tribute could now be paid to him by any part of the British Empire'. She said she was grateful to Monsieur Saby and Mr Pearkes for all they'd done to trace the missing pilot, and believed that the two ceremonies in Italy were sufficient.

> If his name is to be remembered by future generations of Australians, I hope that remembrance will rest on whatever he achieved rather than on the place of his burial. If he is to be forgotten by those future generations, I for one shall be sorry but not surprised, for I shall remember he was also forgotten by his own generation at a time when it might have meant his life.

Katherine apologised for the length of the letter, and said this was a 'painful subject' she wanted 'closed once and forever'.[6]

Later that year, the finalisation of Bert Hinkler's estate in the Queensland courts revealed an amount of £12,000, in the form of bank deposits and war bonds – around £360,000 in today's values. Of this nest-egg, which Hinkler must have slowly built up, Katherine received £1000, along with his personal belongings, and a life interest in the rest of the estate. On her death, the balance of the estate was to pass to Frances Hinkler.

The three women who had featured in Bert Hinkler's life then slipped into the shadows with their thoughts and memories – Frances at Woodbine Villa in Bundaberg, Nance at Mon Repos in Southampton, and Katherine with her sister in Glasgow.

CHAPTER 22

Fighting for a place in the sun

While Katherine, Nance and Frances each mourned the loss of Hinkler in her own way, and dealt with the aftermath, Italian and British aviation authorities were trying to determine the cause of the crash in which he died.

Back in 1915, while he was training with the Royal Naval Air Service in Northumberland, Hinkler had told his mother about the time when he was a passenger in a plane that crashed. 'I knew we were falling and there I was, could do nothing but wait for the crash. Oh, those few moments were terrible, and when the crash did come, the sudden stoppage was awful . . . I was thrown forward, but as I was prepared for it I came off lucky, yes, very lucky indeed.'[1] The scenario in Italy on 7 January 1933 might've been very similar for him, except that this time Hinkler was the pilot, and the sudden stoppage was more awful: he wasn't prepared for it, and his luck had run out.

The Pratomagno range divides the provinces of Florence and Arezzo, and separates the Casentino Valley from the Val di Sieve on the Florence side. At their highest point, the mountains stand at close to 1600 metres above sea level. The Puss Moth's flight direction was estimated as north-west to south-east, which would've been the path that Hinkler followed on his way to Brindisi after passing over Florence, while trying to cross what the locals called 'the summit'.

Despite the number of charts he carried, none was for the area where he crashed, as the official record shows: '14 large geographical maps in English, foolscap format, 60 x 42 cm, of all the Australian, Indian Regions, Asia Minor, Persia, and one of Germany, a map M.I. to 58 of the Australian area, and one 97 x 79 [cm] of the Indian region'.[2]

When the first party of Carabinieri arrived at the scene, they found what one report termed a 'shapeless mass of iron among which only the engine block was distinguishable'.[3] The engine and one blade of the propeller were embedded in the ground. Close by, they found an uninflated yellow rubber raft and pump, the fourteen maps and a shoe; and near some beech trees, the front edge of the plane's right wing and other small pieces of wreckage. The central fuel tank had followed almost the same trajectory as the pilot's body.

The members of this police party had differing views about how the crash happened. A chemist from Strada, who was also a former pilot and current air-force reservist, believed that the right wing collided with high trees due to either 'the limited visibility or fog or the effects of the weather which in that area can come up unexpectedly and violently'.[4] He thought the aircraft had continued on a little before diving into the ground, and didn't think it had crashed into the side of the mountain, because it had gone down *after* going over the mountain pass.

The senior officer of the group, Marshal Aureli, suggested that the plane was 'certainly surprised by a storm with very strong wind squalls which resulted in fragmentation of the wings, and thus the disaster'.[5] He said it was not improbable that the pilot had been thrown from the aircraft at an undetermined height, while the chemist believed that Hinkler was ejected when the DH.80A ploughed into the ground. The attending doctor agreed that one of them was right: the pilot was thrown out either just before the crash or at the time of impact.

The remains of the Puss Moth were carried down the mountain on two donkeys and thence to Pisa for closer examination by Italian authorities. On 23 May, a senior representative from the Ministero dell' Aeronautica advised Britain's Air Attaché in Rome that the cause of the accident was thought to be the loss of the right wing in flight. This conclusion was based on the distance the wing was found from the aircraft (250 yards) and the fact that it couldn't have slid so far if the plane was intact when it hit the ground.

The British authorities were not so sure. An air-crash investigator in the Air Ministry said he'd seen the photos of Hinkler's crashed plane and 'did not think for one moment there is the slightest possibility of this root connection [on the right wing] having failed in the air, at any rate before the wing structure collapsed'.[6] At his request, the Italians sent him the wing root – the part of the wing where it is fixed to the fuselage – in question.

The British asked questions of their Italian counterparts, who responded: there were no photographs taken of the wing where it was found, but the wing joint was smashed at the 'rounded extremity';[7] none of the surrounding trees showed signs of having been struck by the plane – the fabric wing covering was torn, probably from touching the bare branches as the plane fell; the wing was found pointing towards the north, the remainder of the machine was pointing towards the east; the plane couldn't have travelled along the ground after falling because the engine and one blade of the propeller were buried in the ground.

The Ministero dell' Aeronautica also said that bad weather, which was worsening at the time, was probably the main reason the wing broke away, especially when combined with increasingly greater play in the wing joint that caused the slot holding the fastening bolt to break, due to a defect in the soldering.

There had been incidents of wing separation in Puss Moths before Hinkler's crash, including the one he'd apparently discussed with the Royal Canadian Air Force in March the previous year. The first incident was in Australia in 1930, another happened in Africa about the time that Hinkler took delivery of CF-APK, and a third in South Africa while the Queenslander was in Trinidad, on his way to Natal. There were three more in 1932 – two in Europe and one in Australia – in addition to the RCAF crash. Separation of the wing seemed to be associated with the aircraft flying at high speed in a period of violent weather. The RCAF crash, which happened during a high-speed test dive to check for control flutter, was the only one where the pilot survived.

The Air Ministry modifications required balancing the rudder and ailerons to eliminate reported flutter, strengthening and reinforcing the lift struts, and internal bracing of the wings. In the November 1932 recertification of Hinkler's plane, which delayed his departure for Australia, the ministry approved all the modifications and installations as airworthy. But while the Air Ministry's investigator discounted wing separation as a cause of Hinkler's crash, he did seem to allow for the possibility of the 'wing structure' collapsing before the DH.80A hit the ground.

Despite apparently differing opinions at the time about the possible causes of the crash, the remains of CF-APK were destroyed soon after the official report was issued, with the approval of the British Air Ministry and 'the widow'. The reason for the rapid destruction of the Puss Moth was, as the British Air Attaché in Rome explained, that it was 'absolutely against the policy of the Regia Aeronautica to allow the wreckage of a machine to remain at an aerodrome after an examination has been made and a report submitted'.[8]

Whatever the experts concluded about the cause of the crash in which Bert Hinkler died, in her poem 'Vale! Hinkler' in the Brisbane *Sunday Mail* on 30 April 1933, Emily Bulcock offered another explanation:

Like Icarus, he flew too near the sun,
And dared the jealous gods –
The angry, startled gods,
Who, guarding their lone height
Stayed the bold eagle's flight![9]

* * *

Once news of the two charcoal burners' discovery had been wired across the world, commentators had tried to make sense of Hinkler's life and death. Charles Grey, editor of *The Aeroplane* magazine, who had known Bert since the Australian arrived in London in 1913, penniless and looking for work, was quick to quash the rumour that Hinkler had committed suicide because he was at his wits' end. This inference may have been drawn because of his lack of career options, combined with news of the deceased pilot's head injuries and the mention of a gun permit and an empty holster in the police inventory of his personal items, although no gun was found at the crash scene.

Grey spoke to Hinkler the day before he left, and found Hinkler fed up, he said, but not suicidal. 'He was as cheerful and as amusing and as good company as ever, but he had got to the state when he did not care very much about anything,' he said. 'He was far too brave, and far too deeply religious, in the full sense of the word, to commit suicide, but he just did not care. If he got through, all would be well, and if he did not, there would be an end of it.'[10] In any event, the police descriptions of the battered body and the crumpled plane make it clear that it was the crash that killed the flyer, and there is no support from those officials who attended the scene for any alternative view.

Another friend, fellow aviator Frederic Robertson, wrote in the *Manchester Guardian* that Hinkler perhaps shunned publicity 'overmuch'. 'Sometimes he tried to make money, but his motive never was greed or love of gold for its own sake,' Robertson explained. 'He wanted money solely to give practical expression to his own ideas of what a touring aeroplane ought to be.'[11]

The *West Australian* said that Hinkler was 'remembered by all who met him as a modest, unassuming individual, retiring to a degree, and if fault he had, it was his inability to push himself forward'.[12] Under the headline 'Bert Hinkler's martydom', the *Sunday Times* in Western Australia claimed that the pilot's final flight was 'the sad ending to a drawn-out tragedy in which he was fighting for a place in the sun', and said he had to resort to such activities because the Australian Government refused to give him a job in the air force. With his abilities and ambition, Hinkler had to make spectacular flights occasionally, the writer declared, 'to let the world know that he was not played out'.[13]

There was a similar theme in the tribute from the Hobart *Mercury*: 'It is a hard fate, if it must be a fate, that men who have braved so many risks, and have added so much to world knowledge of flying, are to continue what are called "stunts" because there is no place for them in a well-organised system.'[14] *The Times* in London agreed: 'Hinkler, because the world found no steady employment for him, has given his life to an exploit such as might have been left to younger men.'[15] The headline on the *Times* obituary might well have been chiselled on his headstone: 'Mr Hinkler: A great airman lacking a settled task.'

But there were other sides to the Bundaberg-born pilot. There was 'No-news Hinkler', dodging reporters and forever making 'semi-furtive' take-offs, a trait that created confusion following his disappearance; there was 'affable Hinkler', joking and relaxed at official dinners and other public occasions, usually with a few words to say, serious or witty as the occasion demanded; there was 'hard-up' Hinkler, seemingly forever in financial need, from the time he joined Wizard Stone to the time of his final take-off at Great West Aerodrome; there was the Hinkler who irritated civil servants in several countries, resisting their demands and circumventing the regulations; and there was the Hinkler who conducted romances with two women on two different continents, confounding his claim to Nance in 1921 that 'the heart singles out just one and will not be satisfied or even consoled by any other'.[16]

There was also the Hinkler whom Charles Grey knew, the one who didn't always endear himself to prospective employers or partners:

> He was astonishingly good-tempered, but, like all men with quick-working minds, he was impatient with people who were slow to see what he was getting at, or to appreciate his arguments in favour of a certain line of action or a certain change in design. And few important people like being told, and told emphatically, that they are wrong or stupid. And Bert, being an Australian, had a habit of speaking his mind.[17]

It was this belief in his own opinion, in his ability as a pilot and navigator, and in his aptitude for technical innovation, that drove Hinkler to seek to make his mark in the rapidly developing world of aviation in which he grew up. And he did make an impact, with courage and persistence and outstanding flying skills. Nevertheless, the fiercely independent spirit that took him (literally) to such heights of achievement, at the same time constrained his willingness to seek the help of others to achieve his goals. He was always his 'own man', even when circumstances suggested that a manager or publicity agent might better advance his cause.

As a result, although Hustling Hinkler at times became master of his fate in the air, it was his inability to hustle a living that eventually brought him back to earth, and led him to take the chances that led to his untimely death. Like most of the flyers of the interwar period, he was imbued with a passion for aviation that couldn't be extinguished, despite the precariousness of the vocation and the appallingly high loss of life.

Nowhere is Hinkler's passion for flying more evident than in a diversion he made in G-EBOV on his England–Australia flight in February 1928. It was day eleven, and he'd had to contend with fogs, sandstorms, desert landings, a leaking fuel tank, bureaucracy, monotony and loneliness. All he wanted was to reach Australia in the shortest possible time. As he headed towards Rangoon, he saw a sight that surpassed anything he'd ever seen: a massive formation of cirrus and cumulus clouds so thick, they looked as solid as the earth, but this time not the dark, threatening clouds that brought rain, thunder and lightning. Rather, these were soft, cotton-wool clouds lit by the sun.

He later wrote of that moment:

> None but airmen can ever see such a miracle. I looked down the immense cloud gorges, their sides made of solid gold burnished by the sun. Along these narrow defiles I hummed, the sides closing in on me with the effect of falling walls. Over a great escarpment I bounded to see . . . a canyon that seemed to lead me to new beauty. With a whoop I roared along this, the colour changing as I swept up the straight. High precipices yawned before me. With a feeling of pitching myself over in deep security, I rocketed down them, to come racing up again through the shadows into the light, the sun gleaming on my wings. That is the nearest approach to being a bird, to which a man can come.[18]

It was the culmination of a childhood dream. The boy who had once looked with envy at the birds of the air around Bundaberg, had now finally joined them.

Epilogue

Shortly after she'd told the Australian Government in no uncertain terms in October 1933 that she wanted her husband's body to remain exactly where it was, Katherine Hinkler left Glasgow on board the *Tuscania*. This time, she wasn't on her way to New York, her home before her marriage, but to India. The *Tuscania*, refitted to take a smaller number of passengers, had begun autumn and winter sailings from Glasgow to Bombay via Liverpool and return. The voyage to India went through the Suez Canal and took Katherine to parts of the world that Hinkler probably flew over or near on his England-to-Australia flight. When she returned to Glasgow on 13 December 1933, she again stayed with members of her family.

If the trip had been intended to help her get away from recent events, however, it seems it was unsuccessful. According to Katherine's great-nephew, Bill Grimaldi, during this period she suffered a nervous breakdown and spent some time in an institution in Europe. He also believes that at some time she had an audience with the Italian leader, Mussolini. Katherine told Grimaldi that when she went into Mussolini's office in Rome, which had marble columns and a very large desk, he said to her, 'I'm sorry that you've lost him. You're a very beautiful woman.'[1]

Katherine Hinkler finally returned to New York on 17 June 1934, again on the *Tuscania*, using her married name, and travelling cabin class. But she came back to her former home a different woman from the one who'd left Boston alongside her new husband just over two years earlier. She now gave her occupation as 'housekeeper', and her marital status as 'widow'.

In the years up until World War II, Katherine made a number of visits by ship to Glasgow, staying with her sister, Jean, or her cousin Peggy. During that time, she stated her occupation as 'nil', and it seems she didn't begin paid employment again until 1939. According to Grimaldi, during World War II Katherine became involved with a scheme, possibly through the Red Cross, to bring English women who had married American servicemen over to the United States.

Jean Costa, a great-niece of Katherine, recalls as a child visiting her great-aunt in Astoria with her parents. 'Kathy was complaining that what Bert had done was forgotten and a waste of time and he'd died for nothing,' Jean says. 'My father got irate and told her any man would be proud to die a hero's death. This remark seemed to pacify her and please her, and she said no more on the subject. My mother also told me Katherine had Bert's watch on her side table and no one was allowed to dust it or touch it.'[2]

* * *

Hinkler's mother and his brother George visited his grave at Allori, near Florence, in May 1936, as guests of the Italia shipping line and various government agencies. Italy had just successfully invaded Abyssinia (present-day Ethiopia), so Genoa was alive with celebrations when the ship arrived in the harbour. Near the crash site, hundreds of villagers turned out to welcome Mrs Hinkler Senior and some of them produced mementoes: papers, strut wires, a petrol strainer, parts of the cabin, a navigation light. Clearly, not all the parts of CF-APK had reached the crash investigator at Pisa three years before.

Frances Hinkler said that her most prized gift was the plane's registration plate – bearing the inscription DH AEROPLANE TYPE: PUSS MOTH, NO. 2049 – given to her by the doctor who examined the body, Domenico Vettori. In return, Frances and George presented the mayor of Arezzo with packets of seeds of varieties of Australian trees. They were not able to see the nearby memorial because the way was still blocked by snow, a reminder of the circumstances in 1933 that had prevented her son from being found for three months. During World War II, that memorial would be wrecked by Italian partisans (presumably because of the Fascist symbol on it), but it would then be restored in 1968.

From Italy, the Hinklers went on to England. There in June, for the first time, Frances met Katherine, who was in Britain on one of her Atlantic crossings. Although the initial revelation of the marriage must've come as a shock to Hinkler's mother, after their meeting in London, Katherine remembered her as 'the gentle kindly lady who took a strange daughter-in-law into her arms'. At that time, Katherine arranged with Leslie Pearkes that all of Hinkler's medals and mementoes would go to his brother George, or the latter's son or the next male heir bearing the Hinkler name. She had a soft spot for George: 'I think very often of the first time I saw him, and how very kind and brotherly he was to me. And how very like my own dear Bert [he was].'[3]

Katherine corresponded regularly with Hinkler's mother, addressing her as 'little mater', and telling her in June 1939 that she thought of her 'with deep love and gratitude'. Writing from the family home on 37th Street, Astoria, Katherine told Frances that the World's Fair, which had opened in New York the previous month and emphasised futuristic technologies such as television while promoting other consumer goods, appeared to be a 'gigantic failure' because people couldn't even afford the entrance fee.[4]

In the same letter, Katherine said she'd been successful in obtaining a job in advertising and had worked hard on a campaign, but that the advertiser had cancelled at the last moment, because business was too poor to justify the expense. She reported that Jean, her elder sister, who was now also back living in the family home, was undertaking a business course in the hope that economic conditions would improve. Katherine's comments show that some ten years after Hinkler had been seeking backers for the Ibis, the world economy was still struggling.

Notwithstanding the affection she expressed for her mother-in-law, Katherine was a little taken aback by Frances's question about whether she planned to marry again. Then aged thirty-seven, Katherine responded that it was difficult for her to explain what a quiet life she led. 'I have lost all desire for entertainment or company,' she wrote. 'I seldom leave the house except to go to the office. Bert is still as dear to me as when I saw him last and no one could ever take his place. To me he was the best of husbands and the best of companions. If I can't have him, I don't want anyone else.'

Her letter continues:

> As time goes on, one doesn't cry, but nothing can take away that bitter sense of loss. If he had been spared, I think we could have made a good life together; as he was taken, the best I can do is to keep busy. There can be no happiness for me and all I want is peace.[5]

Six years after the burial, Katherine was paying for the maintenance of Hinkler's grave. She did not marry again, and died in October 1976, at the age of seventy-four. Her remains lie alongside those of her parents and her sister, Jean, in Ferncliff Cemetery, Westchester County, New York.

* * *

At the time of the discovery of his body, there was disbelief among his admirers in Australia that a pilot as skilled and as careful as Bert Hinkler could not have extricated himself from the situation he found himself in over the Pratomagno Range unless more malevolent forces were at work. Even his old friend from the 1926 Helvellyn mountain landing, John Leeming, commented: 'Bert Hinkler, who could put a machine down almost on a dinner plate, and who died in the end by flying through clouds into the side of a mountain . . .'.[6] The initial reporting limitations and lack of a clear explanation for the crash only encouraged speculation about what caused it, down to the present day.

In particular, author Ted Wixted was convinced the absence of one blade of the propeller was a key to the mystery, and suggested the airscrew had been interfered with in order to bring about the crash. He related this interference to severe animosity between Katherine Hinkler and Nance, and the involvement of other players, including solicitor Pearkes and 'Dopey' Lingham. The reported smashing of Hinkler's mother's photo during the Mon Repos break-in is part of this scenario. In the 1990s, Wixted pursued this hypothesis by trying to locate the other blade of the propeller through a visit to the Arezzo region and appeals in the Italian press, without success.

However, an Australian aviation engineer and air crash investigator, John Watkins, was convinced that structural failure in wild weather was the culprit. After reviewing reports published in 1937 of nine fatal Puss Moth accidents, including Hinkler's, and having investigated such a crash in North Queensland, Watkins, concluded that it was likely 'Hinkler's crash in the Apennines was due to a geometric peculiarity in the design of his aeroplane that enhanced its susceptibility to wing flutter. The special geometry was intended to facilitate wing-folding on the ground, so that the private owner could garage his plane like a car. But in this and a good many other cases, it appears to have led to catastrophic failure in severe turbulence – a situation quite beyond the pilot's control.'[6] Adventurer Lang Kidby, who retraced Hinkler's England-to-Australia flight in a restored Avro Avian, and who surveyed the crash site in Tuscany from the air, is also reportedly convinced it was a combination of those factors that brought Hinkler's plane down.

* * *

In December 1933, the Australian Government awarded Frances Hinkler a pension of £104 a year, which, the Prime Minister said, 'was intended to be a recognition by the Commonwealth of Squadron Leader Hinkler's splendid contributions to the development of aviation'.[7] It also seems a fitting reward for a mother who was her son's lifelong supporter. Frances Hinkler continued to live quietly in North Bundaberg until her death in September 1953, shortly after her eighty-seventh birthday.

Nance stayed at Mon Repos in Thornhill until 1952, when she sold the property and moved to South Africa with Maida, her daughter. Nance's grand-daughter, Paddy Canavan, later donated letters and other mementoes to the Hinkler Hall of Aviation at Bundaberg. Mon Repos was acquired in 1983 by the Hinkler House Memorial Museum and Research Association, and the house was dismantled brick by brick, slate tile by slate tile, transported to Australia, and then reassembled in Bundaberg North (to use the modern suburb name) as a lasting monument. The Hinkler Hall of Aviation has recently been constructed alongside it, in the Bundaberg Botanic Gardens.

After Nance's departure, the new owner of Mon Repos discovered Hinkler's 'dream machine', the Ibis, still in its shed on the property. An aviation enthusiast bought it, and there was talk of the plane being commercially produced, but, in an echo of the earlier outcome, nothing ever came of the proposal. During an inspection, however, Hinkler's original logbook from his 1928 England–Australia flight was found lodged inside a wing. The blue-covered journal was transported respectfully to Australia by Qantas in June 1953, and is now held at the National Library, Canberra.

The Ibis was reportedly scrapped at Lee-on-Solent, west of Portsmouth in Hampshire, in 1959. Without ceremony, and without due recognition of its significant place in Bert Hinkler's heart and history.

Records and awards

Major record solo flights

1920 London to Turin – 700 miles (1125 kilometres) nonstop in nine-and-a-half hours, on 31 May 1920; flying Avro Baby, G-EACQ

1921 Sydney to Bundaberg – 700 miles (1125 kilometres) nonstop in nine hours, on 11 April 1921; flying Avro Baby, G-EACQ

1927 London to Riga, Latvia – 1200 miles (1930 kilometres) in ten-and-a-half hours, on 27 August 1927; major long-distance flight; flying Avro Avian G-EBOV

1928 England to Australia – 10,000 miles (16,000 kilometres) in 134 flying hours, on 7–22 February 1928; pioneering solo flight; flying Avro Avian G-EBOV

1931 Natal, Brazil, to Bathurst, Gambia – 1800 miles (2900 kilometres) in 22 hours, on 25–26 November 1931, pioneering west-to-east solo South Atlantic crossing, flying de Havilland Puss Moth, CF-APK.

Major awards

1917 Distinguished Service Medal, as aerial gunner in Royal Naval Air Service during World War I in France and Belgium

1920 Britannia Trophy – presented by Royal Aero Club for May 1920 non-stop London–Turin flight

1927 Oswald Watt Gold Medal – presented by Royal Federation of Aero Clubs of Australia for August 1927 non-stop London–Riga flight

1928 J.P. Thomson Gold Medal – presented by Royal Geographical Society of Australasia (Queensland)

Gold Medal – presented by Queensland Institute of Surveyors for role as 'aerial pathfinder'

Air Force Cross – presented by King George V for 1928 England–Australia flight

Britannia Trophy – presented by Royal Aero Club for 1928 England–Australia flight

Oswald Watt Gold Medal – presented by Royal Federation of Aero Clubs of Australia for 1928 England–Australia flight

Fédération Aéronautique International Gold Medal – presented for 1928 England–Australia flight

1931 Moroccan medal [possibly Order of Morocco (Order of Ouissam Alaouite), presented in recognition of exceptional civil and military accomplishments] – for 1931 South Atlantic flight

Oswald Watt Gold Medal – presented by Royal Federation of Aero Clubs of Australia for 1931 South Atlantic flight

Royal Aero Club Gold Medal – presented for outstanding achievement in aviation

Britannia Trophy – presented by Royal Aero Club for 1931 flight New York–London via South America and South Atlantic

1932 Segrave Trophy – presented by British Aeronautical Society for most daring flying feat of 1931

Johnston Memorial Trophy – presented by Guild of Air Pilots and Air Navigators for 1931 South Atlantic crossing

Notes and sources

The main institutional sources for primary documents quoted in the book are as follows: Australian Archives, Canberra and Melbourne; Hinkler Hall of Aviation, Bundaberg, Queensland; National Library of Australia, Canberra; Oxley Memorial Library and Queensland Museum, Brisbane; and the UK Archives, Kew, England. Major electronic sources for published material include the online archives of the Royal Aero Club's *Flight* magazine; and Trove, the newspaper databases of the National Library of Australia. Shipping lists, census records and other personal information were obtained mainly through Ancestry.com.

Notes

Prologue

The re-creation of Bert Hinkler's final flight is based on contemporary accounts and on details provided in *The Last Flight of Bert Hinkler*, by E. P. Wixted.

Chapter 1 – 'A local flying man'

1. 'He was always a boy for machinery': 'Proud mother', *Brisbane Courier*, 24 February 1928, p. 19.
2. 'He would make little models': 'Proud mother', p. 19.
3. 'It seemed to me': B. Hinkler, *Eighteen Years of Flying: Dips into My Diary* (unpublished manuscript), no date, Chapter 1: 'The soaring ambitions of youth', p. 4; OM68-24, Bert Hinkler Papers, John Oxley Library, State Library of Queensland, Australia.
4. 'as one begins his alphabet': B. Hinkler, *Eighteen Years of Flying*, p. 4.
5. 'dreamers and fools': Otto Lilienthal, Inventors Gallery, http://invention.psychology.msstate.edu/i/Lilienthal/Lilienthal.html.
6. 'It is easy to put more tail': B. Hinkler, *Eighteen Years of Flying*, p. 5.
7. 'A local flying man': *Bundaberg Mail*, 25 March 1912.
8. 'like a ride over hurdles': 'W. E. Hart', program for First International Aviation Contest, Sydney, 15 June 1912, National Library, Canberra.
9. 'at a speed': program for First International Aviation Contest, Sydney, 15 June 1912.
10. 'At least one thousand military aeroplanes': 'Australia and the aviator', program for First International Aviation Contest, Sydney, 15 June 1912.
11. 'The pupil leaned over': E.G. Roberts, *Box Kites and Beyond*, Hawthorn Press, Melbourne, 1976, p. 3.
12. 'it was not the kind of flight': B. Hinkler, *Eighteen Years of Flying*, p. 6.
13. 'I resigned myself to patience': B. Hinkler, *Eighteen Years of Flying*, p. 7.

Chapter 2 – The birdman and the Wizard

1. 'It was as if heaven': B. Hinkler, *Eighteen Years of Flying: Dips into My Diary* (unpublished manuscript), no date, Chapter 1: 'The soaring ambitions of youth', p. 8; OM68-24, Bert Hinkler Papers, John Oxley Library, State Library of Queensland, Australia.
2. 'sensational aerial manoeuvres' and 'greatest of American Aviators': advertisement, *Brisbane Courier*, 29 June 1912, p. 2.
3. 'Aviation technique had not': B. Hinkler, *Eighteen Years of Flying*, p. 10.
4. 'an excellent specimen of workmanship': 'Aviation Court', *Brisbane Courier*, 15 August 1912, p. 12.
5. 'The experience I gained': B. Hinkler, *Eighteen Years of Flying*, p. 8.
6. 'having a lovely time' and 'Hope Papa is still doing well': B. Hinkler, letter to Frances Hinkler, 24 April 1913; OM68-24, Bert Hinkler Papers, John Oxley Library, State Library of Queensland.
7. 'all strong', 'I am sure' and 'your opinion has altered': B. Hinkler, letter to Frances Hinkler, 1 June 1913; OM68-24, Bert Hinkler Papers.
8. 'stoney broke' and 'but I hardly fancy it': letter to Frances Hinkler, 15 June, 1913; OM68-24, Bert Hinkler Papers.
9. 'I was happy enough': B. Hinkler, *Eighteen Years of Flying*, p. 10.

Chapter 3 – Disturbing the air, Huns and other insects

1. 'I prowled around the drome': 'Hinkler's flight: Born for wings', *Advocate (Burnie)*, 3 March 1928, p. 6.
2. 'It was only a position': B. Hinkler, *Eighteen Years of Flying: Dips into My Diary* (unpublished manuscript), no date, Chapter 1: 'The soaring ambitions of youth', p. 10; OM68-24, Bert Hinkler Papers, John Oxley Library, State Library of Queensland, Australia.
3. 'I don't know how many', 'the turns are about' and 'whenever it liked': B. Hinkler, letter to Frances Hinkler, 29 March 1914; OM68-24, Bert Hinkler Papers.
4. 'to get far more': B. Hinkler, *Eighteen Years of Flying*, p. 10.
5. 'Love to all and tell Pop': B. Hinkler, letter to Frances Hinkler, 9 October 1914; OM68-24, Bert Hinkler Papers.
6. 'Fair dincum': B. Hinkler, letter to Frances Hinkler, 5 May 1915, OM68-24, Bert Hinkler Papers.
7. 'Oh those few moments', 'Still of course' and 'Now, please Mum, don't worry': B. Hinkler, letter to Frances Hinkler, 5 May 1915.
8. 'as happy as a dog with two tails': B. Hinkler, letter to Frances Hinkler, 1 April, 1916; OM68-24, Bert Hinkler Papers.
9. 'rest assured': B. Hinkler, letter to Frances Hinkler, 1 April 1916.
10. 'By my procedure' and 'As I have often': B. Hinkler, letter to Frances Hinkler, 11 March 1916; OM68-24, Bert Hinkler Papers.
11. 'We had a fine time' and 'One of our chaps': B. Hinkler, letter to Queenie Hinkler, 29 January 1917, Hinkler Hall of Aviation database, Bundaberg.
12. 'Around Ostende, Bruges and Ghent' and 'They also have a[n] idea': B. Hinkler, letter to Frances Hinkler, 27 August 1917; OM68-24, Bert Hinkler Papers.
13. 'Getting leave to Australia': B. Hinkler, letter to Frances Hinkler, 27 August 1917.
14. 'I asked him if he wanted': F.W. Hotson, 'Bert Hinkler and Canada', *The Canadian Aviation Historical Society Journal*, 1992, 30, 1, p. 16.
15. 'On the way back': B. Hinkler, letter to Frances Hinkler, 27 August 1917.
16. 'I am now in a favourable position': F.W. Hotson, 'Bert Hinkler and Canada', p. 16.
17. 'I think if I remember': B. Hinkler, letter to Frances Hinkler, 11 July 1918; OM68-24, Bert Hinkler Papers.
18. 'I climbed to about 4000 feet': B. Hinkler, letter to Frances Hinkler, 11 July 1918.
19. '[T]he birds of prey' and 'I nearly went crazy': B. Hinkler, postcard from Italy to one of his sisters, c. Sept–Oct 1918; OM68-24, Bert Hinkler Papers.
20. 'the wonderful experiences' and 'Wartime Experiences (many excellent)': B. Hinkler, *Eighteen Years of Flying,* p. 11.
21. 'absolutely glorious' and 'Sometime in the future': B. Hinkler, letter to May Hinkler, 2 October 1918; OM68-24, Bert Hinkler Papers.
22. 'We realised quite well': H.C. Biard, *Wings*, Hurst and Blackett, London, 1934, p. 68.

Chapter 4 – 'Get a room ready and air my pyjamas'

1. 'Up till then': 'Flying to Bundaberg', *Daily Mail* (Brisbane), 19 March 1928, p. 1.
2. 'grand little machine': letter to parents, 7 May 1919; OM68-24, Bert Hinkler Papers, John Oxley Library, State Library of Queensland.
3. 'Oh, Queensland is a fine country': B. Hinkler, letter to parents, 22 March 1919, quoted in *Northern Territory Times and Gazette,* 28 June 1919, p. 18.
4. 'Satisfactory in every way', 'We filled out Form Z211' and 'I thought and thought': 'Flying to Bundaberg', p. 1.
5. 'd___ rotten' and 'just about fed up': B. Hinkler, letter to parents, 7 May 1919.
6. 'The publicity value': 'Flying to Bundaberg', p. 1.
7. 'Oh, say, will you': B. Hinkler, letter to parents, 7 May 1919.
8. 'in the neighbourhood of': '£10,000 Prize offered by the Australian Government for a flight from Great Britain to Australia', *Flight*, 29 May 1919, p. 700.
9. 'I . . . learned where': B. Hinkler, letter to Frances Hinkler, 23 September 1919, London; OM68-24, Bert Hinkler Papers.
10. 'Much as I want' and 'Tell me how Papa': B. Hinkler, letter to Frances Hinkler, 23 September 1919.
11. 'Information just received': 'The tragedy at Corfu', *Flight*, 18 December 1919, p. 1621.
12. 'a country of strikes': B. Hinkler, letter to parents, 4 July 1920, quoted in 'Lieut. Bert Hinkler', newspaper clipping (Bundaberg?), n.d.; OM92-114/2, Bert Hinkler Clippings, John Oxley Library, State Library of Queensland.
13. 'but, no, I was': B. Hinkler, letter to Frances Hinkler, 23 September 1919.

Chapter 5 – A pretty battered old Baby

1. 'It was apparent': R. Chadwick, quoted in P. Clegg, *Avro Test Pilots Since 1907*, GMS Enterprises, Peterborough, 1997, p. 77.
2. 'A pretty battered old baby': B. Hinkler, 'Flying to Bundaberg', *Daily Mail (Brisbane)*, 19 March 1928, p. 2.
3. 'a type of pigmy aeroplane': 'Air Pageant', *Illustrated London News*, 10 July 1920.
4. 'I began to think': B. Hinkler, 'Flying to Bundaberg', p. 2.
5. ''but he is a bit of a sport': *Morning Bulletin*, Rockhampton, 2 June 1920, p. 9.
6. 'It was compass or *fini*': B. Hinkler, quoted in E.P. Wixted, *Bert Hinkler and the Avro Baby*, self-published, 1991, p. 5.
7. 'blue bowl': 'Lieutenant Hinkler's flight', newspaper clipping, London (?), c. July, 1921, *Hinkler's worldwide flight*; OM92-114/2, Bert Hinkler Clippings, John Oxley Library.
8. 'I would hate to tell you': B. Hinkler, 'Flying to Bundaberg', p. 2.
9. 'in the direction of': B. Hinkler, letter to parents, 4 July 1920; OM68-24, Bert Hinkler Papers, John Oxley Library.
10. 'among the finest' and 'One scarcely knows': 'Croydon to Turin in 9½ hours', *Flight,* 10 June 1920, p. 614.

11. 'Aviation is, of course': B. Hinkler, letter to parents, 4 July 1920, quoted in 'Lieut. Bert Hinkler', newspaper clipping (Bundaberg?), n.d.; OM92-114/2, Bert Hinkler Clippings, John Oxley Library, State Library of Queensland.
12. 'He was a man': M. Chadwick, quoted in P. Clegg, *Avro Test Pilots Since 1907*, p. 80.

Chapter 6 – A black future or glorious prospects?

1. 'bally Orstrayler': quoted by B. Hinkler in letter to Nance Hinkler from S.S. *Ascanius*, c. 29 January, 1921, Hinkler Hall of Aviation database.
2. 'I must take up something': B. Hinkler, letter to Nance Hinkler from SS *Ascanius*, 11 February 1921, Hinkler Hall of Aviation database, Bundaberg.
3. 'It seems – as I suppose': B. Hinkler, letter to Nance Hinkler from SS *Ascanius*, 5 March 1921, Hinkler Hall of Aviation database, Bundaberg.
4. 'If I don't receive news': B. Hinkler, letter to Nance Hinkler from SS *Ascanius*, 18 February 1921, Hinkler Hall of Aviation database, Bundaberg.
5. 'Say Nance, can you realize': B. Hinkler, letter to Nance Hinkler from SS *Ascanius*, 20 February 1921, Hinkler Hall of Aviation database, Bundaberg.
6. 'Sweetheart, do you know' and 'Here am I': B. Hinkler, letter to Nance Hinkler from SS *Ascanius*, 2 March 1921, Hinkler Hall of Aviation database, Bundaberg.
7. 'Sweetheart my Own': B. Hinkler, letter to Nance Hinkler from SS *Ascanius*, 2 March 1921.
8. 'How peculiar and wonderful': B. Hinkler, letter to Nance Hinkler from SS *Ascanius*, 3 March 1921, Hinkler Hall of Aviation database, Bundaberg.
9. 'I've been thinking': B. Hinkler, letter to Nance Hinkler from SS *Ascanius*, 5 February 1921, Hinkler Hall of Aviation database, Bundaberg.
10. 'Perhaps it must be': B. Hinkler, letter to Nance Hinkler from SS *Ascanius*, 3 March 1921.
11. 'If you don't mind': B. Hinkler, letter to Nance Hinkler from SS *Ascanius*, 19 February 1921, Hinkler Hall of Aviation database, Bundaberg.
12. 'green and shaded lanes': Extract from poem 'My Country' by Dorothea Mackellar.
13. 'When he left home as a lad': quoted in 'Airman's boyhood', *Sydney Morning Herald*, 25 February 1928.
14. '700 miles of perfect lubrication': *Brisbane Courier*, 14 May 1921, p. 10.
15. 'to save the rail fare': 'flying home', *Sydney Sun*, 1 May 1921; OM68-24, Bert Hinkler Clippings, John Oxley Library.
16. 'saw the heavens fill': 'Bert Hinkler's visit', *Isis Recorder*, 29 April 1921.

Chapter 7 – The restless years: test pilot and air racer

1. 'It is really hot stuff': 'Bert Hinkler', newspaper clipping, Bundaberg (?), n.d, *Hinkler's worldwide flight*; OM92-114/2, Bert Hinkler Clippings, John Oxley Library, State Library of Queensland.

2. 'It's rather hard luck': B. Hinkler, letter to E.J. Hart, Sydney, 30 July 1921, National Library, Canberra, M/S 8314.
3. 'If we go flipping around': B. Hinkler, letter to Nance Hinkler from SS *Ascanius*, 5 March 1921, Hinkler Hall of Aviation database, Bundaberg.
4. 'lively brute' and 'the joy of my life': B. Hinkler, letter to E.J. Hart, Sydney, 2 April 1922, National Library, Canberra, M/S 8314.
5. 'They were the sort of thing': B. Hinkler, letter to E.J. Hart, Sydney, 8 March 1923, National Library, Canberra, M/S 8314.
6. 'He goes into these races': 'The King's Cup race', *Flight*, 14 September 1922, p. 527.
7. 'Next time the "Brisbane Mail"': B. Hinkler, letter to parents, 6 December 1922; OM68-24, Bert Hinkler Papers, John Oxley Library, State Library of Queensland.
8. 'From a passenger's point of view' and 'educated up to it': B. Hinkler, letter to E.J. Hart, 8 March 1923.
9. 'He is sending me out': B. Hinkler, letter to E.J. Hart, 26 July 1924, National Library, Canberra, M/S 8314.
10. 'It would be dangerous': 'The British Schneider Cup Team sails for America', *Flight,* 1 October 1925, p. 641.

Chapter 8 – A plane with potential

1. 'We would think nothing': B. Hinkler, 'Barrier of finance', *Daily Mail* (Brisbane), 20 March 1928, p. 2.
2. 'I want to help him': letter, F. Hinkler to Navy Office, Melbourne, 'Bert Hinkler Imperial Service Grant', Australian Archives, Melbourne, MP981/1, item 726103.
3. 'This seems an outrageous action': letter, G. Barber to F. Forde, 'Bert Hinkler Imperial Service Grant'.
4. 'Tho it flies': letter to parents, 14 July 1927; OM68-24, Bert Hinkler Papers, John Oxley Library, State Library of Queensland.
5. 'I flew with him on many occasions': R. Chadwick, quoted in P. Clegg, *Avro test pilots since 1907*, GMS Enterprises, Peterborough, 1997, p. 77.
6. 'He did not seem to 'fly' the machine': John Leeming, *Airdays*, 1936, George G Harrap and Co., London, p. 119.
7. 'That one there' and 'Leave it to me': J.F. Leeming, *Airdays*, George G. Harrap and Co., London, p. 140.
8. 'I hear that tune sometimes': J.F. Leeming, *Airdays*, p. 138.

Chapter 9 – 'My plans are unsettled'

1. 'accompanied by a mechanic': 'British flights to the Antipodes', *Flight*, 24 February 1927, p. 98.
2. 'The response was as good': quoted in 'Insurance plan', newspaper clipping, c. March 1928, *Newspaper clippings: Record of Hinkler's flight, England to*

Australia, 1928; OM92-114/1, Bert Hinkler Clippings, John Oxley Library, State Library of Queensland.

3. 'unsettled' and 'I have not prepared': B. Hinkler, letter to parents, July 1927; OM68-24, Bert Hinkler Papers, John Oxley Library, State Library of Queensland.
4. 'Low black clouds': B. Hinkler, 'Twelve hundred miles non-stop', *Airways*, October 1927, p. 46.
5. 'somewhat hectic dinner' and 'I now fully understand': B. Hinkler, 'Twelve hundred miles non-stop', p. 46.
6. 'I gathered that at the moment': file note (Collins), 5 October 1927, Air Ministry file, 'B. Hinkler, Solo flight England – Australia: Request for permission to fly over certain foreign countries', AVIA 2/284, UK Archives, Kew.
7. 'forcefulness of opinion': H. Penrose, *British Aviation – Widening Horizons 1930–1934*, HMSO, London, 1979, p. 124.
8. '[Hinkler] had such an appreciation': P. Clegg, *Avro Test Pilots Since 1907*, GMS Enterprises, Peterborough, 1997, p. 80.
9. 'Atlantitis': 'British flights to the Antipodes', *Flight*, 24 February 1927.
10. 'It looked as if': quoted in 'Insurance plan'.
11. 'with unfeigned pleasure': 'Editorial comment', *Flight*, 17 November 1927, p. 871.
12. 'the Bristol "Jupiter" engine': 'Editorial comment', *Flight*, 17 November 1927.
13. 'mysterious airmen': F.A. de V. Robertson, 'Aeronautics in Great Britain', *Aircraft*, January 1928, p. 366.
14. 'We were as blind as bats': quoted in 'Glorious failure', *Brisbane Courier*, 5 December 1927, p. 17.
15. 'the 12 hours of flying': quoted in 'India flyers in Poland', *Glasgow Herald*, 21 November 1927, p. 10.
16. 'a glorious failure': quoted in 'Glorious failure', *Brisbane Courier*, 5 December 1927, p. 10.
17. 'chuckling at the success': T.C. Bridges & H.H. Tiltman, *More Heroes of Modern Adventure*, Books for Libraries Press, 1969, p. 65.
18. 'an act of grace': R. Bettiens, *Hinkler: Hyperbole, Hypocrisy and Humbug Versus Authenticity and Accuracy in Australian History*, self-published typescript, 1985, p. 25.
19. 'If he should be able to maintain': 'Hinkler flight', *Times*, 12 December 1927, p. 3.
20. 'especially in view of': file note, 4 January 1928, Air Ministry file, 'B. Hinkler, Solo flight England – Australia: Request for permission to fly over certain foreign countries', AVIA 2/284, UK Archives, Kew.
21. 'As regards Iraq, Persia': letter, Secretary, Air Ministry to B. Hinkler, 4 February 1928, Air Ministry file, 'B. Hinkler, Solo flight England – Australia: Request for permission to fly over certain foreign countries', AVIA 2/284, UK Archives, Kew.

Chapter 10 – On the trail that leads us home

1. 'My common sense': B. Hinkler, 'Barrier of finance', *Daily Mail* (Brisbane), 20 March 1928, p. 9.
2. 'Hang it, I'll go': B. Hinkler, 'Barrier of finance', p. 9.
3. 'I wish you all the best': 'Hinkler leaves for Australia', *Sydney Morning Herald*, 8 February 1928, p. 15.
4. 'I suppose one of those': B. Hinkler, 'Barrier of finance', p. 9.
5. 'At last! At last!': B. Hinkler, 'Flying to Bundaberg', *Daily Mail* (Brisbane), 19 March 1928, pp. 8–9.
6. William Tainsh, 'London Town is a lovesome place': 'Home, airman, home', *The Canberra Times*, 25 February 1928.
7. 'I felt a little blue': B. Hinkler, 'The lights of Rome', *Daily Mail* (Brisbane), 21 March 1928, p. 9.
8. 'Keep her going': B. Hinkler, 'The lights of Rome', p. 9.
9. 'I got a fine view': B. Hinkler, 'Alone in desert', p. 8.
10. 'I was now getting': B. Hinkler, 'Alone in desert', p. 9.
11. 'I might have flown': 'B. Hinkler, 'Alone in desert', *Daily Mail* (Brisbane), 22 March 1928, p. 9.
12. 'Rivers of blood': quoted in R. Collier, *War in the Desert*, Time-Life Books, New York, 2004, back cover.
13. 'great gorges that ran': B. Hinkler, 'Alone in desert', p. 9.

Chapter 11 – Desert sands and a load of anxiety

1. 'I used to sing': B. Hinkler, 'Alone in desert', *Daily Mail* (Brisbane), 22 March 1928, p. 8.
2. 'Twice I said': 'Alone in desert', p. 8.
3. 'Land-keeping people': 'Alone in desert', p. 8.
4. 'I asked him': B. Hinkler, 'Arab visitors help', *Daily Mail* (Brisbane), 24 March 1928, p. 9.
5. 'What excuses': 'Alone in desert', p. 9.
6. 'out of compliment', 'Arab visitors help', *Daily Mail* (Brisbane), 24 March 1928, p. 9.
7. 'as big as a large-sized': B. Hinkler, 'Monotony of flying', *Daily Mail* (Brisbane), 26 March 1928, pp. 8–9.
8. 'What's the good': B. Hinkler, 'Monotony of flying', pp. 8–9.
9. '10,000 feet above the earth': B. Hinkler, 'Monotony of flying', p. 8.
10. 'showed not the slightest': 'Monotony of flying', pp. 8–9.
11. 'It was easy to feel': B. Hikler, 'Monotony of flying', p. 8.
12. 'looked like an unwanted tool' and 'plays the part': B. Hinkler, 'Leaking tank menace', *Daily Mail* (Brisbane), 27 March 1928, pp. 8–9.
13. 'I thought I'd managed': B. Hinkler, 'Leaking tank menace', pp. 8–9.
14. 'Jask has no amusements': B. Hinkler, 'Leaking tank menace', pp 8–9.
15. 'like a doctor taking a pulse': B. Hinkler, 'Leaking tank menace', pp. 8–9.

16. 'in some queer': B. Hinkler, 'Leaking tank menace', pp. 8–9.
17. 'If you want to know': B. Hinkler, 'Leaking tank menace', pp. 8–9.
18. 'Keep it up, Bert': 'Hinkler overtakes himself', *Adelaide Register*, 28 February 1928.
19. 'Sleepy as I was': B. Hinkler, 'Leaking tank menace', pp. 8–9.
20. 'The last thing Hinkler thinks of': 'Hustling Hinkler', *Brisbane Courier*, 16 February 1928, p. 13.
21. 'I am glad to say': B. Hinkler, 'Worst day experienced', *Daily Mail* (Brisbane), 28 March 1928, pp. 8–9.
22. 'I was as near as a touch': B. Hinkler, 'Over dense jungle', *Daily Mail* (Brisbane), 29 March 1928, pp. 8–9.

Chapter 12 – Sticky mud and summer storms

1. 'The water buffaloes': B. Hinkler, 'Over dense jungle', *Daily Mail* (Brisbane), 29 March 1928, pp. 8–9.
2. 'Not a horse of them': B. Hinkler, 'Over dense jungle', pp. 8–9.
3. 'Tiny rice fields': B. Hinkler, 'Over dense jungle', *Daily Mail* (Brisbane), 29 March 1928, pp. 8–9.
4. 'like a gigantic': B. Hinkler, 'Over dense jungle', pp 8–9.
5. 'It was as peaceful': B. Hinkler, 'All night battle waged', *Daily Mail* (Brisbane), 30 March 1928, p. 8.
6. 'I could not help': B. Hinkler, 'All night battle waged', p. 8.
7. 'like bits of cotton': B. Hinkler, 'Over dense jungle', *Daily Mail* (Brisbane), 29 March 1928, pp. 8–9.
8. 'I jolly near holed out': B. Hinkler, 'All night battle waged', p. 8.
9. 'They were generously': 'Over dense jungle', *Daily Mail* (Brisbane), 29 March 1928, pp. 8–9.
10. 'Hinkler coming fast': *Sun-Herald* (Melbourne), c. 19 February 1928, *Newspaper clippings: Record of Hinkler's flight, England to Australia, 1928*; OM92-114/1, Bert Hinkler Clippings, John Oxley Library, State Library of Queensland.
11. 'It appears that Captain Hinkler': letter, British Consul-General, Batavia, to Foreign Office, London, 24 February 1928, Air Ministry file, 'B. Hinkler, Solo flight England – Australia: Request for permission to fly over certain foreign countries', AVIA 2/284, UK Archives, Kew.
12. 'a fly crawling into icing sugar': B. Hinkler, 'All night battle waged', *Daily Mail* (Brisbane), 30 March 1928, p. 8.
13. 'Several times I thought' and 'I didn't sleep': B. Hinkler, 'All night battle waged', p. 8.
14. 'All Australia on tiptoes for Hinkler': *Melbourne Herald*, c. 22 February 1928, *Newspaper clippings: Record of Hinkler's flight, England to Australia, 1928*; OM92-114/1, Bert Hinkler Clippings, John Oxley Library, State Library of Queensland.

15. 'Now that Bert Hinkler': Letter, B. Bonney to Minister for Defence, 10 February 1928, Australian Archives, Melbourne, MP 124/6, item 343071.
16. '*There's an Aussie*': C.J. Dennis, 'The Singing Ace', *Melbourne Herald*, 22 February 1928.
17. 'There was joy': B. Hinkler, 'All night battle waged', *Daily Mail* (Brisbane), 30 March 1928, p. 9.
18. 'I thought I'd arrived': '2FC broadcast', newspaper clipping, c. 11 March 1928, *Hinkler's worldwide flight*, OM92-114/2, Bert Hinkler Clippings, John Oxley Library, State Library of Queensland.
19. 'Hinkle, Hinkle': *Punch*, 28 February 1928.
20. 'the croakers': '2FC broadcast'.
21. 'Some quietly pronounced': 'Hinkler's wonderful feat', newspaper clipping, Melbourne (?), c. 23 February 1928, *Hinkler's worldwide flight*, OM92-114/2, Bert Hinkler Clippings.
22. 'out of the heated' and 'as light as a feather': '2FC broadcast'.

Chapter 13 – The conquering hero

1. 'Thank you very much': 'Darwin's welcome', newspaper clipping, c. 23 February 1928, *Newspaper clippings: Record of Hinkler's flight, England to Australia, 1928*, OM92-114/1, Bert Hinkler Clippings, John Oxley Library, State Library of Queensland.
2. 'Bravo beloved': telegram, N. Hinkler to B. Hinkler, 23 February 1928, OM68-24, Bert Hinkler Papers, John Oxley Library, State Library of Queensland.
3. 'You ball of muscle' and 'The Humble Avro': telegrams, Bert Hinkler Papers, John Oxley Library.
4. 'the hazardous undertaking': 'Mr Bruce's message', newspaper clipping, c. 23 February 1928, *Newspaper clippings: Record of Hinkler's flight, England to Australia, 1928*, OM92-114/1, Bert Hinkler Clippings.
5. 'The earlier difficulties': file note, Air Ministry file, 'B. Hinkler, Solo flight England – Australia: Request for permission to fly over certain foreign countries', AVIA 2/284, UK Archives, Kew.
6. 'He is very keen': quoted in 'British public stirred', newspaper clipping, London, 23 February 1928, *Newspaper clippings: Record of Hinkler's flight, England to Australia, 1928*, OM92-114/1, Bert Hinkler Clippings.
7. 'It was difficult': 'Courier fund', *Brisbane Courier*, 9 March 1928.
8. 'It requires a finer nerve': 'Home', *Sydney Morning Herald*, 28 February 1928.
9. 'the same enthusiastic': 'Still "Our Bert" to Bundaberg', newspaper clipping, 2 March, 1928, *Newspaper clippings: Record of Hinkler's flight, England to Australia, 1928*, OM92-114/1, Bert Hinkler Clippings, John Oxley Library.
10. 'It is the proudest': 'Still on top', newspaper clipping, c. 27 February 1928, *Hinkler's worldwide flight*, OM92-114/2, Bert Hinkler Clippings, John Oxley Library, State Library of Queensland.

11. 'dark days of depression': quoted in 'Still on top', newspaper clipping, c. 27 February 1928, Hinkler's worldwide flight, OM92-114/2, Bert Hinkler Clippings, John Oxley Library.
12. 'Bert and I were more like pals': 'Invasion begun', newspaper clipping, c. 24 February 1928, *Hinkler's worldwide flight*, OM92-114/2, Bert Hinkler Clippings.
13. 'put your receivers down': 'Broadcast arranged to Britain', newspaper clipping, c. 28 February 1928, *Newspaper clippings: Record of Hinkler's flight, England to Australia, 1928*, OM92-114/1, Bert Hinkler Clippings, John Oxley Library.
14. 'I counted the days': 'Mother's message', newspaper clipping, c. 28 February 1928, *Newspaper clippings: Record of Hinkler's flight, England to Australia, 1928*; OM92-114/1, Bert Hinkler Clippings, John Oxley Library.
15. 'convey to the intrepid aviator': 'Hinkler thanksgiving service', *Mercury* (Hobart), 26 March 1928, p. 3.
16. 'very wonderful accomplishment' and 'By that accomplishment': '£2000 granted: Commonwealth tribute', newspaper clipping, c. 24 February 1928, *Hinkler's worldwide flight*, OM92-114/2, Bert Hinkler Clippings.
17. 'sunburnt and smiling': 'His unassuming manner', 'Special coverage: Bert Hinkler's visit 6 March 1928', *Brisbane Courier*, 7 March 1928.
18. 'disciple of flying': 'Special coverage: Bert Hinkler's visit 6 March, 1928', *Brisbane Courier,* 7 March 1928.
19. 'the idol of the whole empire': 'special coverage: Bert Hinkler's visit 6 March 1928'.
20. 'fill the back blocks': 'Courier fund', *Brisbane Courier*, 9 March, 1928.
21. *'Now 'e's the sort'*: *Loxton Courier*, 15 March 1928, p. 6.

Chapter 14 – Modesty is seldom rewarded

1. 'indefinite' and 'It seems to me': 'Knightly feat: Returned soldiers' welcome', newspaper clipping, c. 11 March 1928.
2. 'practically certain' and 'Most sincerely appreciate': telegrams, OM68-24, Bert Hinkler Papers, John Oxley Library, State Library of Queensland.
3. 'With a keen appreciation of his services': letter, Stanley Bruce to A.H. Burnett, 6 April 1928, National Archives, Canberra, 'Mr Bert Hinkler', CP 103/11.
4. 'The Smith brothers and Cobham': C. Power, 'Honouring Hinkler', *Brisbane Courier*, 15 March 1928, p. 23.
5. 'Understand government have refused': telegram, Sydney *Daily Guardian* to Prime Minister, 1 March 1928, Australian Archives, Canberra.
6. 'Answer is in the affirmative': telegram, Prime Minister of Australia to Secretary of State for Dominion Affairs, 4 March 1928, Air Ministry file, 'Award of AFC to Mr B Hinkler, DSM, in recognition of his flight from England to Australia', 830264/28. Air 2/331, UK Archives, Kew.
7. 'certain agitation' and 'agitation for': telegram, Prime Minister of Australia to Secretary of State for Dominion Affairs, 7 March 1928, Air Ministry file, 'Award of AFC to Mr B Hinkler, DSM . . . '.

8. 'distinguished service rendered': telegram, Secretary of State for Dominion Affairs to Prime Minister of Australia, 10 March 1928, Air Ministry file, 'Award of AFC to Mr B. Hinkler, DSM, in recognition of his flight from England to Australia', 830264/28. Air 2/331, UK Archives.
9. 'I am handing': quoted in 'Progress of aviation', newspaper clipping, c. 11 March 1928, *Hinkler's worldwide flight*, OM92-114/2, Bert Hinkler Clippings, John Oxley Library, State Library of Queensland.
10. 'personal consideration': letter, F., Forde to Prime Minister, 1 March 1928, NAA: A458, AB314/4, Aviation flights to Australia: Bert Hinkler.
11. 'very unusual circumstances under which': 'Bert Hinkler Imperial Service Grant', Australian Archives Melbourne, MP981/1, item 726103.
12. 'a shy retiring woman': 'Mrs Hinkler arrives', *Sydney Morning Herald*, 4 April 1928, p. 17.
13. 'Of course, I am tremendously': 'Mrs Hinker arrives', p. 17.
14. '25 to the mile': 'The airman's wife', *Advertiser*, 16 April 1928, p. 9.
15. 'in her demure black frock': 'Escorting Hinkler', *Mail*, 14 April 1928, p. 1.
16. 'If the Australian Government': 'Hinkler family', *Mercury*, 16 April 1928, p. 7.
17. 'the unsatisfactory nature': B. Hinkler, letter to E.J. Hart, 11 July 1928, National Library, Canberra, M/S 8314.
18. 'At a time': 'Hinkler's wonderful feat', newspaper clipping, Melbourne?, Kew, c. 23 February 1928, *Hinkler's worldwide flight*; OM92-114/2, Bert Hinkler Clippings, John Oxley Library, State Library of Queensland.
19. 'without a cork': 'Hinkler', *Sunday Times* (WA), 2 December 1928, p. 6s.
20. 'There was nothing doing here': letter, Frances Hinkler to P. Deane, Prime Minister's Department, 20 October 1928, 'Flight of Mr Bert Hinkler to Australia', NAA, Canberra, 406/1/101, Part 1.

Chapter 15 – Flight of the Ibis

1. 'pleasant, restful and monotonous': B. Hinkler, letter to Frances Hinkler, 10 December 1928; OM68-24, Bert Hinkler Papers, John Oxley Library, State Library of Queensland.
2. 'I am a freelance': 'Air service', *Sydney Morning Herald*, 30 October 1928, p. 11.
3. 'While Sir Alan Cobham': 'Bert Hinkler: Unheralded and unsung', *Sydney Morning Herald*, 5 December 1928, p. 22.
4. 'Since our return': B. Hinkler, letter to Frances Hinkler, 10 December 1928.
5. 'I had no further use': B. Hinkler, letter to Frances Hinkler, 28 August 1929, OM68-24, Bert Hinkler Papers.
6. 'I call my machine': B. Hinkler, letter to Frances Hinkler, 28 August 1929, OM68-24, Bert Hinkler Papers.
7. 'priceless lessons learned': 'Hinkler honoured', *Brisbane Courier*, 29 June 1929, p. 17.
8. 'They are two really dinky': B. Hinkler, letter to Frances Hinkler, 30 October 1929, OM68-24, Bert Hinkler Papers.

9. 'the year the Moth': F.W. Hotson, 'From Moth to Mosquito', *Canadian Aviation Historical Society Journal*, 1978, vol. 16, no. 2, p. 39.
10. 'as an unbeaten' and 'warm tribute': '"Southern Cross" makes record flight', *Flight*, 18 July 1929, p. 736.
11. 'the centre of a whirlpool': 'Miss Amy Johnson honoured', *Flight*, 6 June 1930, p. 607.
12. 'Squadron Leader Bert Hinkler': 'Hinkler coming', *Northern Territory Times*, 9 May 1930, p. 3.
13. 'may very well be': 'An amphibian owner from France', *Flight*, 27 December 1929, p. 1345.
14. 'not very co-operative': H. Penrose, *British Aviation – Widening Horizons 1930–1934*, HMSO, London, 1979, p. 124.
15. 'perhaps the most noteworthy': 'The race to Australia', *Flight*, 24 October 1930, p. 1156.
16. 'We prefer to regard': 'Editorial comment', *Flight*, 24 October 1930, p. 1154.

Chapter 16 – The lone wanderer

1. 'I was hoping to resurrect': letter, B. Hinkler to E.J. Hart, June 1931, National Library, Canberra, M/S 8314.
2. 'My finances being what they are': letter, B. Hinkler to E.J. Hart, June 1931, National Library, Canberra, M/S 8314.
3. 'dark haired little guy': F.W. Hotson, 'Bert Hinkler and Canada', *Canadian Aviation Historical Society Journal*, 1992, vol. 30, no. 1, p. 18.
4. 'Whenever I use my plane': 'In cloud of mystery', newspaper clipping, c. 20 October 1931, *Hinkler's worldwide flight*, OM92-114/2, Bert Hinkler Clippings, John Oxley Library, State Library of Queensland.
5. 'Hinkler plans flight': *Advocate* (Burnie), 7 May 1931, p. 1.
6. 'What an awful looking': F.W. Hotson, 'Bert Hinkler and Canada', p. 19.
7. 'When you worked for Bert': quoted in F.W. Hotson, 'Bert Hinkler and Canada', p. 20.
8. 'Until the aircraft': quoted in F.W. Hotson, 'Bert Hinkler and Canada', p. 19.
9. 'semi-furtive departure': H. Penrose, *British aviation – widening horizons 1930–1934*, HMSO, London, 1979, p. 124.
10. 'Mr Hinkler did not advise': letter, 'Mr Bert Hinkler', Official Secretary, Office of the Commissioner-General of Australia in the USA, to Secretary, Prime Minister's Department, 20 November 1931, memo PM/31/460, NAA:A458, BS 314/4.
11. 'My airship, *Karohi*': 'Bert Hinkler: Record non-stop flight – future plans', *Mercury* (Hobart), 31 October 1931, p. 11.
12. '[Hinkler's] detention': letter, 'Mr Bert Hinkler', Official Secretary, Office of the Commonwealth-General for Australia in New York, 20 November 1931, NAA: A458, BSS 14/4.

13. 'Here's hoping': 'Mrs Hinkler surprised and thrilled', *Advertiser (*Adelaide), 30 November 1931, p. 9.

Chapter 17 – A bold, bad little pilot

1. 'It was like being in a glass box': 'Hinkler's blind flying', *Morning Bulletin*, 9 December 1931, p. 7.
2. 'Mr Hinkler – Flight across South Atlantic', *Sydney Morning Herald*, 28 November 1931, p. 13.
3. 'For all I knew' and 'It is not a question': 'Mrs Hinkler surprised and thrilled', *Advertiser* (Adelaide), 30 November 1931, p. 6.
4. '*un exploit sensationnel*' and 'a destination he wants': 'H. J. Hinkler le vainquer de l'Atlantique Sude atterit á Casablanca', newspaper clipping, MG92-114/2, Bert Hinkler clippings, John Oxley Library, State Library of Queensland.
5. 'Proud of your achievement': 'Acclaim: Hinkler home', *The Sun*, 8 December 1931.
6. 'most becomingly in black', 'somewhat the worse' and 'One cannot imagine': F.A. de V. Robertson, 'The return of Bert Hinkler', *Flight,* 11 December 1931, p. 1207.
7. 'This latest flight': 'Airport News – Croydon', *Flight*, 4 December 1931, p. 1197.
8. 'We do not know': F.A. de V. Robertson, 'The return of Bert Hinkler', p. 1208.
9. 'May it please your Majesty': letter, W.B. Stephenson to 'The King's Most Excellent Majesty', c. December 1931, 'Award of AFC to Mr B Hinkler, DSM, in recognition of his flight from England to Australia', 830264/28. Air 2/331, UK Archives, Kew.
10. 'harebrained stunt' and 'Haven't I been saying': 'London notes', *Mercury* (Hobart), 13 January 1932, p. 7.
11. 'joy ride', 'I don't know' and 'a brother Aussie': quoted in F.A. de V. Robertson, 'The return of Bert Hinkler', p. 1209.
12. 'He has been almost': 'Editorial comment', *Flight*, 4 December 1931, p. 1183.
13. 'nowadays the arrangement': 'Hinkler's "Ibis"', *Flight,* 1 January 1932, p. 8.
14. 'I hate the idea': 'Ultimatum: Hinkler to Britain', *Canberra Times*, 21 December 1931, p. 1.

Chapter 18 – Fallen onto hard facts

1. 'One Schneider winner': H.C. Biard, *Wings*, Hurst and Blackett, London, 1934, p. 216.
2. 'If I am too old': 'Hinkler's retort', *Northern Standard* (Darwin), 12 February 1932, p. 7.
3. 'He was as keen on success': quoted in 'Looking for trouble', *Barrier Miner*, 19 January 1933, p. 2.
4. 'What I had expected': B. Hinkler, 'Worst day experienced', *Daily Mail* (Brisbane), 28 March 1928, p. 8.
5. 'I've got a chance': quoted in H.C. Biard, *Wings*, p. 217.

6. 'Squadron Ldr. Hinkler's plans': quoted in F.W. Hotson, 'Bert Hinkler and Canada', *Canadian Aviation Historical Society Journal*, 1992, vol. 30, no. 1, p. 21.
7. 'There is no telling': 'Hinkler and his famous "Karohi"', *Flight*, 15 December 1932, p. 1191.
8. 'As Hinkler prepared to depart': 'Dramatic departure', *Cairns Post*, 11 January 1933, p. 9.

Chapter 19 – Wrapped in a shroud of snow

1. 'including acceptance of': 'Mr Hinkler: No request made', newspaper clipping, c. 12 January, 1933. *Newspaper clippings: Record of Hinkler's flight, England to Australia, 1928*; OM92-114/1, Bert Hinkler Clippings, John Oxley Library, State Library of Queensland.
2. '[he] took a tremendous': 'Looking for trouble', *Barrier Miner* (Broken Hill), 19 January 1933, p. 2.
3. 'the amazing position': 'Mr Hinkler still missing', newspaper clipping, *Daily Mail,* c. 10 January, 1933. *Newspaper clippings: Record of Hinkler's flight, England to Australia, 1928*; OM92-114/1, Bert Hinkler Clippings, John Oxley Library, State Library of Queensland.
4. 'I am going': quoted in 'No word of Hinkler', newspaper clipping, 13 January, 1933. *Newspaper clippings: Record of Hinkler's flight, England to Australia, 1928*; OM92-114/1, Bert Hinkler Clippings, John Oxley Library.
5. 'My husband's mother': 'Mrs Hinkler arrival in Sydney', newspaper clipping, c. mid January 1933, *Newspaper clippings: Record of Hinkler's flight, England to Australia, 1928*; OM92-114/1, Bert Hinkler Clippings, John Oxley Library, State Library of Queensland.
6. 'with the face' and 'would be of': 'Hinkler robbed', newspaper clipping, c. 10 January, 1933, *Newspaper clippings: Record of Hinkler's flight, England to Australia, 1928*; OM92-114/1, Bert Hinkler Clippings, John Oxley Library.
7. 'The obvious conclusion': report, M. Saby, Sens, France, 24 April 1933, Air Ministry file 207862/32, UK Archives Avia 2/606.
8. 'Although the sun was shining': quoted in 'Report submitted to the Government of the Canton de Vaud by the Chef de Port of the Lausanne Aerodrome "Le Blecherette", on Captain Hope's expedition to trace the lost Australian, Squadron Leader Bert Hinkler, January 17 to January 21, 1933', Air Ministry file 207862/32.
9. 'For six hours we continued': quoted in 'Report submitted to the Government of the Canton de Vaud . . .', Air Ministry file 207862/32.
10. 'was done with': 'Airman's wife critical of government', newspaper clipping, c. 26 January, 1933, Newspaper clippings: Record of Hinkler's flight, England to Australia, 1928, OM92-114/1, Bert Hinkler Clippings, John Oxley Library.

11. 'carelessness and lack of consideration': 'Copy of decisions of the Committee of the Royal Aero Club reached at a special meeting held under the provisions of club rule 59 on 21st April, 1933', folio 78A, Air Ministry file 207862/32.
12. 'in case you have any means': letter, Director of Civil Aviation, to L.V. Pearkes, 3 February 1933, Air Ministry file 207862/32.
13. 'In spite of': Letter, Lt de V Albertas to Wing Commander Harris, Air Ministry, 24 April 1933, Air Ministry file 207862/32, UK Archives Avia 2/606.
14. 'I cannot believe': 'Missing airman', *Mercury* (Hobart), 29 March 1933, p. 8.
15. 'through which we identified him': public prosecutor, 'Transcript of proceedings concerning the recognition of the objects and letters found upon the body at Pratomagno', 29 April 1933, Strada, Italy, Queensland Museum Library.
16. '*High on the shoulders*': B. Southey, 'Hinkler in Italy', *Bulletin*, 13 September 1933.

Chapter 20 – Vale, Hinkler!

1. 'I never gave up hope': 'Wife's distress,' *Cairns Post*, 2 May 1933, p. 7
2. 'The fruy of the wind': Marshal Romeo Aureli & Carabinieri Giovanni Polini, 'Proceedings into the death of Herbert John Hinkler, 41, following an air accident, 31 May 1933', Strada, Italy, Queensland Museum Library.
3. '1. A wallet of black leather': 'Transcript of proceedings concerning the recognition of the objects and letters found upon the body discovered on Mt Pratamagno, 29 April 1933,' Royal Carabinieri, Strada, Italy, Queensland Museum Library.
4. 'THE RESERVE PERSONNEL': memorandum, attachment to letter, British Ambassador, Rome, to British Foreign Secretary, 4 May 1933, Air Ministry file 207862/32, UK Archives Avia 2/606.
5. 'The service was simple': P. Cox, 'Vale Hinkler!', newspaper clipping, c. 1 May 1933, *Newspaper clippings: Record of Hinkler's flight, England to Australia, 1928*; OM92-114/1, Bert Hinkler Clippings, John Oxley Library, State Library of Queensland.
6. 'for reasons which': memo, British Ambassador, Rome, to British Foreign Secretary, 4 May 1933, Air Ministry file 207862/32.

Chapter 21 – The secret of Karohi

1. 'I think he has done wonderfully': 'Mr Hinkler: Successful flight', *Sydney Morning Herald*, 30 November 1931, p. 5.
2. 'To the long-distance airman' and 'a very clear testimony': memorandum, 'Hinkler Memorial', British Military Attaché to Mr Murray, British Embassy, Rome, 19 September 1933, Air Ministry file 207862/32, UK Archives Avia 2/606.
3. 'In memory of my beloved husband': 'Hinkler: Memorial unveiled', *Sydney Morning Herald*, 19 September 1933, p. 7.

4. 'Some time before': letter, Katherine Hinkler to Australian Government official, 2 October 1933, quoted in E.P. Wixted, *The Last Flight of Bert Hinkler*, Vantage Press, New York, 1992, pp. 87–88.
5. 'it was my feeling': letter, Katherine Hinkler to Australian Government official, 2 October 1933, quoted in E.P. Wixted, *The Last Flight of Bert Hinkler*, pp. 87–88.
6. 'any worthwhile tribute': letter, Katherine Hinkler to Australian Government official, 2 October 1933, quoted in E.P. Wixted, *The Last Flight of Bert Hinkler*, p. 87.

Chapter 22 – Fighting for a place in the sun

1. 'I knew we were falling': B. Hinkler, letter to Frances Hinkler, 5 May 1915, OM68-24, Bert Hinkler Papers, John Oxley Library, State Library of Queensland.
2. '14 large geographical maps': public prosecutor, 'Transcript of proceedings concerning the recognition of the objects and letters found upon the body at Pratomagno', 29 April 1933, Strada, Italy, Queensland Museum Library.
3. 'shapeless mass of iron': Marshal Romeo Aureli and Carabinieri Giovanni Polini, 'Proceedings into the death of Herbert John Hinkler, 41, following an air accident, 31 May, 1933', folio 7, Strada, Queensland Museum Library.
4. 'the limited visibility or fog': G. Ghedini, 'Proceedings into the death of Herbert John Hinkler, 41, following an air accident, 31 May, 1933', folio 7, Strada, Queensland Museum Library.
5. 'certainly surprised by a storm': Marshal Romeo Aureli and Carabinieri Giovanni Polini, 'Proceedings into the death of Herbert John Hinkler, 41, following an air accident, 31 May, 1933', folio 22, Strada, Italy, Queensland Museum Library.
6. 'did not think for one moment': memo, J.P.C. Cooper, accident investigator, British Air Ministry, to D.D.T.D., 22 June 1933, Air Ministry file 207862/32, UK Archives Avia 2/606.
7. 'rounded extremity': letter, Ministero Dell'Aeronautica to British Military Attaché, Rome, 6 November 1933, Air Ministry file 207862/32.
8. 'absolutely against the policy': T.G. Hetherington, memo, 'Disposal of the remainder of the later Squadron Leader Hinkler's machine', 11 November 1933, Air Ministry file 207862/32.
9. '*Like Icarus*': 'Vale! Hinkler', *Sunday Mail* (Brisbane), 30 April 1933, p. 1.
10. 'he was as cheerful': quoted in 'Looking for trouble', *Barrier Miner* (Broken Hill), 19 January 1933, p. 2.
11. 'overmuch' and 'Sometimes he tried': F. de V. Robertson, *Manchester Guardian*, quoted in E.P. Wixted, *The Last Flight of Bert Hinkler*, Vantage Press, New York, 1992, p. 139.
12. 'remembered by all': 'Universal favourite', *West Australian*, 2 May 1933, p. 9.
13. 'the sad ending' and 'to let the world he was not played out': 'Bert Hinkler's martydom', *Sunday Times* (Western Australia), 7 May, 1933.
14. 'It is a hard fate': 'The end of Hinkler', *Mercury* (Hobart), 1 May 1933, p. 6.

15. 'Hinkler, because the world': obituary, 'Mr Hinkler: A great airman lacking a settled task', *Times* (London), 29 April 1933.
16. 'The heart singles out': B. Hinkler, letter to Nance Hinkler from S. S. Ascanius, 3 March 1921, Hinkler Hall of Aviation database.
17. 'He was astonishingly': quoted in 'Looking for trouble', *Barrier Miner* (Broken Hill), 19 January 1933, p. 2.
18. 'None but airmen': B. Hinkler, 'Worst day experienced', *Daily Mail* (Brisbane), 28 March, 1928, p. 8.

Epilogue

1. 'I'm sorry that you've lost him': quoted in personal communication, William Grimaldi, 25 February 2011.
2. 'Kathy was complaining': Jean Costa, email, 28 February 2011.
3. 'the gentle kindly lady' and 'I think very often': letter, Katherine Hinkler to Frances Hinkler, 18 June 1939, Hinkler Hall of Aviation database, item 200-335.
4. 'little mater': letter, Katherine Hinkler to Frances Hinkler, 18 June 1939.
5. 'I have lost all desire': letter, Katherine Hinkler to Frances Hinkler, 18 June 1939.
6. 'Bert Hinkler, who could put a machine down': John Leeming, *Airdays*, George G. Harrap and Co., London, 1936, p. 119.
7. 'Hinkler's crash in the Apennines': J.L. Watkins, 'Hinkler and fifty years beyond', *Talk to be delivered before a joint meeting of the Institution of Engineers, Australia, Canberra Division and the Australian Division of the Royal Aeronautical Society, Canberra Branch, 28 September 1977*; typescript held at Flinders University Library, Adelaide.
8. 'was intended to be a recognition': quoted in 'Hinkler's mother; Federal pension', *Mercury* (Hobart), 14 December 1933, p. 9.

Bibliography

Printed sources

'147 Air conquerors dead', Program for First International Aviation Contest, Sydney, 15 June 1912, National Library, Canberra.

Ralph Barker, *Verdict on a Lost Flyer: The Story of Bill Lancaster and Chubbie Miller*, Fontana/Collins, Sydney, 1986.

A.S. Berg, *Lindbergh*, Macmillan, London, 1998.

R. Bettiens, *Hinkler: Hyperbole, Hypocrisy and Humbug versus Authenticity and Accuracy in Australian History*, self-published typescript, 1985.

H.C. Biard, *Wings*, Hurst and Blackett, London, 1934.

H. Bolitho, *King Edward VII: An Intimate Biography*, J.B. Lippincott Company, London, 1937.

R. Bonds, *The Illustrated Directory of a Century of Flight*, Salamander, London, 2003.

T.C. Bridges & H.H. Tiltman, *More Heroes of Modern Adventure*, Harrap, London, 1930.

P. Clegg, *Avro Test Pilots Since 1907*, GMS Enterprises, Peterborough, 1997.

R. Collier, *War in the Desert*, Time-Life Books, New York, 2004.

L. Edmonds, *Airmindedness – Selling a New Kind of Technology to the Australian Public*, Airways Museum/Civil Aviation Historical Society, Industry Regulation & Aviation Policy, n.d., www.airwaysmuseum.com.

L. Edmonds, *Problems of Defence, Isolation and Development: What Civil Aviation Could Do to Help*, Airways Museum/Civil Aviation Historical Society, Industry Regulation & Aviation Policy, n.d., www.airwaysmuseum.com.

N. Ellison, *Flying Matildas*, Angus & Robertson, Sydney, 1957.

'A Famous Skywriter Tells of His Job', *Popular Science Monthly*, March 1929, p. 140.

P. Fitzsimons, *Charles Kingsford Smith and Those Magnificent Men*, HarperCollins, Sydney, 2009.

F. Gardam, 'Bert Hinkler – what we didn't know', *Devonport Times*, vol. 7, no. 10, 2004, p. 32.

T. Gwynn-Jones, *Pioneer Aviator: The Remarkable Life of Lores Bonney*, University of Queensland Press, Brisbane, 1988.

T. Hall, *Flying High*, Methuen, Sydney, 1979.

J. Haynes & J. Dellit, *Great Australian Aviation Stories*, ABC Books, Sydney, 2006.

Hinkler's Sydney Visit, Souvenir booklet, 10 March 1933; held at National Library, Canberra.

H. Holmes, *Avro: The History of an Aircraft Company*, Crowood Press, Marlborough, 2004.

M. Hooper, *God 'elp All of Us*, Methuen, Sydney, 1986.

D. Hopwood, 'British relations with Iraq', *Iraq: Conflict in Context*, www.bbc.co.uk/history/recent/iraq/britain_iraq (UK), www.southernlife.org.uk/hinkler.htm.

F.W. Hotson, 'Bert Hinkler and Canada', *Canadian Aviation Historical Society Journal*, 1992, vol. 30, no. 1, pp. 14–22.

F.W. Hotson, 'From Moth to Mosquito: The Early History of de Havilland in Canada', *Canadian Aviation Historical Society Journal*, 1978, vol. 16, no. 2, pp. 37–51.

H. Irwin, 'Showmen, Stars, Larrikins and Pioneers', *Australian Journal of Communication*, vol. 25, no. 1, 1998, pp. 19–40.

F.C. Kelly, *The Wright Brothers: A Biography*, Dover Publications, New York, 1989.

R. Lee, *Linking a Nation: Australia's Transport and Communications 1788–1970*, Chapter 8: 'The rise of civil aviation to 1970', Australian Heritage Council, www.environment.gov.au/heritage/ahc/publications/commission/books/linking-a-nation/index.html

A. Lunn, *The Man Who Flew the Aldershot*, Southern Life, www.southernlife.org.uk/hinkler.htm

R.D. McKenzie, *Solo: The Bert Hinkler Story*, Jacaranda Press, Brisbane, 1962; 2nd edn, Ure Smith, Dee Why, NSW, 1979.

J. D. Murphy, *Military Aircraft, Origins to 1918: An Illustrated History of Their Impact*, ABC-CLIO Inc, Santa Barbara California, 2005.

D. Nevin & the Editors of Time-Life Books, *The Pathfinders*, Caxton, London, 2004.

Nine Network Australia, *Hinkler the Aviator* (25 mins), 1990; copy from Queensland Museum.

H. Penrose, *British Aviation – Widening Horizons 1930–1934*, HMSO, London, 1979.

D.A. Pisano & F.R. Van Der Linden, *Charles Lindbergh and the Spirit of St Louis*, Harry N. Abrams, New York, 2002.

C. Prendergast, *The First Aviators*, Time-Life Books, Alexandria, VA, 1981.

M. Pugh, 'Wish You Were Here? Britain Between the Wars', *History Today*, vol. 58, no. 8, 2008, www.historytoday.com/martin-pugh/wish-you-were-here-britain-between-wars.

E.G. Roberts, *Box Kites and Beyond*, Hawthorn Press, Melbourne, 1976.

T. Sheehy, 'Hawker, Harry George (1889–1921)', *Australian Dictionary of Biography*, vol. 9, Melbourne University Press, 1983, pp. 233–34.

Southern Cross Productions, *Hinkler, the Lone Eagle*, video (50 mins), 198?; copy from Queensland State Library, record no. 314211.

J. Spenser, *The Airplane,* HarperCollins, New York, 2008.

M. Taylor, *The Aviators: A History in Photographs*, Times Books, London, 2003.

J.L. Watkins, 'Hinkler and fifty years beyond', *Talk to be delivered before a joint meeting of the Institution of Engineers, Australia, Canberra Division and the Australian Division of the Royal Aeronautical Society, Canberra Branch, 28 September, 1977*; typescript held at Flinders University Library, Adelaide.

'W. E. Hart', Program for First International Aviation Contest, Sydney, 15 June 1912.

E.P. Wixted, *Bert Hinkler and the Avro Baby*, self-published, 1991.

E.P. Wixted, *Bert Hinkler Comes Home*, self-published, 1991.

E.P. Wixted, *The Bettiens Tome: To the 37 Known Recipients*, self-published typescript, 1985.

E.P. Wixted, 'Hinkler, Herbert John Louis (Bert) (1892–1933)', *Australian Dictionary of Biography*, vol. 9, Melbourne University Press, 1983, pp. 305–07.

E.P. Wixted, *The Last Flight of Bert Hinkler*, Vantage Press, New York, 1992.

E.P. Wixted, *Spotting the Poseurs*, self-published, 1991.

'Wizard Stone', program for First International Aviation Contest, Sydney, 15 June 1912, National Library, Canberra.

Websites

A. V. Roe & Co Limited Production, www.ab-ix.co.uk/avian.pdf.

A.V. Roe and Company, Ltd. In *Encyclopædia Britannica*, Encyclopædia Britannica Online: http://www.britannica.com/EBchecked/topic/45324/AV-Roe-and-Company-Ltd.

All the world's air races, Society of Air Racing Historians, www.airrace.com/Chronology.htm.

ANZAC Day Commemoration Committee (Qld) , *World War I – The Western Front*, 1998, www.anzacday.org.au/history/ww1/overview/west.html, adapted from Matt Anderson, *'Don't forget me, cobber!': Australia and the first world war*, 1997.

Australian Army Aviation Association, 'From Boxkite to Black Hawk: A Brief History of Australian Army Aviation', www.fourays.org/history/history_1.htm.

Australian National Aviation Museum, Early Australian Aviation, http://www.aarg.com.au/Aviation-EarlyAustralian.htm.

'British civil aviation in 1932', Royal Air Force Museum, www.rafmuseum.org.au/milestones-of-flight/british_civil/1932.

'Charles Kingsford Smith and the first trans-Pacific flight, 1928', National Museum of Australia Exhibitions, www.nma.gov.au/exhibitions/now_showing/the_hall_exhibitions/charles_kingsford_smith_flight_1928.

Colin DeFries, Australian Aviation Pioneer, www.ctie.monash.edu.au/hargrave/biography1.html#defries.

Commercial aviation 1920 to 1930, *Century of Flight*, www.century-of-flight.net.

Commercial flight in the 1930s, *Century of Flight*, www.century-of-flight.net.

Croydon Airport, www.croydononline.org/history/places/airports.asp.

Early aviation cigarette cards guide, ebay.co.uk/Aviation-Cigarette-Cards.

T. Finch, 'HMAT Ascanius', from *Merchant Fleets* by Duncan Haws, vol. 6, Blue Funnel Line, www.oulton.com/cwa/newsships.nsf/.

Gaston Cugnet, Australian Aviation Pioneer, www.ctie.monash.edu.au/hargrave/biography1.html#cugnet.

Herbert John Louis Hinkler, Detail ID 1533732, NYPL Digital Gallery, www.digitalgallery.nypl.org.

'History notes', Powerhouse Museum, 2001, D*Hub, www.dhub.org/object/11575, http://queenslandplaces.com.au/bundaberg-suburbs.

NASA, History of flight, 2009, www.ueet.nasa.gov/StudentSite/historyofflight.html.

National Library of Australia, Digital collection – Music, http://nla.gov.au/nla.mus-an6160986.

NSW State Library, Hustling Hinkler, *Aviation in Australia*, www.sl.nsw.gov.au/discover_collections/history_nation/aviation/crossing_oceans/hinkler.html.

B. Pearson, *More than would reasonably be anticipated: The story of No. 3 Wing*, RNAS, www.overthefront.com/WWI-Aviation-No-3-Wing-Royal-Naval-Air-Service.

Phillip Treweek, Kiwi Aircraft Images, Bleriot XI, 2001, http://www.kiwiaircraftimages.com/bleriot.html.

Powerhouse Museum, Sydney, *Bleriot XI monoplane, 1914, History notes*, www.powerhousemuseum.com/m/collection/database/?irn=288461&img=101155.

Reaching Down Under: Record Setting Flights to Australia, US Centennial of Flight Commission, www.centennialofflight.gov/essay/Explorers_Record_Setters_and_Daredevils/Australia/EX9.htm.

J. Reilly, *Renfrew aviation*, http://www.myrenfrew.com/renaviation.htm, accessed 13 November, 2009.

Royal Air Force: *28 Squadron*, www.raf.mod.uk/history/shorthistoryoftheroyalairforce.cfm.

Royal Air Force: *Short History of the RAF*, www.raf.mod.uk/history/shorthistoryoftheroyalairforce.cfm.

Schneider Trophy, *Absolute astronomy*, www.absoluteastronomy.com/topics/Schneider_Trophy; 'Doolittle wins in Baltimore', *Airpower*, 1 November 2005.

Short Calcutta, *The flying boats*, www.centuryof-flight.net.

Sir Hudson Fysh – photograph of W.E. Hart in his Boxkite biplane, 1911, General note, State Library of NSW, PXA 1063/276, a1378001.

The beginnings of Soviet civil aviation, US Centennial of Flight Commission, www.centennialofflight.gov/essay/Commercial_Aviation/soviet_air/Tran17.htm.

The first decade of flight – 1909, 1910. State Library of NSW, www.sl.nsw.gov.au/discover_collections/history_nation/aviation/aviatorrs/first-decade.html.

The inspiration, History, Qantas, www.qantas.com.au/info/about/history/details1.

The Wright Brothers: Inventing a flying machine, Smithsonian Institute, Washington, www.nasm.si.edu/wrightbrothers/fly/1903/triumph.cfm.

UK Parliament, Hansard, 24 April, 1917. http://hansard.millbanksystems.com/commons/1917/apr/24/freiburg-air-raid.

J. Wientjens, 'Incidents in Holland', http://sites.google.com/site/hinklerresearch/news/incidentsinholland, 2010.

Wizard Stone's flight, Aviation, *Explore Te Ara: The Encyclopedia of New Zealand*, www.teara.govt.nz/EarthSeaAndSky/SeaAndAirTransport/Aviation/2/ENZ-Resources/Standard/1/en#breadcrumbtop.

Acknowledgements

This book has been several years in the making, and many people have helped bring it to the point of publication. It was my agent, Sophie Hamley, who first encouraged me to write a biography of Bert Hinkler. Since that time, I've benefitted from the help and advice of many people, including Chris and David at Hampshire Life, Michael Rodgers of the Canadian Aviation Historical Society, Meg Lloyd at the Queensland Museum, and professional staff at the Queensland State Library, National Archives of Australia in Canberra and Melbourne, National Library, Canberra, UK National Archives, Kew, and the RAF Museum. Dr Laurent Filliettaz assisted with translation from a French newspaper.

At the Hinkler Hall of Aviation, Bundaberg, Colleen Foglia facilitated access to their records, and I am grateful for ongoing advice from Lex Rowland OAM, the driving force behind the relocation of Hinkler's house from England, and the establishment of the present museum in 2008. I am also indebted to Bill Grimaldi,

Katherine Hinkler's great nephew, and to Jean Costa, her great niece, for sharing their special knowledge of 'Aunt Kathy'.

The book underwent further development when it was selected for the 2010 Queensland Writers Centre/Hachette Australia manuscript development program, and benefited from advice from a number of people, including Kim Wilkins, whose earlier workshops also helped me develop a better understanding of the writing process. I warmly remember, too, the support from my fellow writers at those events. *Hustling Hinkler*'s evolution since that time has been enhanced by the efforts at Hachette Australia of Vanessa Radnidge in particular, but also of Kate Ballard and Roberta Ivers, as well as the painstaking editing of Jon Gibbs. Thanks to everyone at Hachette Australia for your ongoing support.

While writing is mostly a singular activity, books are rarely developed in a vacuum, and I want to thank my family and friends for believing in me while I have been working on this project. In particular, I want to thank my Griffith University colleague, Dr Ann Kelly, and my eldest son, Mark Dymock, for their frank critique of the manuscript at a time when it was in need of a careful appraisal.

No acknowledgements would be complete without a mention of the support and patience shown by my wife, Cheryl, over the period I have been writing this book. Not always by choice, she probably knows as much about Bert Hinkler's life as I do.

Darryl Dymock
Brisbane, Australia

Index

C

D

E